SOCIOMETRY IN THE CLASSROOM

EDUCATION FOR LIVING SERIES

UNDER THE EDITORSHIP OF

H. H. REMMERS

NORMAN E. GRONLUND
UNIVERSITY OF ILLINOIS

SOCIOMETRY IN THE CLASSROOM

HARPER & BROTHERS
NEW YORK

SOCIOMETRY IN THE CLASSROOM

Printed in the United States of America

For information address Harper & Brothers
49 East 33rd Street, New York 16, N. Y.
D-I

Library of Congress catalog card number: 58-7026

TO MARIE, JIM, AND DICK

CONTENTS

PART III
APPLYING SOCIOMETRIC RESULTS TO EDUCATIONAL PROBLEMS

TABLES

FIGURES

EDITOR'S FOREWORD

Man's relations with his fellows are crucially important for his personal and social survival. From Aristotle's observation that man is a political (i.e., social) animal, the Christian Scripture's "Ye are members one of another," John Donne's "No man is an Island . . ." to the title of one of the first publications on sociometry, *Who Shall Survive?* it is clear that prophets, poets, and thinkers generally have been fundamentally concerned with the problems inherent in these relations. The recent development of sociometric concepts and tools has yielded new and important insight into and understanding of the complex social microcosms that are the classroom and the school.

In this book Professor Gronlund has made available for the first time a comprehensive integration and interpretation of sociometric research literature and its meaning for education from reports chiefly scattered throughout technical professional journals not generally available to school personnel. His evaluation of this literature from the point of view of the prospective "consumers" of this research is competent, thoughtful, and clear. This would be expected in view of the fact that he has himself been a notable contributor to this research literature.

The influence of the classroom and the school on personal and social development of children has now been sufficiently explored to make clear the great responsibility that formal education shares especially with the home. It is no longer possible to view this responsibility as consisting merely of teaching the cognitive functions. Indeed, the learning of these is conditional upon the sociometric status of the learner. Where this is optimal, effective learning takes place; where it is not, the corroding effects of interpersonal and intergroup conflicts and cleavages make for ineffective learning, tension, and unhappiness.

Not only does Professor Gronlund make clear the effects of numerous factors that impinge upon the individual, but he also provides excellent guides on "how to do it" for the teacher, the supervisor, the counselor, and the administrator in the use of this relatively new and powerful tool. These guides are not only for measurement but also for what to do about the results of measurement.

As Professor Gronlund makes clear, sociometry is not a panacea. It is, however, an easily used additional aid for the appraisal of vitally important aspects of the educational process. The modern school uses a variety of tools for this purpose, and sociometric "tests" are an important addition to the educator's tool kit.

With our knowledge of man still largely *terra incognita,* it follows that much research is needed. The teacher and the researcher will find this book both a guide to the use of this new technique and a compendium of hypotheses—both implicit and explicit—that need to be tested. Its contents are an important addition to the literature on education for living.

H. H. REMMERS

PREFACE

The modern teacher's increasing concern with the social and emotional development of his pupils has resulted in the need for an objective approach to improved social relations in the classroom. Sociometry has provided the basis for such an approach. Through sociometric testing the teacher is able to analyze the social relations among class members, to organize classroom groups which have a beneficial effect on pupils' social relations, and to evaluate the social development of individual pupils. When combined with other educational procedures, the sociometric test can also make constructive contributions to the solution of many of the educational problems faced by teachers, supervisors, counselors, and administrators.

The aim of this book is to provide teachers, and other educational practitioners, with the principles and procedures of sociometry that have implications for educational practice. Although the book was written in a how-to-do-it vein, the points of view and suggestions are supported throughout by sociometric theory and research. In fact, the findings of the majority of research studies pertinent to sociometry in the classroom have been incorporated into the text. This extensive reference to sociometric research literature should be of special value to those persons who are interested in further exploring the potentialities of sociometry in educational practice.

Although this book was written especially for teachers, much of the material will be of interest to students of psychology, sociology, and social psychology. For such students, the book should provide a useful introduction to the theory and methods of sociometric testing and to the research literature on children's social relations. The several hundred references cited in the text will enable the serious student to pursue areas of individual interest in his own major field.

The book is organized into three parts, following an introductory chapter which presents a description of the sociometric technique. The first part is devoted to the methods of sociometric testing. Step-by-step procedures are provided for constructing and administering the sociometric test, and for analyzing, interpreting, and recording sociometric results. Typical sociometric results, for pupils from the third-grade level through college, are presented to illustrate the patterns of sociometric choice at various age levels. The second part of the book presents an integrated interpretation of the research literature which is pertinent to the reliability and validity of sociometric choices and to the personal and social factors related to sociometric results. Although this is probably the most difficult part to read, it provides the basic information for understanding the meaning of sociometric results. The final part of the book is devoted to the educational applications of sociometric results. In the chapters concerned with social relations in the classroom, supplementary methods for improving pupils' social relations were included so that sociometric procedures could be viewed in proper perspective. In the final chapter, the possible uses of sociometric results throughout the school are indicated, and a systematic procedure for applying sociometric results in educational practice is described.

As noted throughout the text, the writer is indebted to the inspirational writings of J. L. Moreno, the father of sociometry, and to the numerous research workers and classroom teachers who have explored the value of sociometry in educational practice. Gratitude is also expressed to Mrs. Julia Snyder who took the major responsibility for clerical work on the manuscript.

NORMAN E. GRONLUND

January, 1959

SOCIOMETRY IN THE CLASSROOM

CHAPTER 1

THE SOCIOMETRIC TECHNIQUE

In 1932, in a public school in Brooklyn, New York, all of the pupils from the kindergarten through the eighth grade were requested to choose the two classmates they preferred to have sit near them. Some pupils received a large number of choices as seating companion, some received no choices, and others ranged in between these extremes. A further analysis of the choices revealed an underlying social structure of which the teachers were only partly aware. Mutual friendships, small pupil cliques, a sexual cleavage between boys and girls, and other facets of interpersonal relations among pupils were apparent from the choosing. This technique for evaluating the extent to which pupils were accepted by their peers and for determining the internal social structure of the group was called a *sociometric test* by its originator, Jacob L. Moreno (*42*).[1] The term sociometry was derived from Latin and means social or companion measurement. The sociometric test, itself, is not a test, in the sense that the term is commonly used but rather a technique. It was designated a test by Moreno, to prevent confusing it with the various other methods of diagnosis he developed in the general area of sociometry.

Since Moreno's original use of the sociometric test in the public schools, its use has spread to prisons, industry, summer camps, and

[1] The italicized numbers in parentheses apply to the references to be found at the end of each chapter. See p. 32 for the references for this chapter.

various other places where interpersonal relations are considered important. Entire communities have been studied by means of the sociometric technique. Institutes of sociometry have been developed in several countries and an international journal of sociometry was founded recently. Despite this widespread use and acceptance of sociometry, the most extensive use of the sociometric test has been in school settings. Teachers and research workers alike have used this technique to study the extent to which individual pupils were accepted by their peers and to analyze the social structure of classroom groups. They have found it a simple and convenient device for measuring aspects of social relations that previously were neglected or were evaluated by teacher judgment. The ease with which it can be constructed and administered makes it a practical instrument for use by the regular classroom teacher.

In addition to the simplicity and the convenience of the sociometric test, its increased use in school settings is due to several merging forces. The recent stress modern education has placed on social adjustment has made the classroom teacher more conscious of the social development of his pupils. Findings from small group research (*12, 23*) have pointed out the implications of group structure for the effective functioning of groups. Studies of group leadership (*2, 40*) have indicated the influence of the emotional climate of groups on the learning and behavior of individuals. Authorities in human development (*25, 49*) have stressed the value of social relations in the normal development of personality. Likewise, mental hygienists (*38, 50, 51*) have emphasized the importance of being accepted by others in the attainment of good personal and social adjustment. Recent textbooks in educational psychology (*5, 15, 37*) have pointed out the inextricable relationship between the learning and adjustment of individual pupils and their position in the group structure. These merging forces have created a need for a practical instrument to study the structure of classroom groups. The sociometric test, to a large extent, is satisfying this need.

SOCIOMETRIC TESTING AND TERMINOLOGY

The sociometric test requires individuals to choose a given number of associates for some group situation or activity. For example, pupils may be requested to indicate the five classmates with whom they most prefer to work on classroom projects. The basis of the choice is commonly called the *sociometric question* or the *sociometric criterion.* This sociometric question may be very general, such as the example given, or it may be very specific, such as asking the pupils to indicate the five classmates with whom they most prefer to study spelling. The number of choices allotted to each pupil also varies. Sometimes the number of choices is unlimited, but usually each pupil is limited to a fixed number. Other variations in the technique include the use of negative choices, where the pupils are requested to indicate those classmates they least prefer for the activity.

Regardless of variations in the sociometric test, it is basically a method of evaluating the feelings of the group members toward each other with respect to a common criterion. The number of choices that each individual receives is referred to as his *sociometric status,* his *social status,* or his *group status.* The first and last terms are preferred since *social status* is frequently used in other situations, such as "social status in the community." The pattern of choices to and from individuals, revealing the network of interpersonal relations among group members, is called the *sociometric structure,* the *social structure,* or the *group structure.* This structure of choice patterns is commonly presented in the form of a diagram, with the group members represented by small circles or triangles and the choices represented by lines drawn between the figures. Such a graphic representation of the sociometric structure of a group is referred to as a *sociogram* (see p. 73 for an illustration of a sociogram). The term sociogram is frequently confused with the term sociometric test and is used as a synonym for it. However, the sociometric test is the method used to evaluate the group structure, and the sociogram is merely one method of presenting the results.

In addition to the above sociometric terms, there is other specialized terminology associated with the sociometric test. The following list of terms will acquaint the beginner with the basic vocabulary necessary to comprehend the sociometric literature pertaining to the use of sociometry in the classroom. Most of these terms were coined by J. L. Moreno, the founder of sociometry, and are unique to sociometric measurement.

STAR

The term star refers to an individual who receives a large number of choices on a sociometric test. In his original use of the sociometric test, Moreno (*42*) reported that some of the pupils "attracted so many choices that they captured the center of the stage like stars." Bronfenbrenner (*10*) later made the definition more specific by indicating that a star was any individual who received more choices on the sociometric test than could be expected by chance alone. He developed a table of scores indicating the number of choices it would be necessary to receive, with various choice limits, in order to be placed in the star category. For example, where five choices are used with one sociometric criterion, any individual receiving nine or more choices would be designated a star. The complete table may be found on p. 67.

ISOLATE

The isolate is an individual who receives no choices on a sociometric test. Although he is a physical member of the group, he is psychologically isolated from the other group members. He is also sometimes referred to as an "outsider" or a "social island," although these designations are not as common as the term isolate.

NEGLECTEE

This term is used to identify the individual who receives relatively few choices on the sociometric test. Although he receives some choices, he tends to be neglected by the majority of the group members. Bronfenbrenner (*10*) also clarified this term by indicating that a neglectee was any individual who received fewer sociometric choices than could be expected by chance. His table of scores indicates the number of choices which identifies a neglectee. Where five choices are used with one sociometric criterion, any individual receiving one choice would be classified as a neglectee. Other limits for use with fewer than five choices and more than one criterion are indicated in the table on p. 67. Neglectees are also referred to as "fringers," since they are located on the fringe of the group. However the term neglectee is preferred since it is more definitive.

REJECTEE

The rejectee is an individual who receives negative choices on a sociometric test. Negative choices are those resulting from a sociometric question requesting individuals to indicate those whom they *least prefer* for a group activity. This term is commonly confused with the term isolate. However the isolate receives neither positive nor negative choices on a sociometric test. In short, he is truly isolated from the group, since he attracts no attention from the group members. The rejectee on the other hand may receive no positive choice from the group, but he does receive negative or rejection choices. Thus he attracts attention from the group members, but the attention is of a rejective nature. The confusion between these terms has probably arisen from the fact that negative sociometric choices are seldom used. Consequently, some of the individuals receiving no positive choices are true isolates, whereas others would be rejectees if a negative sociometric question were introduced. Without the use of a negative question the rejectees cannot be identified. Therefore, where only positive sociometric questions are used, the isolates would include some unidentified rejectees. The two terms, however, have distinct meanings and should not be used interchangeably.

MUTUAL CHOICE

This term indicates that two individuals have chosen each other on the same sociometric criterion. This is also called a reciprocated choice or a pair. The important aspect of the definition is that the choice must be reciprocated on the same criterion, thus indicating a mutual desire to associate together in the same group activity.

SOCIOMETRIC CLIQUE

This indicates a situation where a number of individuals choose each other on the same sociometric criterion, but give relatively few choices to individuals outside of their closely knit group. Thus the sociometric clique forms a subgroup within the larger group.

SOCIOMETRIC CLEAVAGE

This phenomenon refers to the lack of sociometric choices between two or more subgroups. An example of a sociometric cleavage may be found between the sexes at the elementary school level where the boys seldom choose girls and the girls seldom choose boys. In addition to this sexual cleavage, the sociometric test may reveal cleavages between racial groups, cleavages between rural-urban populations, cleavages between socioeconomic groups, and the like.

There are many other terms unique to the area of sociometry. However most of them are technical terms associated with the development of sociometric theory and need not be introduced here.

USING THE SOCIOMETRIC TEST

While the sociometric test has become a useful tool in the hands of the classroom teacher, its simplicity of construction and administration has led to the frequent misuse and misinterpretation of sociometric results. Since it is an informal evaluation instrument constructed by the person using it, the skill and understanding of the teacher are of paramount importance. Like all informal evaluation techniques, the more informal and the less structured the instrument the more knowledge required in its use. Thus an understanding of sociometric theory and method is essential if sociometric results are to be properly interpreted and applied.

An analysis of sociometric theory has indicated a number of qualifications concerning the use of the sociometric test. Probably foremost in Moreno's (*43*) writings has been his insistence that sociometric choices should be based on a criterion which reflects an actual situation or activity in which the group members have a real opportunity for participation. Requesting pupils to choose associates on criteria related to living in close proximity (i.e., seating companions, roommates, etc.), working in close proximity (i.e., study groups, working on classroom projects, etc.), and spending leisure time together (i.e., play companions, school parties, etc.) would meet this requirement. It is assumed that individuals will be motivated to give more spontaneous and valid choices if the situation or activity is meaningful to them and they can see the consequences of their choices. This, of course, implies that the teacher will follow through and arrange or rearrange the groups in accordance with the sociometric choosing.

In terms of the above limitations, asking pupils "Whom do you like best?" or "Who are your best friends?" could not be considered sociometric questions. The lack of a clear-cut criterion of choice and the absence of any implied action would not assure valid responses. Tests using such questions have been labeled "near-sociometric" tests. Although these tests may serve useful purposes in research settings (*41*), they are of limited value to the classroom teacher. In classroom situations requiring such "near-sociometric" questions, the teacher must utilize special motivational techniques, beyond the test itself, to assure sincere and accurate responses.

Effective use of the sociometric test also requires that every group member be familiar with the choice situation or activity and that they all are free to participate in it. This implies that the sociometric questions will be adapted to the age level of the pupils and to the nature of the group. None of the pupils should be left out of the choosing because of limitations in the criterion itself or because of factors extraneous to the sociometric situation. For example, choice of classmates for playing some special game would be ineffective if some of the pupils did not know how to play the game; choice of teammates for basketball would provide distorted results if some pupils were physically handicapped; and choice of classmates for the school dance would be inappropriate if some of the pupils were unable to attend because they lived on a farm and lacked transportation.

The sociometric choosing should place no limits on the pupils in the group who may be chosen, so that the test will provide a measure of the group members' acceptance or rejection of each individual. Of course, the nature of the group should be clearly defined to the chooser. Indicating that pupils may choose anyone in this room, in the fourth grade, in this high school, etc., will provide the limits within which the choices must be made. However, once the limits of the group are set, the teacher must make certain that every pupil within the group has an equal opportunity to participate in the situations or the activities included in the sociometric test.

A corollary to the above restriction is that the group members should have had sufficient opportunity to become acquainted with each other before the sociometric test is administered. Although

Barker (*4*) has shown that even the sociometric choices of complete strangers have some stability, other studies (*27*) have shown that more stable results will be obtained if group members have had several weeks to get acquainted. This does not mean, however, that each pupil must know every other pupil in the group before the test is administered. A recent study (*19*) has shown that the number of choices an individual receives on a sociometric test is not influenced by the number of group members that he knows or by the number of group members that know him. These results were based on groups which had been together one hour each day for seven weeks. Consequently, the opportunity for association is necessary to stabilize the sociometric choices, but merely increasing the acquaintance span of individuals does not necessarily modify the sociometric structure. Thus, providing for sufficient interaction among the pupils and making a special effort to introduce new pupils to the other class members should precede the administration of the sociometric test.

An equally important consideration in sociometric testing is that of assuring the group members that their choices will be kept strictly confidential. Individuals are reluctant to record the names of preferred associates if they suspect that their choices will be revealed. This is especially true if their desired associations in the group are widely different from their actual associations. Since the sociometric test measures the feelings and attitudes of individuals toward the other group members, it reflects the internal structure of the group. These feelings and attitudes may be directed toward individuals who are unavailable for actual association either due to environmental restrictions or lack of a reciprocal feeling of preference. In contrast, the individual's actual associations are as much a result of how others feel toward him, his formal placement in the group, and the limitations of the environment. For example, a pupil generally walks to school and plays after school with those children living in his neighborhood. These may not be his preferred associates, but environmental circumstances have placed them together. A similar illustration may be taken from the classroom itself. In one study (*45*) of fourth- and fifth-grade classes, only 10 percent of the pupils chose their present neighbors when asked to record the names of pupils they preferred to sit near. This discrepancy between preferred and actual association will make pupils fearful of recording their real choices unless they have complete assurance that the confidence of their choices will be protected.

TEACHER JUDGMENT VS. SOCIOMETRIC RESULTS

Teachers have always been aware that patterns of friendship, mutual dislike, and feelings of indifference existed among the pupils they were teaching. These observations, however, are based on expressed feelings of pupils in actual situations. This is the external structure of the group which may or may not reflect the real feelings of the pupils. There is no question concerning the value of observational techniques in studying the interaction of group members. Valuable information is obtained concerning interpersonal conflicts and mutual attractions of pupils. Observational techniques also reveal clues to the internal structure of the group. However, when teachers first use the sociometric test they are usually surprised to find that some of the pupils they thought were leaders are only moderately accepted by the group; or that some of the pupils they were certain would attract no choices receive a relatively large number; or that the small group of pupils which seemed inseparable on the playground do not choose each other on the sociometric test. The internal structure of the group is frequently quite different from the external structure, and the sociometric status of individual pupils is sometimes in striking contrast to his apparent group status.

A number of studies (*6, 8, 17, 18, 20, 21*) have investigated the extent to which teachers are accurate in judging the sociometric status of their pupils. Both student teachers and experienced teachers at the elementary and the secondary school level have been included in the studies. In general, the teachers' judgments have ranged from "near zero" to "near perfect" with an average accuracy score of approximately .60.[2] Although some teachers seemed to have more ability than others in judging the sociometric status of their pupils, even the best judges made rather large errors in judging individual pupils. This was found to be partly due to the tendency of teachers to over-judge the sociometric status of the pupils they themselves preferred and to under-judge the sociometric status of pupils they least preferred (*18*). The difference between the internal structure of the group, measured by the sociometric test, and the external structure of the group, which provided the clues for the teachers' judgments, is, of course, also a major factor contributing to the inaccuracy of the teachers' judgments (*8*). It is interesting to note that neither the size of the class (*17, 18*) nor the training and experience of the teachers could account for the differences among the teachers in the accuracy of their judgments.

Although the studies of teacher judgment reflect a moderate degree of accuracy in perceiving the social relations of pupils, the general inaccuracy of some teachers and the specific inaccuracies in judging individual pupils, shown by most teachers, indicate the importance of using the sociometric test for a complete picture of the classroom social structure. The need for an objective measure of interpersonal relations in the social sphere is roughly equivalent to the need for an intelligence test in the academic area. Teachers' ability to judge the intelligence of their pupils is approximately equivalent to their ability to judge the sociometric status of their pupils. In a recent study (*22*) comparing the ability of expe-

[2] This correlation coefficient indicates a moderate positive relationship between the teachers' judgments and the sociometric results. Zero relationship would be indicated by a correlation coefficient of .00. A perfect positive relationship would be indicated by a correlation coefficient of +1.00.

rienced elementary teachers in these two areas, it was reported that the teachers' average accuracy in judging their pupils' intelligence was represented by a correlation of .73, while their average correlational accuracy score for judging their pupils sociometric status was .70. With the widespread use of intelligence tests in schools, few teachers depend solely on their judgments of pupils for an evaluation of their scholastic aptitude. It would seem equally important for teachers to supplement their judgments of pupils' interpersonal relations with an objective measuring instrument such as the sociometric test.

VALUES AND USES OF THE SOCIOMETRIC TEST

It has been pointed out that using the sociometric test will make teachers more aware of the importance of interpersonal relationships among their pupils (*9*). A study of the internal structure of the group will provide hunches concerning the pattern of classroom interaction, the emotional climate of the group, and the problems of learning and adjustment of individual pupils. It will also provide a basis for organizing classroom groups and for evaluating attempts to improve the social structure of the group or the group status of individual pupils. Within this general framework there are a number of specific purposes for which the sociometric test is especially useful in a school setting.

IMPROVING THE SOCIAL ADJUSTMENT OF INDIVIDUAL PUPILS

Although the sociometric test does not indicate how to improve the social adjustment of pupils, it does identify those needing help in their social relationships and thus provides a basis for further diagnosis and remedial action. Pupils who are isolated or rejected by the group are generally characterized as possessing socially ineffective behavior patterns or withdrawal tendencies which interfere with their social adjustment (*7, 35, 48*). The patterns of choice to and from such pupils will provide clues as to their best placement in the group. Organizing the group so that the isolated and rejected pupils are in the most favorable position for developing social relationships with others and applying appropriate remedial action will frequently improve their adjustment to the group. Specific techniques for improving the social acceptance of individual pupils will be considered in a later chapter. It will suffice here to point out the value of the sociometric test in identifying those pupils who are having difficulty in their social adjustments.

Another important aspect of social adjustment that can be measured by the sociometric test is the individual's drive for social interaction with group members. When the pupil is permitted to use an unlimited number of choices, the number of choices he actually gives will provide clues to his desire for social contact. The number of group members to whom an individual is attracted on a sociometric test is called his *social* or *emotional expansiveness* (*28, 31, 43*), and it varies considerably among individuals. A clinical study (*48*) of pupils with low acceptance on a sociometric test has shown that some of them were uninterested in social contact. Although it is not clear whether lack of acceptance contributes to reduced drive for social adjustment or disinterest in social interaction is a cause of low social acceptance, measuring the social expansiveness of individual pupils will provide further information concerning a pupil's difficulties in adjusting to the group.

Analyzing the choices an individual pupil gives and receives on a sociometric test can also assist in evaluating the development of social maturity (*5*). Choices to and from members of the opposite sex will provide clues concerning the development of heterosexual interests. Choices of younger or more immature pupils will reveal possible difficulties in adjusting to his own age group. Choices, or the absence of choices, toward minority group members will provide additional evidence concerning the presence or absence of prejudice. A study of an individual's sociometric choice pattern can provide valuable supplementary data concerning his problems of social adjustment and his present level of social development.

Using the sociometric test to improve the social adjustment of individual pupils is by no means restricted to those pupils having difficulty in adjusting to the group. Identifying leadership potential in the classroom and assisting pupils in the development of this potential ability is equally as important as helping the isolate or rejectee gain status. In general, the leader identified by the sociometric test is the "popular leader" who has the personality and social skills necessary to maintain effective interpersonal relationships with a large number of group members. His effectiveness in influencing group members and his ability to provide actual leadership in school activities do not necessarily parallel his skill in social relations. Moreno and others (*29, 43*) have pointed out the possible discrepancy between "popular leaders" who receive a large number of choices on the sociometric test and actual leaders who may or may not be highly accepted by the group members. Thus, the "popular leader" may be considered an individual who has leadership potential. Helping him develop the skills necessary for actual leadership in school situations should be of vital concern to teachers and school administrators alike.

IMPROVING THE SOCIAL STRUCTURE OF THE GROUP

Through the measurement of the attractions and rejections between individual group members the sociometric test is uniquely adapted to the study of the social structure of groups. When the network of choices is presented in the form of a sociogram, the pattern of interpersonal relations becomes readily apparent. Mutual friendships, small cliques of pupils, cleavages between subgroups, and general patterns of group integration or disintegration are easily identified by the classroom teacher. Thus, the sociometric test provides an objective basis for identifying interpersonal conflicts and for improving the interpersonal relations of group members. Recognizing that a closely knit clique of pupils is disrupting the efficiency of the classroom, regrouping procedures may be utilized. Identifying cleavages between racial, religious, rural-urban, or socioeconomic status groups may indicate the necessity of putting special emphasis on programs to integrate the divided factions. A general lack of mutual attraction among pupils and a disintegrated group structure might reflect a highly competitive and hostile classroom atmosphere arising from autocratic teaching procedures. Better integration may result from the introduction of group work and teacher-pupil planning.

It is, of course, recognized that the sociometric test does not indicate why the resulting social structure is present in the classroom. Neither does it specify the therapeutic procedures necessary for improving interpersonal relations. Like any diagnostic tool it merely identifies the present situation. However, it does provide a graphic representation of interpersonal relations among pupils which is not available by other methods. Combined with classroom observation and other diagnostic information, the sociometric test serves as a firm base for improving the social structure of groups.

ORGANIZING GROUPS

Basic to the theory of sociometric testing is the application of the sociometric results in actual arrangement or rearrangement of the groups. Knowing that results will be put into effect in organizing groups, the individual recognizes an opportunity to participate in the arrangement and control of his social environment (*30, 43, 44*). In addition to eliciting more valid and spontaneous sociometric responses, the organization of sociometric groups serves another valuable purpose. It is assumed (*41*), and there is some evidence (*47*) to verify the assumption, that a social group is most effective when individuals within the group are placed in proximity to those with whom they prefer to associate. Participating in activities with chosen associates provides a feeling of personal security by freeing the individual of interpersonal tensions, thus resulting in more spontaneous and creative activity. Although one of the original purposes in the development of the sociometric test was that of improving the effectiveness of groups through rearrangement along sociometric lines, this basic procedure has been frequently neglected in the application of sociometric techniques to educational problems.

The classroom offers numerous opportunities for sociometric grouping. Arranging seating in the classroom, organizing work groups or classroom committees, selecting companions for classroom games or parties are some of the more obvious classroom situations that are adapted to the use of sociometric grouping. Groups for field trips and other out-of-class projects can also be organized on the basis of pupils' choices. Schools have used sociometric results at the junior high and senior high school levels in organizing entire grade levels into classroom sections and homerooms (*1, 36*). The possibilities of sociometric grouping are only limited by the need for arranging pupils into groups and the ingenuity of the user of the sociometric test.

In addition to improving the working effectiveness of groups, sociometric grouping has therapeutic values. Numerous studies at the elementary (*30, 34, 52*), secondary (*1, 11*), and college (*54, 55*) levels have indicated how sociometric grouping has improved the social structure of the group and the social adjustment of individual pupils. Generally, sociometric grouping is not used as a single technique but is combined with other methods of remedial action. Consequently, it is difficult to evaluate its individual contribution in the improvement of group structure and individual status. Nevertheless, it is considered an important procedure when supplemented by other therapeutic practices.

The organization of sociometric groups is seldom based on

sociometric choices alone. It is obvious that the members of an undesirable clique should not be placed together if they are disturbing the classroom group, even though they have chosen each other. Likewise, classroom cleavages should not be encouraged, although the sociometric choices do not cross between sex, race, rural-urban, or socioeconomic groups. Thus, sociometric results form the basis for sociometric grouping, but other factors such as the pupils' characteristics, the purposes of the group, and the objectives of the school must be considered before the most effective grouping is attained.

SOCIOMETRY AND SPECIAL SCHOOL PROBLEMS

There are a number of special school problems where sociometric results will contribute to more sound educational decisions. Determining the best placement of exceptional children in the school program can be aided by the use of the sociometric test. For example, some studies (*32, 33*) have shown that mentally handicapped children are not socially accepted in the regular classroom. Since one of the reasons for placing these pupils in with their age mates of normal intelligence is to improve their social adjustment, these studies raise questions concerning the effectiveness of such procedures. Nevertheless, sociometric results can provide evidence on the relative influence of special classroom experiences and regular classroom experiences on the social adjustment of the exceptional child. In addition, the sociometric test can be used to identify those exceptional children needing special help with their social relationships and can be used again later to evaluate the effectiveness of the remedial steps taken.

Using sociometric results to evaluate the effectiveness of school practices can be applied to a variety of areas. Where special effort is made to integrate new pupils into class, and extra-class groups, the sociometric test will provide valuable evidence on how well the orientation procedures are working. The effectiveness of programs directed toward integrating minority groups into the school can be evaluated by observing the increase in choices to and from the minority group members. When a new school is consolidated, sociometric results will aid in determining how well the pupils from various areas are relating to each other and thus the extent to which a unified school population is developing. In some rural schools there is a distinct cleavage between transported and non-transported pupils. The extent to which this cleavage exists, as well as the effectiveness of procedures directed toward reducing this cleavage, can be determined by the use of the sociometric test. Thus, wherever special school programs are developed to bring about a better integration of individuals or groups, sociometric results can be used to evaluate the effectiveness of the programs.

The sociometric test can also provide information which is useful to the classroom teacher and the principal in dealing with pupils who are disciplinary problems. Knowing a pupil's social position in the group may partly explain his attention-seeking behavior. Identifying his chosen associates may provide clues to the attitudes and values underlying his difficulty in abiding by the school's regulations. Recognizing that a pupil is rejected by his peers may make it easier to understand his frequent truancy from school and his delinquent tendencies. Besides helping to clarify the behavior of disciplinary cases, sociometric results also provide a basis for determining the pupil's most favorable position in the group. Placing him with associates who will have a desirable influence on his behavior and assisting him to gain greater acceptance among the group members are important adjuncts to other remedial techniques.

In addition to using the sociometric test in dealing with special school problems pertinent to pupils, the sociometric technique can also be effectively applied to school personnel (*13*). Evaluating the integration of new teachers into the school system, organizing teacher committees, identifying leaders for supervisory positions, and evaluating procedures designed to develop a unified faculty, all lend themselves to the use of the sociometric test. Similarly, the school administrator will find the sociometric technique a useful research tool in studying problems of staff relationships, communication patterns, problems of morale and factors related to teaching effectiveness.

SOCIOMETRY AND ACTION RESEARCH

Recent emphasis on the desirability of having classroom teachers and supervisors use research techniques in the study of school problems has led to the importance of action research (*14*). In general, action research refers to the systematic study of practical school problems by those in a position to put the findings into action. It is not expected that the results of such research will be general enough to apply to similar situations in other schools. However, it is hoped that the findings will provide a general understading of how to cope with similar problems in the same school setting, in addition to solving the immediate problem being investigated. Thus, action research should contribute to the professional growth of the teacher as well as to improved school practices.

The sociometric test has a number of unique characteristics that makes it especially valuable and practical for use in action research. *First,* sociometric measurement can contribute to the study of a variety of school problems. As indicated above, it can play a useful role in studies of social adjustment, interpersonal relations, grouping procedures, integration of minority groups, learning and discipline problems, and many other areas where social relations are involved. *Second,* the simplicity with which the sociometric test can be constructed and the brief time required for administration increases its utility to the busy teacher and school administrator. The sociometric test can be administered in a relatively few minutes. Although the time required for analyzing and interpreting the results is a little longer than the construction and administration of the device, these procedures do not involve the pupils and therefore do not interfere with their school programs. *Third,* the flexible nature of the sociometric test makes it readily adaptable to a local school situation. In fact, proper use of the technique requires that it be adapted to the situation in which it is used. Thus, the directions, sociometric questions, and time of administration can be fit naturally into the school routine. *Fourth,* the sociometric test serves several specific purposes. The results of one administration of the sociometric test can be used both to diagnose the present social structure of a group and to serve as a basis for restructuring or rearranging the group. The same sociometric test can again be administered later to evaluate the effect of the rearrangement on the group structure. Thus the sociometric test can serve diagnostic, therapeutic, and evaluative functions while contributing to both instructional and research purposes. *Fifth,* since the sociometric test is a teacher-made instrument, there is no cost except the paper on which it is printed. This seems to be a special asset during this time of budget-conscious school personnel. *Sixth,* considerable research on the application of the sociometric test to school problems is already available in published form. Consequently, suggestions concerning research design and procedural techniques are readily available. This also makes it possible to compare local results with the findings on similar problems in other schools. Several of the later chapters in this book will present the research studies pertinent to the application of sociometric techniques to school problems.

LIMITATIONS OF THE SOCIOMETRIC TEST

In stressing the values and uses of the sociometric test in school settings the limitations of this technique are frequently overlooked. As with all innovations in school practice, the innovators are usually more enthusiastic than cautious, more positive than objective, and more optimistic than factual. A survey of the literature on the application of sociometry to schools will reveal relatively few articles (*16, 39, 41*) which mention the limitations of the sociometric test. Such uncritical acceptance of this relatively new technique will only hinder its effective use in school settings.

The limitations of the sociometric test and the necessary cautions in applying it to educational problems can be classified into several categories. First, the technique itself is limited in the kinds of information it can provide. Second, there are limitations or cautions in the construction and administration of the test. Third, there are limitations or cautions in the interpretation and application of the results. As noted, some of these limitations are inherent in the technique itself and can be recognized and taken into account only when the sociometric test is used. Others are limitations which can be controlled or corrected through basic understanding of sociometric procedures and skill in the interpretation and application of the results.

LIMITATIONS INHERENT IN THE SOCIOMETRIC TEST

The sociometric test measures the extent to which individuals are accepted by the other group members, and it reveals the internal social structure of the group. It presents this information with respect to certain selected criteria of choice, a fixed (or unlimited) number of choices, and for a given point in time. It does *not* indicate why some individuals are highly chosen and others are isolated, nor does it indicate the reason this particular social structure evolved rather than some other. Likewise, the sociometric results, by themselves, do not indicate how the sociometric status of individuals or the social structure of the group can be improved. Certainly, sociometric data provide clues for remedial action, but supplementary data are necessary if therapeutic procedures are to be effective. In short, sociometric measurement reveals the present status of individuals and groups and does not indicate how they got that way or what should be done to change the situation.

In addition, the sociometric results obtained from any one administration of the test reveal status and structure with regard to that specific test and that specific group. Variations in individual status and group structure are obtained when the directions vary, the number of choices is changed, different criteria of choice are used, when the same test is repeated later, or when the membership of the group is changed. This does not mean that interpretations beyond the immediate situation cannot be made. Research studies (*46*) have revealed the degree of stability that is obtained with varying numbers of choices, different criteria of choice, a repetition of the same test over varying periods of time, and a variation of group membership. Thus, within limits, certain interpretations and inferences can be drawn from the results of one sociometric test. However, it should be recognized that these interpretations and inferences are based on generalizations derived from sociometric research and are not applicable unless the sociometric procedures used are sufficiently controlled to provide somewhat comparable results. Thus, care in the construction and administration of the sociometric test is essential if the results are to be meaningful.

LIMITATIONS OF OR CAUTIONS IN THE CONSTRUCTION AND ADMINISTRATION OF THE SOCIOMETRIC TEST

These limitations are more aptly attributed to the users of the sociometric test than to the technique itself. Probably the most important and, surprisingly, the most neglected aspect of sociometric testing is that of selecting appropriate sociometric criteria of choice. Somehow the attitude has developed that as long as individuals are choosing associates for some purpose sociometric procedures are adequate. Thus, pupils have been asked to indicate with whom they would like to live on a South Sea Island, whom they like best, whom they respect most, and the like. Although choices based on such questions may have implications for social relations, interpretations of the choices are complicated by the fact that neither sociometric theory nor sociometric research reveals evidence which can provide meaning for the results. Consequently, sociometric results are of limited value unless the criteria of choice are carefully selected. A large part of the next chapter is devoted to this topic.

Although no standard procedure has been developed for administering the sociometric test, sociometric theory indicates cautions to be observed. These will also be considered in the next chapter. It will suffice here to point out that the interpretations that can be made from sociometric results are limited by the directions used and the administration procedures followed.

LIMITATIONS OF OR CAUTIONS IN INTERPRETING AND APPLYING SOCIOMETRIC RESULTS

Although some of the limitations associated with the interpretation and application of sociometric results have been stated or implied above, several others warrant consideration. Like the limitations mentioned under the construction and administration of the sociometric test, these limitations are due in large part to the uncritical acceptance of sociometric procedures and can be either eliminated or controlled. Below are some of the more common misinterpretations deriving from oversimplification of sociometric results and ignorance of the inherent limitations in the sociometric technique.

1. An individual who receives a large number of choices on a sociometric test (star) is frequently considered to be a leader and to have good personal adjustment. However, the sociometric results merely indicate that he is highly chosen by his associates for certain activities and presents no evidence concerning his emotional stability or his ability or power as a leader. To be sure, sociometric research has revealed that in general individuals with

high sociometric status are characterized as possessing those personal qualities associated with leadership and good personal adjustment. But to apply generalizations, based on inferred qualities related to a category of status, to individuals is at best a dubious procedure. In summary, an individual's sociometric status indicates his relation to the other group members. Supplementary evidence is needed to verify his leadership ability and his personal adjustment.

2. Receiving no choices on a sociometric test is commonly equated with maladjustment. Although such an individual has not established social relations with his peers, the sociometric test does not indicate why he is isolated. Here again sociometric research has indicated that, on the average, the isolate tends to be unhappy and to have problems of personal adjustment. However, in individual cases the isolate may be new to the group and, thus, has not had time to develop relations with other group members. In other instances isolated individuals may have constructive individual interests and not have the same personal needs for close social relations that other individuals have. Although social relations with others and status among peers is highly valued by the majority in our society, these values need not be universally accepted by all individuals. Nevertheless, to equate the sociometric position of isolation with personal maladjustment is invalid without supporting evidence.

3. Characterizing the highly rejected individual as a person of doubtful character or undesirable personal qualities is another hasty generalization not revealed directly by sociometric data. Rejection by peers may be due to lack of personal grooming, lack of social skill, the social position his family holds in the community, membership in a minority group, or similar factors not directly related to his personality. An individual may also be rejected if he has the courage to take an individual position which is opposed to the values and beliefs of the group. As with the isolate, equating the sociometric position of the rejectee with

preconceived notions of the characteristics of rejected individuals is extremely dangerous. Supplementary data are essential for adequate interpretation of the basis for rejection by peers.

Other limitations in the interpretation and application of sociometric results to educational problems may be attributed to untested assumptions in sociometric theory and to the limited amount of systematic research in educational settings. The assumption that certain types of social structure are better than others for educational purposes needs to be verified by more carefully controlled studies. Likewise, the specific influence of group status and structure on pupils' behavior, emotional problems, attitudes, and responsiveness to learning situations warrants extensive investigation. These are not limitations in the technique itself, but rather limitations in our knowledge of how to use the sociometric test most effectively in solving educational problems and in improving school practices.

SUPPLEMENTARY TECHNIQUES

Many of the limitations of the sociometric test arise from sole dependence on sociometric data as a means of studying group status and structure. Thus, these limitations can be eliminated or minimized by supplementing sociometric results with other sources of information. The desirability of supplementing sociometric procedures with other techniques of evaluation is not unique to sociometric measurement. Any method of measurement is limited in its applications and should be supported by other evidence, for its most effective use. In addition, combining sociometric data with supplementary techniques is in harmony with sound sociometric theory. Moreno (*43*) has consistently pointed out the desirability and, in many cases, the necessity of such a practice. Supplementary data are essential if sociometric results are to contribute effectively to the solution of educational problems and to improved school practices.

A number of related techniques are particularly well adapted to the study of group status and structure. These vary from controlled observation of the external structure and functioning of the group to carefully developed instruments designed to measure the social stimulus value of the personality of individual group members. Although some of these techniques are occasionally classified as sociometric procedures, they were not derived directly from sociometric theory and are therefore more aptly considered as related techniques. In many situations, however, they provide essential supplementary data which aid in the interpretation of sociometric results.

TEACHER-OBSERVATION METHODS

The skilled observer can learn a great deal about the external structure and functioning of a group through the use of systematic observational methods. One technique commonly used is that of making an interaction analysis chart. This chart indicates which members of the group participated in a designated activity, with whom they interacted both physically and verbally, and the nature of the interaction that took place. Categories of individual response and types of interaction have been developed (*26*) which simplify the process of recording and analyzing the interaction of group members. Although the complexities of this technique limit its use by the busy classroom teacher, combining it with time sampling procedures would make it a feasible classroom technique. This simply means that the classroom teacher would systematically observe and record the interaction of the group members for brief periods of time at regular intervals throughout the day. This technique assumes that the observations will cover various situations and activities so that the samples of interaction are typical of the external structure and functioning of the group. An interaction analysis chart will provide clues to the formation of the internal structure of the group, as well as information concerning the actual associations of individual pupils with various sociometric positions.

A more common observational technique used by classroom teachers is the anecdotal record. This is merely a record of the teacher's observations of a pupil's behavior in a given situation. Usually the teacher records exactly what the pupil said and did that was significant to the purpose of the observation. Where anecdotal records are used as a supplement to sociometric data, incidents that clarify a pupil's relations with his peers would be especially pertinent. Does he withdraw from the group? Is he overly aggressive in his social relations? With whom does he play or share hobbies? Is he a good sport in group games? How effectively does he participate in group work? These and similar questions can be answered by careful observation and objective recording of pertinent incidents of behavior in specific situations. A systematic record of such observations helps clarify the reasons an individual is accepted or rejected by his peers and provides data for future remedial action.

A standardized record of teachers' observations may be obtained through the use of various types of rating scales. Since the behavior to be observed is defined by items in the rating scale, this method has the obvious advantage of presenting comparable data from several teachers. The average ratings of a number of teachers on items like the following will provide fairly reliable information concerning a pupil's participation in groups.

To what extent does this pupil participate in group discussions?

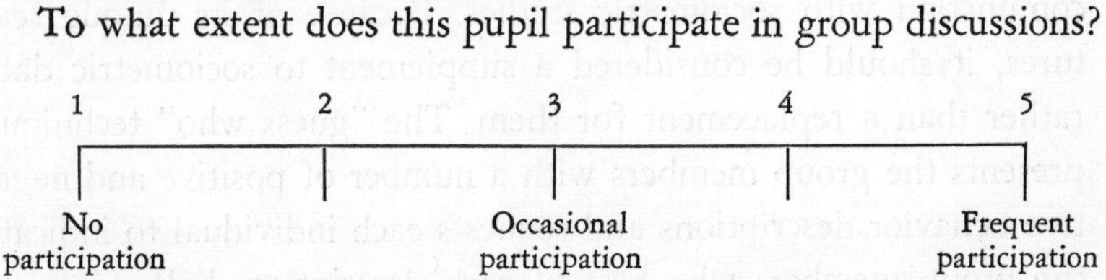

The rating scale differs from anecdotal records in that the categories of behavior are predetermined. Although this restricts the type of information obtained, judgments concerning the pupil's social relations in various groups can be compared. Thus, the rating scale provides unique, supplementary data which are useful in interpreting and applying sociometric results.

PUPIL-REPORT METHODS

In addition to the observational methods used by teachers, there are some supplementary techniques which depend on pupils for their information. One of the least structured methods is the personal interview. It is sometimes helpful to follow up the administration of the sociometric test with an interview of each person. Such an interview could provide information on the reasons certain pupils were chosen as associates while others were rejected or ignored. Although the reported reasons for choice are limited by the individual's conscious awareness of his reasons for choosing and his ability to report accurately, the interview does provide clues concerning the acceptance and rejection choices of individual group members.

A more systematic method of determining the reasons for an individual's sociometric status in a group is that of the "guess who" technique. The procedures used in this technique are very similar to sociometric procedures and thus, the technique is frequently confused with sociometric testing. However, this method was originally developed by Hartshorne, May, and Maller (*24*) for use in their character studies. Its development was independent of the sociometric movement and only recently has it been used in conjunction with sociometric studies. Because of its unique features, it should be considered a supplement to sociometric data rather than a replacement for them. The "guess who" technique presents the group members with a number of positive and negative behavior descriptions and requests each individual to indicate the group members who best fit each description. Following are positive and negative behavior descriptions for *friendliness* (*36*) taken from a form used in a research study at the sixth- and seventh-grade levels.

1. "Here is someone who is very friendly, who has lots of friends, who is nice to everybody."
2. "Here is someone who does not care to make friends, who is bashful about being friendly, or who does not seem to have many friends."

Similar items may be developed for cheerfulness, sportsmanship, enthusiasm, and the like. Any behavior description that seems pertinent to the purpose of using this technique may be incorporated into the items. For each positive and negative behavior description, individuals are usually permitted to name as many group members as they desire. Young children are usually asked to "guess who" the description best fits. However at the junior and senior high school levels, and at the college level, it is more appropriate to leave out the "guess who" aspect and merely ask the pupils to indicate which group members best fit the description.

The "guess who" technique is usually scored by totaling the number of mentions each pupil receives on each of the behavior descriptions. Since the positive descriptions indicate socially desirable characteristics and the negative descriptions indicate socially undesirable characteristics, the number of mentions on positive and negative descriptions are usually summed algebraically to provide one score for each behavior characteristic. The extent to which each characteristic is descriptive of an individual is determined by the resulting score. The strength of the characteristic is assumed to be roughly equivalent to the number of mentions received on that characteristic. Thus, the data obtained by the "guess who" technique provide a measure of each individual's reputation among the other group members. Combining such results with sociometric data will provide valuable insights concerning the reasons for the acceptance and rejection of individual pupils.

In addition to the above techniques, there are numerous adaptations and modifications of the sociometric test. A common one is that of asking group members *with whom they do associate* for a given activity rather than *with whom they would like to associate.* This modification is designed to obtain a measure of the existing social structure, which would serve as a check on the teacher's observation of the functioning of the group. Another common modification of sociometric procedures is that of having individuals rate each of the other group members on a five-point scale indicating the extent to which they would like them as a friend. This is a combination of near-sociometric procedures and rating techniques. Although this method is similar to the sociometric test, it has been reported (*3*) that the resulting data do not correspond closely with sociometric results. A recent adaptation and extension of the sociometric test is that of relational analysis (*53*). This includes the regular choosing on a sociometric question, as well as predictions by the chooser, as to who will choose him. Measuring the ability of an individual to perceive his sociometric position in the group and the feelings of acceptance and rejection directed toward him provides useful information on his ability to perceive the social characteristics of self and others. Although relational analysis was developed for use in social perception studies, it should also provide valuable clues concerning the problems of social adjustment experienced by individual group members.

The above adaptaions and modifications of the sociometric test, as well as others, have resulted from a desire to broaden the scope of sociometric measurement. This is a desirable and necessary move, if all of the complexities of group status, structure, and development are to be uncovered. However, the experimental nature of such modifications and the lack of supporting theory limit their value as tools for the classroom teacher. Thus, until further evidence is obtained, the classroom teacher might consider them experimental techniques, supplementary to the regular sociometric test.

In this section only those techniques uniquely adapted to an evaluation of group status and structure have been discussed. Of course evaluation techniques such as measures of intelligence, achievement, and the like, will present additional information concerning an individual's characteristics and, thus, provide further hunches about his acceptance or rejection by group members. In special cases the classroom teacher may want to make a complete case study in order to identify factors contributing to an individual pupil's sociometric position in the group. Although this section has been limited to the more obvious supplementary techniques, the classroom teacher should make use of any source of information that contributes to a more effective interpretation and application of sociometric results.

SUMMARY

The sociometric test is a technique for measuring the extent to which individuals are accepted by other group members and for determining the internal structure of a group. In its administration, it requires individuals to choose a given number of associates for some group situation or activity. The sociometric test was first administered in a school setting by the founder of sociometry, Jacob L. Moreno. An analysis of the results revealed an underlying social structure which was not readily apparent to the teachers. Since that original application of sociometric data to school problems, the sociometric test has found widespread use in educational settings. Both theoretical and research findings have contributed to the need for methods of measuring group structure. The simplicity and convenience of the sociometric test have made it an ideal tool for the study of group structure in the classroom.

Proper use of the sociometric test requires an understanding of specialized terminology and the theoretical assumptions underlying its use. When properly applied the sociometric test can contribute to the solution of many types of educational problems. Sociometric data provide the basis for improving the social adjustment of individuals, for improving the social structure of groups, for organizing classroom groups, and for dealing with specific school problems. In addition, the sociometric test serves as an excellent tool for action research in the classroom.

As with any technique of evaluation, the sociometric test has limitations which should be recognized if it is to be used most effectively. The majority of these limitations, however, can be minimized or eliminated by combining sociometric results with data obtained from supplementary techniques. It is also possible to control the limitations of this technique by careful construction and administration of the sociometric test. A detailed description of the most effective procedures for constructing and administering the sociometric test will be found in the following chapter.

REFERENCES

1. Amundson, C. L., "Increasing Interpersonal Relationships in the High School with the Aid of Sociometric Procedures," *Group Psychotherapy,* 1954, *6:*183–188.
2. Anderson, H. H., and Brewer, J. E., "Studies of Teachers' Classroom Personalities II (Effects of Teachers' Dominative and Integrative Contacts on Children's Classroom Behavior)," *Applied Psychological Monographs,* No. 8, American Psychological Association, Stanford University Press, 1946.
3. Ausubel, D. P., Schiff, H. M., and Gasser, E. B., "A Preliminary Study of Developmental Trends in Sociempathy: Accuracy of Perception of Own and Others' Sociometric Status," *Child Development,* 1952, *23:*111–128.
4. Barker, R. G., "The Social Interrelations of Strangers and Acquaintances," *Sociometry,* 1942, *5:*169–179.
5. Blair, G. M., Jones, R. S., and Simpson, R. H., *Educational Psychology,* New York, The Macmillan Company, 1954.
6. Bonney, M. E., "The Constancy of Sociometric Scores and Their Relationship to Teacher Judgments of Social Success and to Personality Self-Ratings," *Sociometry,* 1943, *6:*409–424.
7. Bonney, M. E., "Personality Traits of Socially Successful and Socially Unsuccessful Children," *Journal of Educational Psychology,* 1943, *34:*449–472.

8. Bonney, M. E., "Sociometric Study of Agreement Between Teacher Judgments and Student Choices," *Sociometry,* 1947, *10:*133–146.

9. Bonney, M. E., "Values of Sociometric Studies in the Classroom," *Sociometry,* 1943, *6:*251–254.

10. Bronfenbrenner, U., "The Measurement of Sociometric Status, Structure and Development," *Sociometry Monographs,* No. 6, New York, Beacon House, 1945.

11. Buck, J. V., "The Sociometric Technique and the Teaching of General Science," *School Science and Mathematics,* 1952, *52:*456–461.

12. Cartwright, D., and Zander, A., *Group Dynamics,* Evanston, Illinois, Row, Peterson and Company, 1953.

13. Cooper, D. H., "The Potentialities of Sociometry for School Administration," *Sociometry,* 1947, *10:*111–121.

14. Corey, S. M., *Action Research to Improve School Practices,* New York, Teachers College, Columbia University, 1953.

15. Cronbach, L. J., *Educational Psychology,* New York, Harcourt, Brace and Company, 1954.

16. Dahlke, H. O., and Monahan, T. O., "Problems in the Application of Sociometry to Schools," *School Review,* 1949, *57:*223–234.

17. Gage, N. L., Leavitt, G. S., and Stone, G. C., "Teachers' Understanding of Their Pupils and Pupils' Ratings of Their Teachers," *Psychological Monographs,* No. 21, American Psychological Association, Washington, D.C., 1955.

18. Gronlund, N. E., "The Accuracy of Teachers' Judgments Concerning the Sociometric Status of Sixth-Grade Pupils," *Sociometry Monographs,* No. 25, New York, Beacon House, 1951.

19. Gronlund, N. E., "Acquaintance Span and Sociometric Status," *Sociometry,* 1955, *18:*62–68.

20. Gronlund, N. E., "The General Ability to Judge Sociometric Status: Elementary Student Teachers' Sociometric Perceptions of Classmates and Pupils," *Journal of Educational Psychology,* 1956, *47:*147–157.

21. Gronlund, N. E., "The Relative Ability of Homeroom Teachers

and Special Subject Teachers to Judge the Social Acceptability of Pre-Adolescent Pupils," *Journal of Educational Research,* 1955, *48:*381–391.

22. Gronlund, N. E., and Whitney, A. P., "The Relation Between Teachers' Judgments of Pupils' Sociometric Status and Intelligence," *Elementary School Journal,* 1958, *59:*264–268.
23. Hare, A. P., Borgatta, E. F., and Bales, R. F., *Small Groups,* New York, Alfred A. Knopf, 1955.
24. Hartshorne, H., May, M. A., and Maller, J. B., *Studies in the Nature of Character,* New York, The Macmillan Company, 1929.
25. Havighurst, R. J., *Developmental Tasks and Education,* New York, Longmans, Green and Company, 1950.
26. Heyns, R. W., and Lippitt, R., "Systematic Observational Techniques," Chapter 10, in G. Lindzey (ed.), *Handbook of Social Psychology,* Cambridge, Massachusetts, Addison-Wesley Publishing Company, 1954.
27. Hunt, J. McV., and Solomon, R. L., "The Stability and Some Correlates of Group-Status in a Summer-Camp Group of Young Boys," *American Journal of Psychology,* 1942, *55:*22–45.
28. Jennings, H. H., *Leadership and Isolation,* New York, Longmans, Green and Company, 1950.
29. Jennings, H. H., "Leadership and Sociometric Choice," *Sociometry,* 1947, *10:*32–49.
30. Jennings, H. H., "Sociometric Grouping in Relation to Child Development," Chapter 13, in C. M. Tryon (ed.), *Fostering Mental Health in Our Schools,* Washington, D.C., Association for Supervision and Curriculum Development, N.E.A., 1950.
31. Jennings, H. H., "A Sociometric Study of Emotional and Social Expansiveness," Chapter 30, in R. G. Barker, J. S. Kounin, and J. F. Wright (eds.), *Child Behavior and Development,* New York, McGraw-Hill Book Company, 1943.
32. Johnson, G. O., "A Study of the Social Position of Mentally Handicapped Children in the Regular Grades," *American Journal of Mental Deficiency,* 1950, *55:*60–89.
33. Johnson, G. O., and Kirk, S. A., "Are Mentally Handicapped

Children Segregated in the Regular Grades?" *Journal of Exceptional Children,* 1950, *17:*65–68, 87–88.

34. Kerstetter, L. M., and Sargent, J., "Reassignment Therapy in the Classroom," *Sociometry,* 1940, *3:*293–306.
35. Kuhlen, R. G., and Lee, B. J., "Personality Characteristics and Social Acceptability in Adolescence," *Journal of Educational Psychology,* 1943, *34:*321–340.
36. Laughlin, F., *The Peer Status of Sixth- and Seventh-Grade Children,* New York, Bureau of Publications, Teachers College, Columbia University, 1954.
37. Lindgren, H. C., *Educational Psychology in the Classroom,* New York, John Wiley and Sons, Inc., 1956.
38. Lindgren, H. C., *Psychology of Personal and Social Adjustment,* New York, American Book Company, 1953.
39. Lindzey, G., and Borgatta, E. F., "Sociometric Measurement," Chapter 11, in G. Lindzey (ed.), *Handbook of Social Psychology,* Cambridge, Massachusetts, Addison-Wesley Publishing Company, 1954.
40. Lippitt, R., and White, R., "The Social Climate of Children's Groups," Chapter 28, in R. G. Barker, J. S. Kounin, and J. F. Wright (eds.), *Child Behavior and Development,* New York, McGraw-Hill Book Company, 1943.
41. Loomis, C. P., and Pepinsky, H. B., "Sociometry, 1937–1947; Theory and Methods," *Sociometry,* 1948, *11:*262–287.
42. Moreno, J. L., *Who Shall Survive?* Washington, D.C., Nervous and Mental Disease Publishing Company, 1934.
43. Moreno, J. L., *Who Shall Survive?* New York, Beacon House, 1953.
44. Moreno, J. L., and Jennings, H. H., "Sociometric Methods of Grouping and Regrouping with Reference to Authoritative and Democratic Methods of Grouping," *Sociometry,* 1944, *7:*397–414.
45. Moreno, J. L., Jennings, H. H., and Stockton, R., " Sociometry in the Classroom," *Sociometry,* 1943, *6:*425–428.
46. Mouton, J. S., Blake, R. R., and Fruchter, B., "The Reliability of Sociometric Measures," *Sociometry,* 1955, *18:*7–48.

47. Mouton, J. S., Blake, R. R., and Fruchter, B., "The Validity of Sociometric Responses," *Sociometry,* 1955, *18:*181–206.
48. Northway, M. L., "Outsiders: A Study of the Personality Patterns of Children Least Acceptable to Their Age Mates," *Sociometry,* 1944, *7:*10–25.
49. Olson, W. C., *Child Development,* Boston, D. C. Heath and Company, 1949.
50. Redl, F., and Wattenberg, W. W., *Mental Hygiene in Teaching,* New York, Harcourt, Brace and Company, 1951.
51. Shaffer, L. F., and Shoben, E. J., *The Psychology of Adjustment,* Boston, Houghton Mifflin Company, 1956.
52. Shoobs, N. E., "Sociometry in the Classroom," *Sociometry,* 1947, *10:*154–164.
53. Tagiuri, R., "Relational Analysis: An Extension of Sociometric Method with Emphasis upon Social Perception," *Sociometry,* 1952, *15:*91–104.
54. Thrasher, F. M., and Kerstetter, L. M., "Sociometry and an Activity Program on the University Level," *Sociometry,* 1947, *10:*178–185.
55. Zeleny, L. D., "Status: Its Measurement and Control in Education," *Sociometry,* 1941, *4:*193–204.

PART I

THE METHODS AND TECHNIQUES OF SOCIOMETRIC TESTING

CHAPTER 2

CONSTRUCTING AND ADMINISTERING THE SOCIOMETRIC TEST

The relative ease with which the sociometric test can be constructed and administered has contributed to its widespread use by classroom teachers. Basically the construction of the sociometric test involves the selection of appropriate choosing situations (sociometric criteria), a determination of the number of choices to allot for each criterion, and the development of directions that will assure valid responses. Although little time and skill are required for these procedures, it is important that the implications of the procedures be carefully considered. For example, some sociometric criteria may be satisfactory for organizing classroom groups but still provide little information on the extent to which individuals are socially acceptable to the group. Likewise, asking pupils to give their first choice only may provide an indication of their strongest preference but may not provide sufficient information to give a clear picture of the classroom social structure. Thus the use to be made of the results must be considered when developing a sociometric test. Care in construction usually leads to sociometric results that serve several useful purposes (*25*).

IMPORTANCE OF SOCIOMETRIC CRITERIA

Since the crux of the sociometric technique is based on the individual's *choice* of associates, the selection of *criteria of choice* is the most important consideration in the development of a sociometric test. Unfortunately, this aspect of sociometric testing has too frequently been neglected by users of sociometry. With little thought given to the selection of criteria, some investigators have measured superficial and fleeting aspects of the group structure. Others have used such general and vague criteria that the nature of the choosing situation was not clear. Part of this lack of concern with the selection of sociometric criteria has been due to misinterpretations of sociometric theory and part of it has been due to the lack of research evidence on the value of different criteria. It has been consistently stressed by sociometrists that any group activity or situation may provide the basis for a sociometric criterion. Although this is true, some situations and activities provide for the measurement of more permanent aspects of group structure, and elicit more spontaneous and truthful responses (*22*). The selection of such criteria will increase the meaningfulness and the general usefulness of the sociometric results.

TYPES OF SOCIOMETRIC CRITERIA

The numerous and varied opportunities for pupils to choose associates is sometimes confusing to the classroom teacher who is trying to select the most appropriate criteria for a sociometric test. Keeping in mind the purpose for which the test is to be given, a consideration of the following contrasting types of criteria may be helpful in making the selection.

GENERAL VS. SPECIFIC CRITERIA

A general criterion is one that indicates an area of activity but does not specify the particular bases of interaction. The most widely used criteria in this category are those based on choice of *seating companion, work companion,* and *play companion.* In fact these three choice situations are general enough to be used at any grade level and encompass most activities included in the school day. In a dormitory situation, such as at a boarding school or college, general criteria based on choice of *roommate* and *dining companion* have also been used. It will be noted that choices on general criteria imply a desire for social proximity in the major areas of the pupil's life sphere.

In contrast to general criteria, a specific criterion is one that indicates a very limited basis for social interaction. Illustrations of such criteria would include choice of associates to work with on arithmetic problems, to play basketball with, to dance with, to review history with, and the like. The number of available specific criteria is as numerous as the diverse situations and activities that occur in the pupil's daily life. It should be recognized, however, that the specific nature of such criteria often restricts the interpretations that can be made of the sociometric results.

STRONG VS. WEAK CRITERIA

Although this classification is closely related to the one above, there are some important differences. A strong criterion reveals the more basic and permanent social relationships existing in a group, whereas a weak criterion reflects the superficial and fleeting aspects of the group structure (*22*). The illustrations used for general criteria, above, would likewise serve as examples of strong criteria, since they generally measure basic and permanent aspects of the social relationships among pupils. The situation also influences the strength of the criterion, however, and therefore must be considered. Choice of work companions, for example, would not serve as a strong criterion of choice where students were not permitted to work together. Thus the choice situations must be realistic as well as basic if sociometric criteria are to be strong.

Weak criteria are those based on temporary situations or those concerned with activities where choice of associates is of little interest to the group members. Temporary situations would include such activities as the "school party." Criteria on which group members have little desire to choose associates are usually those where the individuals lack the social development or the experience to make such choices. Asking fifth-grade pupils to choose companions for social dancing would illustrate a weak criterion in this area. Sociometric results based on weak criteria are usually of little value and may actually be harmful if misinterpreted.

ACTUAL VS. HYPOTHETICAL CRITERIA

The main distinction between these contrasting types of criteria is whether the situation is "real" or "assumed." For most classroom and school situations it is possible to use real choice situations. This implies, of course, that the sociometric results will be used to rearrange the groups. Thus, choices for seating companion will result in a new seating arrangement, choices for work companion will result in pupils working with chosen classmates, and the like. Although the use of actual criteria is highly desirable, and expected in terms of sociometric theory, there are times when it is necessary for diagnostic or research purposes to use hypothetical criteria. In this instance it is especially important that the criteria at least reflect choice situations that are highly probable. Asking pupils to indicate those classmates they would prefer in their section *if* the class were divided into two groups is realistic in terms of probability, even though it is hypothetical. Many similar choice situations may provide valid sociometric data. However, the farther the choices get from actual situations the less assurance there is that the pupils will be motivated to give conscientious responses.

PERSONAL VS. SOCIAL CRITERIA

The writings of Jennings (*16, 17*) have suggested that there may be two aspects to group structure: one based on personal criteria related to informal situations and the other based on social, and less personal, criteria related to more formal situations. Examples of personal criteria include choices of *seating companions, roommates, associates for leisure-time activities,* and similar situations where no goal-directed activities are indicated. The resulting group structure is called *psychegroup* and is assumed to represent choices mainly on personal bases. In contrast, social criteria reflect common goal-directed activities such as *working together on a group project.* It is assumed that choices on such criteria are influenced more by the contributions individuals can make to group work and less by their personal qualities. This type of social structure is called a *sociogroup.*

Although some criteria call for choices on a more personal basis while others reflect goal-oriented activities, there is a question (*21*) as to whether the resulting social structures represent different types of groups. Choices on personal and social criteria have shown considerable overlap (*11*) when used in educational settings. This would seem to indicate that in school situations personal and social criteria represent directions of emphasis rather than measures of distinct aspects of the group structure. Consequently, in the selection of sociometric criteria, it should be recognized that personal and social factors operate together in any sociometric choosing situation and that their relative influence varies with the nature of the criterion. Probably both types of criteria should be used when a comprehensive analysis of the group structure is desired.

TWO-WAY VS. ONE-WAY CRITERIA

A distinction in sociometric criteria that has been frequently overlooked is that between two-way criteria and one-way criteria (*8*). A two-way criterion is one on which mutual association is possible. Any of the common criteria having to do with living, working, or playing together would fit into this category. The important characteristic is that individuals can choose each other for the same activity and mutual relationships are revealed.

One-way criteria do not request choices for mutual association, but rather choices of representation. Having individuals indicate their preferences for student council representatives, class officers, and other leadership positions would be included in this category. There is some evidence that choices on one-way criteria provide different results than choices on two-way criteria (*10, 14*). It has been suggested (*4*) that choices on one-way criteria are based more on the individual's ability to "get things done," whereas skill in interpersonal relationships has greater influence on two-way criteria. Nevertheless, it should be pointed out that mutual relationships cannot be determined from one-way criteria, since mutual association is neither implied nor necessary in the choice process.

Other contrasting types of sociometric criteria may exist but these are the main ones suggested by the literature. Some teachers have used such questions as "Whom do you like best?" or "Who are your friends?" These questions are not truly sociometric, however, since they do not indicate a clear criterion of choice. They are commonly referred to as *near-sociometric* procedures. Although they might serve useful purposes in certain research studies, they are of doubtful value to the classroom teacher.

SELECTION OF SOCIOMETRIC CRITERIA

Which of the above types of criteria to select for a sociometric test depends mainly on the purposes for giving the test and on the opportunities for social interaction available to the group members. If the sociometric results are to be used for organizing temporary classroom groups, such as for an art project, school party, trip to a museum, a specific criterion limited to the activity could be used. The resulting choices would provide a basis for organizing the classroom groups. However, because of the temporary nature of the groups and the specific characteristics of the choosing situations, generalizations concerning the social structure of the group or the social acceptability of individual group members would be unwarranted. Criteria based on specific and transitory situations tend to have little diagnostic value, even though they are based on realistic choosing situations. Their diagnostic value can be increased by using a large number of such criteria, but the results are cumbersome to work with if the choices on each criterion are analyzed separately and there is some question concerning the validity of combining choices based on diverse specific situations.

General criteria based on the more permanent aspects of the group structure tend to provide the most stable and generally useful results. Such criteria as *work companion, play companion,* and *seating companion* have provided measures of group structures that changed very little over a period of several months (*6*). Other studies (*11, 12*) have also shown that results based on such criteria provide a fairly stable and general measure of an individual's acceptance by the group. It seems that sociometric choices on general criteria are less influenced by temporary, situational factors usually associated with specific activities.

In using general criteria there is some danger of having the choices seem less "real" to the individual. However, this can be avoided by careful wording of the directions. Before choosing work companions, for example, the pupils could be told that they will work in groups from time to time on different aspects of the course work. The fact that the results will be used to form work groups makes the choices realistic, even though the specific work activity is not indicated. Thus the strength and reality of the choosing situation are maintained without the limiting qualities of a specific criterion.

Several other general criteria might be used, in addition to those on seating, work, and play. If field trips are a common occurrence, the pupils could be asked to indicate which classmates they would prefer as companions on field trips. If classroom committees are used, the pupils could select companions for committee work. In general, any choosing situation requiring social proximity could serve as a basis for a sociometric test. However a sociometric criterion will provide the most valid results for both interpreting the social structure of the group and for evaluating the social acceptability of individual group members, if it possesses the following characteristics:

1. Clearly indicates the nature of the activity or situation for which the individual is choosing associates.
2. Is based on an activity or situation familiar to the group members and one on which they have real opportunity for association.
3. Is general enough to minimize the influence of situational factors and skills associated with specific activities.
4. Is based on relationships that are strong, fundamental, and relatively permanent.
5. Provides for reciprocal choice and mutual association among the group members.

In addition, the criterion should be little influenced by environmental factors, unless environmental influence is being specifically investigated. Choice of week-end house guests, for example, would be strongly influenced by socioeconomic status. Choice of companions to attend the local theater would be affected by social proximity in the community. Environmental factors will, of course, influence choices on any sociometric criterion. However, careful selection of the criterion will minimize the extent to which sociometric results are contaminated by such extraneous factors.

NUMBER OF CRITERIA TO USE

Generally, the use to be made of the sociometric results plus the nature of the criteria will aid in determining the number of criteria to use. For sociometric grouping (*18*) or for research purposes (7) one criterion may be sufficient. However, for evaluating interpersonal relationships and for determining the group acceptance of individual pupils several criteria are usually necessary. An attempt should be made to include criteria which cover the main aspects of the group members' personal and social relationships. Thus, if general criteria such as seating, play, and work are used, three criteria may be sufficient. Where highly specific criteria are necessary, a much larger number would be required to obtain the same coverage. Although there is no research evidence on this point, it would be expected that the use of fewer criteria would result in more spontaneous and discriminating responses.

USE OF NEGATIVE CRITERIA

Asking individuals to indicate those whom they would *least* prefer as associates for some activity or situation has generally been avoided in the classroom. It has been pointed out (*24*) that the use of such criteria has resulted in expressed resentment among group members. If negative criteria make individuals more conscious of their feelings of rejection, neither the emotional development of the individuals nor the social development of the group will be benefited. Consequently, the use of such rejection choices should be eliminated from most classroom testing situations.

The use of negative criteria is sometimes essential, however, for certain teaching and research purposes. For example, locating conflicts among individuals may be a necessary step in understanding and coping with classroom hostility. Likewise, detecting unexpressed feelings of rejection might be needed in the evaluation of attempts to integrate minority group members. Where such situations require the use of negative criteria, it is best to permit rather than to require rejection choices. This approach saves pupils from feeling that they must reject someone, and it provides a more realistic measure of the extent to which feelings of rejection are present in the classroom. The disturbing effects of negative criteria can be further reduced by asking the pupils to indicate which pupils they would choose *last* for the activity, rather than have them indicate which pupils they do *not* want as associates.

SELECTING NUMBER OF CHOICES TO USE

The number of choices allotted to each sociometric criterion may be fixed or unlimited. Where an evaluation of the emotional or social expansiveness of individuals is important, the use of an unlimited number is required. Here the emphasis is on the chooser and the number of choices he gives to others, rather than the number of choices he receives from others. Such information is useful in evaluating the individual's desire and drive for social interaction. Except for such special purposes, however, using a fixed number of choices has both statistical and practical advantages (*6*).

The question of how many choices to allot for each sociometric criterion is influenced partly by the age of the subjects but mainly by the stability of the sociometric results. Studies at the nursery school (*9, 19, 20*) and kindergarten (*1*) levels have indicated that there is very little discrimination beyond the first choice with these age groups. During the early elementary school years, children have been able to make at least three choices for each criterion (*2, 3*). From the third grade on, experience has shown that five choices can be made without difficulty. Since studies have also reported that five choices provide the most stable sociometric results (*12, 13, 23*), it is suggested that this number be used at the later elementary school, high school, and college levels.

Moreno's (*22*) original use of two choices for seating companion in his study of school children led to the suggestion that the number of choices should fit the situation. That is, three choices should be allotted if groups of four are being formed, while two choices should be allotted when forming groups of three. Although this seems to make the choices more realistic, in actual practice it does not. Attempting to arrange groups on the basis of two or three choices makes it difficult, and at times impossible, to satisfy even one choice for all pupils. Studies show that a large number of pupils tend to choose the same few highly chosen individuals

(5). The greater flexibility provided by five choices enables the teacher to organize groups in which all pupils have some choices satisfied, and the majority can be placed with two or more of their chosen associates. If the reason for five choices is made clear to the pupils, the reality of the choosing is easily maintained and the general usefulness of the results is actually increased.

THE SOCIOMETRIC FORM

The sociometric test is a flexible procedure which does not require a formalized test form. Some teachers prefer to give oral directions and to have the pupils record their choices on a blank sheet of paper. Others provide the pupils with an alphabetical list of the class members and ask them to merely check the pupils whom they would choose. Both of these methods are entirely satisfactory, as long as the directions and the choice criteria are carefully developed and clearly presented. However, such informal methods frequently lead to careless or incomplete directions and to unclear statements of choice. This can be prevented by the development of a sociometric form which may be administered directly to the pupils or which may serve as a guide to the teacher's more informal procedures.

The sociometric form should contain detailed directions, clear statements of choice, and a place for the pupils to record their responses. The directions and the choice criteria, of course, must be adapted to the age level of the group and to the situation in which the form is to be used. Figure 1 (page 50) illustrates a form that has been used at the later elementary school level.

Although this sociometric form was designed for a specific situation, the directions illustrate several important points. First it should be noted that the word "test" is not mentioned. Any reference to testing in the directions would probably distort the meaning of the choices to the pupils. Instead the directions indicate to the pupils the opportunity they have for helping in the arrange-

Name .... Date ....

During the next few weeks we will be changing our seats around, working in small groups and playing some group games. Now that we all know each other by name, you can help me arrange groups that work and play best together. You can do this by writing the names of the children you would like *to have sit near you, to have work with you,* and *to have play with you.* You may choose anyone in this room you wish, including those pupils who are absent. Your choices will not be seen by anyone else. Give first name and initial of last name.

Make your choices carefully so the groups will be the way you really want them. I will try to arrange the groups so that each pupil gets at least two of his choices. Sometimes it is hard to give everyone his first few choices so be sure to make five choices for each question.

Remember!

1. Your choices must be from pupils in this room, including those who are absent.
2. You should give the first name and the initial of the last name.
3. You should make all five choices for each question.
4. You may choose a pupil for more than one group if you wish.
5. Your choices will *not be seen* by anyone else.

I would choose to *sit near* these children:

1. .... 3. ....
2. .... 4. ....
5. ....

I would choose to *work with* these children:

1. .... 3. ....
2. .... 4. ....
5. ....

I would choose to *play with* these children:

2. .... 3. ....
1. .... 4. ....
5. ....

FIGURE 1. Sociometric Form Used at Later Elementary School Level.

ment of classroom groups. Thus it becomes a natural part of the classroom planning, and the possibility of spontaneous and truthful responses is increased.

In addition to indicating what use will be made of the choices, the directions also state when the choices will be put into effect, what the restrictions are on the choosing situation (i.e., anyone *in this room*), and how the choices are to be recorded. Equally important is the stress on the confidential nature of the responses and the importance of making all five choices for each question. These general points should be included in the directions for any sociometric test. However, the exact wording of the directions is to be determined by the specific situation and by the age of the pupils being tested. All promises made to pupils in the directions (i.e., arranging groups, keeping choices confidential, etc.), of course, must be kept.

Care in the construction of the sociometric form will result in ease of administration and will increase the probability of obtaining valid and useful sociometric data.

ADMINISTERING THE SOCIOMETRIC TEST

The classroom teacher is usually in the best position to administer a sociometric test to his pupils. He knows the extent to which they are acquainted with each other, and he has already developed working relations with them. Thus it is just a matter of incorporating the test administration into the daily schedule. If the pupils are accustomed to making some choices in the planning of classroom activities, they will consider responding to the sociometric test part of the classroom routine. Under such conditions, no special attention needs to be directed toward the administration of the sociometric test. Making sure the directions are clearly understood is generally sufficient to obtain spontaneous and truthful responses.

For certain purposes, such as for a research study or for a schoolwide testing program, it may be necessary to have someone other than the classroom teacher administer the sociometric test. When this is done, the test takes on special significance in the eyes of the pupil. He realizes that it is not a part of the normal classroom routine and he may feel reluctant to express his choices to a stranger. This reluctance is increased if the classroom contains minority groups or other bases for social cleavage (*22*).

When an outside examiner administers the test, it is important that a warm-up period precede the making of sociometric choices. This warm-up period should be devoted to developing rapport with the pupils; to explaining the purpose of the sociometric test and the use to be made of the results; to stressing the confidential nature of the choices; and to encouraging the pupils to make spontaneous and truthful responses. Time should be allowed for questions and discussion. The length of the warm-up period varies with different groups but generally lasts about ten or fifteen minutes. It should not be terminated until the examiner thinks that he has developed a feeling of mutual confidence with the pupils and that they feel free to respond to the sociometric test.

TEST PROCEDURES

Individual interviews are necessary in testing pupils below the fourth-grade level. This is generally done by having the pupils come to the teacher's desk one at a time. Although the procedure should be kept informal and casual, the teacher must be careful to give each child the same directions for choosing. This can be facilitated by using the sociometric form as an interview guide.

Group testing is generally used at, and beyond, the fourth-grade level. The pupils may record their choices on a sociometric form, on an alphabetical list of class members, or on a blank sheet of paper. Regardless of the procedure used, the teacher should be certain that the directions and the statements of choice are clear to the pupils. It is usually desirable to give the directions orally and to permit the pupils to ask questions, even if written directions are stated on the sociometric form. This will clarify the procedure and help allay fears concerned with the expression of preferences toward others.

WHEN TO ADMINISTER SOCIOMETRIC TESTS

The use to be made of the results determines, to some extent, when a sociometric test should be administered. If the results are to be used for sociometric grouping only, the test should be given when realistic grouping situations arise. However, if changes in the social structure of the group or the social acceptability of individual pupils is to be evaluated, the sociometric test needs to be administered periodically.

The first sociometric test should not be administered until the group members have had an opportunity to become acquainted with each other and the group structure has achieved some stability. This usually takes from four to eight weeks (*15*), but varies considerably with the nature of the group and the teaching procedures used.

How frequently to administer sociometric tests is somewhat arbitrary, but Jennings (*16*) has recommended an interval of seven or eight weeks between tests. This, she suggests, is long enough to make the choosing realistic to the pupils and short enough to keep up with changes in the group structure. When sociometric tests are given at regular intervals, special effort is necessary to fit them into the classroom routine.

SUMMARY

In the construction of a sociometric test the selection of criteria of choice is an important consideration. Any classroom activity or situation may provide the basis of choice in a sociometric criterion. However, choices for some situations and activities reflect more basic and permanent aspects of the group structure. A consideration of the various types of sociometric criteria suggests selecting criteria of choice that have the following characteristics: clearly indicates the nature of the activity or situation; is familiar and realistic to the group members; is general enough to minimize extraneous factors; is based on fundamental and permanent relationships; and provides for reciprocal choice and mutual association among group members. The number of criteria to use and the use of negative criteria must be determined by the situation in which the sociometric test is to be used and by the purposes for giving the test.

When the sociometric criteria have been selected, it is necessary to decide how many choices should be allotted for each criterion. There may be an unlimited number of choices or a fixed number. Except when social expansiveness is being investigated, a fixed number of choices is suggested. Up to the third-grade level, no more than three choices should be allotted. At the later elementary school level, the junior and senior high school level, and the college level the use of five choices for each criterion is recommended. This recommendation is based on the increased stability of sociometric results with five choices.

The administration of the sociometric test will be facilitated by the use of a sociometric form. This form contains detailed directions, clear statements of choice, and a place for the pupils to record their responses. The administrative procedures should be adapted to the age group being tested. Children at the early elementary school level should be interviewed individually, whereas older pupils may be tested in groups. Although there is little evidence on the frequency with which sociometric tests should be administered, an interval of seven or eight weeks between tests has been suggested. This, of course, will vary with the nature and purpose of the sociometric test and with the use to be made of the results.

REFERENCES

1. Biehler, R. F., "Companion Choice Behavior in the Kindergarten," *Child Development*, 1954, *25:*45–50.

2. Bonney, M. E., "Differences in Social Behavior Between Sociometrically High and Sociometrically Low Children," *Journal of Educational Research,* 1953, *46:*481–495.

3. Bonney, M. E., "Social Behavior Differences Between Second-Grade Children of High and Low Sociometric Status," *Journal of Educational Research,* 1955, *48:*481–495.

4. Bonney, M. E., "Sociometric Study of Agreement Between Teacher Judgments and Student Choices," *Sociometry,* 1947, *10:*133–146.

5. Bonney, M. E., "A Study of the Sociometric Process Among Sixth-Grade Children," *Journal of Educational Psychology,* 1946, *37:*359–371.

6. Bronfenbrenner, U., "A Constant Frame of Reference for Sociometric Research: Part II, Experiment and Inference," *Sociometry,* 1944, *7:*40–75.

7. Byrd, E., "A Study of Validity and Constancy of Choice in a Sociometric Test," *Sociometry,* 1951, *14:*175–181.

8. Criswell, J. H., "Sociometric Concepts in Personnel Administration," *Sociometry,* 1949, *12:*287–300.

9. Frankel, E. B., "The Social Relationships of Pre-School Children," *Sociometry Monographs,* No. 11, New York, Beacon House, 1947, 15–30.

10. Gibb, C. A., "The Sociometry of Leadership in Temporary Groups," *Sociometry,* 1950, *13:*226–243.

11. Gronlund, N. E., "Generality of Sociometric Status over Criteria in the Measurement of Social Acceptability," *Elementary School Journal,* 1955, *56:*173–176.

12. Gronlund, N. E., "The Relative Stability of Classroom Social Status with Unweighted and Weighted Sociometric Status Scores," *Journal of Educational Psychology,* 1955, *46:*345–354.

13. Gronlund, N. E., and Barnes, F. P., "The Reliability of Social-Acceptability Scores Using Various Sociometric-Choice Limits," *Elementary School Journal,* 1956, *57:*153–157.

14. Hollander, E. P., and Webb, W. B., "Leadership, Followership, and Friendship: An Analysis of Peer Nominations," *Journal of Abnormal and Social Psychology,* 1955, *50:*163–167.

15. Hunt, J. McV., and Solomon, R. L., "The Stability and Some Correlates of Group-Status in a Summer-Camp Group of Young Boys," *American Journal of Psychology,* 1942, *55:*33–45.

16. Jennings, H. H., "Sociometric Grouping in Relation to Child Development," Chapter 13, in C. M. Tryon (ed.), *Fostering Mental Health in Our Schools,* Washington, D.C., Association for Supervision and Curriculum Development, N.E.A., 1950.

17. Jennings, H. H., "Sociometry of Leadership," *Sociometry Monographs,* No. 14, New York, Beacon House, 1947.

18. Kerstetter, L. M., and Sargent, J., "Re-Assignment Therapy in the Classroom," *Sociometry,* 1940, *3:*292–306.

19. Lippitt, R., "Popularity Among Pre-School Children," *Child Development,* 1941, *12:*305–332.

20. Moreno, F. B., "Sociometric Status of Children in a Nursery School Group," *Sociometry,* 1942, *5:*395–411.

21. Moreno, J. L., "Progress and Pitfalls in Sociometric Theory," *Sociometry,* 1947, *10:*268–272.

22. Moreno, J. L., *Who Shall Survive?* New York, Beacon House, 1953.

23. Newstetter, W. I., Feldstein, M. J., and Newcomb, T. M., *Group Adjustment: A Study in Experimental Sociology,* Cleveland, Western Reserve University, 1938.

24. Northway, M. L., *A Primer of Sociometry,* Toronto, University of Toronto Press, 1952.

25. Smith, W. D., "Sociometric Measurements in the School," *High School Journal,* 1957, *41*:103–107.

CHAPTER 3

ANALYZING AND PRESENTING SOCIOMETRIC RESULTS

When a sociometric test has been administered to a classroom group, the resulting data will include the list of choices each pupil has made on each sociometric criterion. The teacher now faces the task of analyzing and presenting the results in a manner that is most useful to him. This analysis may vary from a simple tally of the number of choices each pupil received to a comprehensive statistical analysis of the results. Although the method used is determined somewhat by the nature of the problem being investigated, tabulating the data into a matrix table is usually the first step in analyzing sociometric results. This is merely a twofold table which reveals the choices each pupil has given and received.

USING THE MATRIX TABLE

For the purpose of discussion let us assume that Mr. Young, a fifth-grade teacher at Central School, has administered a sociometric test to his twenty pupils. The pupils were requested to name the five classmates they most preferred as work companions. Each pupil was also told to indicate any of the pupils with whom he would rather not work. Thus, Mr. Young had twenty sociometric forms. Each form indicated five choices for work companion, and some of the forms indicated rejection choices. The complete tabulation of Mr. Young's sociometric data can be recorded in the matrix table presented in Table 1. This is a modified version of the matrix table used originally by Jennings (*16*) in her study of leadership. Although this table may appear complicated at first glance, it is actually simple to construct and easy to use.

CONSTRUCTING THE MATRIX TABLE

The following steps will aid in the construction of the matrix table.

1. Select a large piece of graph paper that is divided into small squares like those in Table 1. The number of squares both vertically and horizontally should be at least ten greater than the number of pupils in the group.

2. Four squares in from the left-hand margin of the paper list the boys' names down the sheet in alphabetical order. Follow this with a list of the girls' names in alphabetical order. Then number the pupils consecutively from top to bottom.

3. Place the same numbers, corresponding to the pupils' names, in consecutive order across the top margin of the table.

4. Draw a heavy line both horizontally and vertically between the list of boys and the list of girls. This divides the matrix table into four parts which makes cross-sex choices readily apparent.

5. A diagonal line should also be drawn from the upper left-hand corner of the table to the lower right-hand corner, as illustrated in Table 1. This line cuts through squares that are not used in the tabulation of choices, since pupils do not choose themselves on the sociometric test. The main purpose of this diagonal line is to serve as a guide in identifying mutual choices.

6. At the left of the names, vertical columns are used for summarizing information on choices given. In Table 1 these columns

are to be used for totaling the number of choices given to pupils of the same sex and the opposite sex, and the number of rejections given to pupils of the same sex and the opposite sex. These summary columns may be varied to fit the purpose of the investigation.

7. At the bottom of the matrix table the rows are used for summarizing information on choices received. In Table 1 these summary rows are to be used for totaling the number of choices, rejections, and mutual choices received from pupils of the same sex and the opposite sex. As with the columns, these summary rows may be modified for special purposes.

When the matrix table is constructed, it consists of a twofold table, with the names of the pupils down the left side of the table and the numbers corresponding to the pupils' names across the top of the table. Thus the sociometric results can be quickly recorded by placing the choices and rejections made by each individual in the proper column opposite the chooser's name.

TABULATING SOCIOMETRIC DATA IN THE MATRIX TABLE

To illustrate the recording and tabulation of sociometric data, let us consider the procedure used by Mr. Young in Table 1. John A., the first pupil in Table 1, made the following choices:

Prefer as work companion
1. Bill H.
2. George L.
3. Mike A.
4. Betty A.
5. Pete V.

Would rather not work with
1. Henry D.
2. Bob F.

These choices were recorded in Table 1 by placing, across from John A's name, number 1 in column six to indicate Bill H. as his first choice; number 2 in column seven to indicate George L. as his second choice; number 3 in column two to indicate Mike A. as his third choice; number 4 in column twelve to indicate Betty A.

TABLE 1. Matrix Table Used for Tabulating Sociometric Data

Rejections Given		Choices Given				Pupils Chosen																			
OS	SS	OS	SS	Name		1	2	3	4	5	6	7	8	9	10	11	12	13	14	15	16	17	18	19	20
				John A.	1		3		X	X	1	2			5		4								
				Mike A.	2																				
				Jim B.	3																				
				Henry D.	4																				
				Bob F.	5																				
				Bill H.	6																				
				George L.	7																				
				Dick N.	8																				
				Dale P.	9																				
				Pete V.	10																				
				Mary A.	11																				
				Betty A.	12																				
				Karen B.	13																				
				Lois C.	14																				
				Sharon J.	15																				
				Ann K.	16																				
				Margie M.	17																				
				Sue R.	18																				
				Pat S.	19																				
				Carol W.	20																				
Central (School)				Choices Received	SS																				
					OS																				
5A (Class)				Rejections Received	SS																				
					OS																				
F. R. Young (Teacher)				Mutual Choices	SS																				
					OS																				

NOTE: SS = Same Sex. OS = Opposite Sex. X = Rejection.

as his fourth choice; and number 5 in column ten to indicate Pete V. as his fifth choice. His rejection of Henry D. and Bob F. as work companions was indicated by placing an X in column four and column five. Thus, looking across the table from John A.'s name, his choices and rejections are readily apparent. The use of the symbol X for rejection is merely to prevent confusion with the positive choices. Some teachers prefer to use numbers for the rejections, since this indicates more clearly the degree of rejection. When this is done, different colors are used to distinguish clearly the positive choices from the rejections.

The choices and rejections of the remaining nineteen pupils were recorded in the matrix table in the same manner as those for John A. The complete tabulation of Mr. Young's sociometric data is presented in Table 2. It will be noted in this table that all twenty pupils made five positive choices; some of them made two rejection choices; several made one rejection choice; and the remainder did not reject anyone. This is in harmony with Mr. Young's policy of permitting but not requiring rejection choices.

With all of the choices and rejections recorded in Table 2, it can readily be seen that the choices given go across the table and the choices received go down the table. Before summarizing these columns and rows the mutual choices are usually identified. This is done by starting at the diagonal in the upper left-hand corner and going down column one to determine if any of the pupils whom John A. chose also chose him. In column one, it can readily be seen that John A. received only one choice. This was from Dick N. (number 8). Going across row one from the diagonal line it can be seen that John A. did not choose number 8. Consequently, John A. has no mutual choices. Starting at the diagonal line again and going down column two it will be noted that Mike A. (number 2) received choices from Jim B. (number 3), George L. (number 7), and Dale P. (number 9). Going across row two from the diagonal line indicates that Mike A. has also chosen pupils number 3, 7, and 9. Since these are mutual choices, the choices

TABLE 2. Matrix Table Showing Choices and Rejections of Work Companions (5 choices allotted)

Rejections Given		Choices Given		Name		Pupils Chosen																			
OS	SS	OS	SS	Name		1	2	3	4	5	6	7	8	9	10	11	12	13	14	15	16	17	18	19	20
0	2	1	4	John A.	1		3		X	X	1	2			5		4								
0	2	0	5	Mike A.	2			(2)	X	X		(1)	4	(3)	5										
0	0	0	5	Jim B.	3		(3)				1	(2)		(4)	5										
0	0	1	4	Henry D.	4					(1)	2		3		4		5								
1	0	1	4	Bob F.	5				(1)		2	3	4				5	(X)							
1	0	3	2	Bill H.	6							(2)	(1)			(3)	X		4				(5)		
0	2	0	5	George L.	7		(2)	(4)	5	X	(1)		X	(3)											
0	0	1	4	Dick N.	8	4					(1)	3			(2)		5								
0	1	0	5	Dale P.	9		(2)	(3)		5	4	(1)	X												
0	0	1	4	Pete V.	10					5	2		(1)	3					4						
0	0	2	3	Mary A.	11						(5)		4				(1)		(3)				(2)		
0	0	0	5	Betty A.	12											(1)		(5)	(2)				(3)		(4)
1	1	1	4	Karen B.	13					(X)					5		(2)		X		(1)	(3)	4		
0	1	1	4	Lois C.	14								5			(2)	(1)						(4)	X	(3)
0	1	0	5	Sharon J.	15											1	2	4	3					X	5
0	0	2	3	Ann K.	16					5	3					4		(2)				(1)			
0	0	1	4	Margie M.	17										2	4	5	(1)			(3)				
0	1	1	4	Sue R.	18						(4)					(2)	(1)		(3)					X	(5)
0	0	0	5	Pat S.	19											2	1	3				4	5		
0	1	1	4	Carol W.	20						5						(1)	4	(2)				(3)	X	
Central (School)				Choices Received	SS	1	4	3	2	3	8	7	5	4	5	7	8	6	5	0	2	3	6	0	4
					OS	0	0	0	0	1	4	0	2	0	2	1	4	0	2	0	0	0	1	0	0
5A (Class)				Rejections Received	SS	0	0	0	2	3	0	0	2	0	0	0	0	0	1	0	0	0	0	4	0
					OS	0	0	0	0	1	0	0	0	0	0	0	1	1	0	0	0	0	0	0	0
F. R. Young (Teacher)				Mutual Choices	SS	0	3	3	1	1	2	4	2	3	1	3	5	3	4	0	2	2	4	0	3
					OS	0	0	0	0	0	2	0	0	0	0	1	0	0	0	0	0	0	1	0	0

NOTE: SS = Same Sex. OS = Opposite Sex. X = Rejection.

Mike A. has given to pupils number 3, 7, and 9 are circled and the choices Mike A. has received from pupils number 3, 7, and 9 (in column two) are also circled. This procedure of starting at the diagonal line and going down each column and across each corresponding row to identify and circle the mutual choices is continued until all mutual choices are identified. Thus, all circled numbers in Table 2 indicate a choice that was reciprocated by the individual chosen. The two X's that are circled indicate a mutual rejection. In this specific case pupil number 5 rejected pupil number 13 and pupil number 13 rejected pupil number 5.

When the pupils' choices and rejections have been recorded and the mutual choices identified, the data can be quickly summarized. This summary is aided by the heavy horizontal and vertical lines between the list of boys and the list of girls. Looking at Table 2 it will be noted that the boys' choices of boys are all recorded in the upper left-hand quarter of the table, since the boys' numbers range from 1 to 10. The boys' choices of girls are all recorded in the upper right-hand quarter of the table, since the girls' numbers range from 11 to 20. This pattern is reversed in the lower half of the table with the girls' choices of boys in the lower left-hand quarter and the girls' choices of girls in the lower right-hand quarter. The diagonal line aids in identifying the proper quarter, since it goes through the quarter where choices of the same sex are recorded. This division of the matrix table into four parts makes the relatively few cross-sex choices readily apparent and easy to tabulate.

The choices given are summarized by going across the rows after each name. These totals are recorded in the summary columns to the left of the pupils' names. For example, John A. (number 1) has given four choices to boys (SS), one choice to a girl (OS), two rejections to boys (SS), and no rejections to girls (OS). When summarizing the choices given by girls, it is important to remember that the quarters in the lower part of the table are reversed, to prevent recording the totals in the wrong summary columns. For example, Mary A. (number 11) has given three choices to girls (SS) and two choices to boys (OS).

The choices received are summarized by totaling the choices in each column and placing them in the summary rows at the bottom of the table. For example, Mike A. (number 1) received one choice from a boy (SS) and no other choices or rejections. Mary A. (number 11) received seven choices from girls (SS), one choice from a boy (OS), and no rejections. Three of her choices from girls and her single choice from a boy were mutual choices, as indicated by the circled choices in her column (number 11).

WEIGHTING OF SOCIOMETRIC CHOICES

It will be noted that no distinction was made between first, second, third, fourth, or fifth choice when summarizing the choices received, in Table 2. All choices were given a value of one regardless of level of choice. This is in contrast to the practice of some investigators (*26*) who assign arbitrary weights to the various choice levels. Where weights are used the first choice is usually given a value equal to the total number of choices allotted and each succeeding choice decreases in value by one. For example, with five choices a first choice would be given a value of five points, a second choice four points, a third choice three points, etc. This is based on the assumption that a first choice has more social significance and, therefore, should count more. Although this assumption may have some validity, it should be pointed out that there is no experimental evidence to justify any particular system of weights and assigning arbitrary weights is, therefore, a dubious practice. Studies (*2, 15*) have shown that the stability of sociometric results is not improved by the weighting of sociometric choices. Thus, until evidence is presented to justify the assigning of weights to sociometric choices, it is suggested that each choice be given a value of one regardless of level of choice.

The level of choice should still be recorded in the matrix table, however, since it does serve a useful purpose when the sociometric results are used to organize classroom groups.

INTERPRETING THE MATRIX TABLE

Although interpretations of the matrix table were implied during the discussion of the tabulation of sociometric results, a more detailed analysis of the data will clarify the type of information that is readily obtained from the matrix table.

CHOICES RECEIVED. A glance across the summary rows in Table 2, for the total number of choices received, it will be noted that two pupils (numbers 15 and 19) received no choices and two pupils (numbers 6 and 12) received a total of twelve choices (8 SS + 4 OS) each, as work companion. The remaining pupils received between one and eight choices. These pupils can be placed in the sociometric categories indicated below, based on the number of choices they received on the sociometric test. Thus, it may be noted that one boy and one girl are stars of the group; one boy is neglected by the group; and two girls are isolated. The other pupils received an average number of choices. Both the leadership potential (stars) and those needing help with their social adjustments (neglectee and isolates) are easily identified.

Category	*Number of Choices Received*	*Boys (by No.)*	*Girls (by No.)*
Star	9-up	6	12
Above Av.	5-8	7, 8, 10	11, 13, 14, 18
Below Av.	2-4	2, 3, 4, 5, 9	16, 17, 20
Neglectee	1	1	
Isolate	0		15, 19

The method of classifying the pupils into the sociometric categories given here was obtained from Table 3 based on Bronfenbrenner's (5) fixed frame of reference. This table indicates the critical sociometric status scores for varying numbers of choices with up to three sociometric criteria. In the sociometric data analyzed above, five choices were used with one sociometric criterion. Consequently, the average number of choices that could be expected was five. The lower limit, which identifies neglectees, was one choice. The upper limit, which identifies stars, was nine or more choices. The average, or expected values, and the upper and lower limits for other sociometric choosing situations may be obtained directly from Table 3. It should be noted that all of the sociometric status score values in this table are based on unweighted sociometric choices.

The lower and upper limits presented in Table 3 are actually limits of statistical significance at the .02 and .03 level. Receiving as few choices as the value indicated in the lower limit or as many choices as the value indicated in the upper limit would be expected less than two, or three, times out of a hundred by chance alone. In other words, the teacher can be fairly confident that pupils classified as neglectees (lower limit) and stars (upper limit) have been placed in the proper sociometric category.

The values for the lower and upper limits, presented in Table 3, may be applied to any group which contains no fewer than ten persons and no more than fifty persons. Thus, the frame of reference remains fixed for groups of varying size. The obvious advantage of such a fixed frame of reference is that the number of stars and neglectees in different groups can be compared directly even though the size of the groups is different. Thus, the total number of stars and neglectees in an entire school system could be determined by administering the same sociometric test in individual classrooms. This would assume, of course, that the criteria used and the number of choices allotted remained the same for all classroom groups. It would also assume that all of the classroom groups contained between ten and fifty pupils.

REJECTIONS RECEIVED. Referring back to Table 2 it will be noted in the summary rows of the matrix table that pupil number 19 received four rejection choices and no positive choices. Although the seriousness of this rejection cannot be determined

TABLE 3. Critical Raw Status Scores for Diverse Sociometric Situations

Number of Choices Allotted to Each Person for Each Criterion	One Criterion			Two Criteria			Three Criteria		
		Critical Scores			Critical Scores			Critical Scores	
	Expected Value	Lower Limit	Upper Limit	Expected Value	Lower Limit	Upper Limit	Expected Value	Lower Limit	Upper Limit
1	1	none	4	2	none	6	3	0	8
2	2	none	6	4	0	9	6	1	12
3	3	0	7	6	1	11	9	3	15
4	4	0	8	8	2	13	12	5	18
5	5	1	9	10	4	16	15	9	22

NOTE: Reprinted from Bronfenbrenner (5), by permission.

from the sociometric data alone, it should alert the teacher to the need for observing pupil number 19 and seeking the causes of her rejection by the group members. Other pupils receiving rejection choices should likewise receive further study by the teacher.

MUTUAL CHOICES. With the exception of a few pupils, the number of mutual choices recorded in Table 2 seem to be fairly evenly distributed among the class members. It will be noted that there are very few mutual choices between members of the opposite sex. This is common among pupils at this age level, since the number of cross-sex choices is usually relatively small.

CROSS-SEX CHOICES. Of the 100 positive choices given in Mr. Young's class, only seventeen (17 percent) went to members of the opposite sex. This information may be readily obtained from the "choices given" column or the "choices received" row in Table 2.

As suggested by the above analysis, the matrix table provides for quick and easy interpretation of sociometric data. It also organizes the sociometric results into a convenient form for further analysis and study. Thus, the matrix table is a convenient and desirable first step in analyzing sociometric results. For certain purposes, such as determining the sociometric status of individual pupils, the matrix table may be sufficient. However, where a clear picture of the social structure of the group is desired, a graphic presentation of the data is more effective. For this purpose the data in the matrix table is usually converted into a sociogram.

USING THE SOCIOGRAM

The sociogram is a graphic picture of the underlying social structure of a group. In its original use by Moreno (*23*), group members were indicated by symbols, and lines and arrows were used to indicate the direction of choice. Although these basic features of the sociogram have been retained, numerous modifications have been made by other investigators. One of the most useful improvements is that of Northway's (*24*) target diagram which contains four concentric circles similar to an archery target. In her procedure the stars are placed in the center of the target and the isolates in the outside circle. Other group members are placed between these extremes in terms of the number of choices received. Thus, when the sociogram is plotted on this diagram, the sociometric status of individual group members as well as the social structure of the group is depicted.

The concentric circles in Northway's (*24*) target diagram divided the sociometric status scores into quartiles. Although this is a convenient division of scores, sociograms based on groups of varying size cannot be compared directly. To remedy this factor Bronfenbrenner (*4*) suggested the use of his fixed frame of reference for identifying the position and the values of the concentric circles in the target diagram. This would make the sociometric levels, represented by the concentric circles, comparable from group to group.

The sociograms presented and discussed in this book will be based on Northway's (*24*) and Bronfenbrenner's (*4*) refinements of the original sociogram. It is felt that the "target sociogram" based on Bronfenbrenner's (*5*) fixed frame of reference is the most generally useful for classroom teachers.

CONSTRUCTING THE SOCIOGRAM

For illustrative and practice purposes a blank target diagram is presented in Figure 2. This diagram is ready for the plotting of Mr. Young's (Table 2) sociometric data and was constructed in the following manner. The concentric circles were drawn equal distance apart except for the outer circle. This depicts the variation in the sociometric levels indicated by Bronfenbrenner's fixed frame of reference. The vertical line through the center of the diagram provides for a separation of the boys and girls. The numbers along this line below each circle indicate the choice levels for each of the concentric circles. Thus, pupils receiving nine or more choices on the sociometric test (stars) would be placed in the smallest circle in the center of the diagram; pupils receiving one choice (neglectees) or none (isolates) would be placed in the outer ring of the diagram; pupils between these extremes would be placed in the two middle rings indicating below average or above average sociometric status depending on the number of choices received. It will be noted that these sociometric categories and choice levels are the same ones used in the analysis of data in the matrix table. The choice levels for the concentric circles were obtained from the

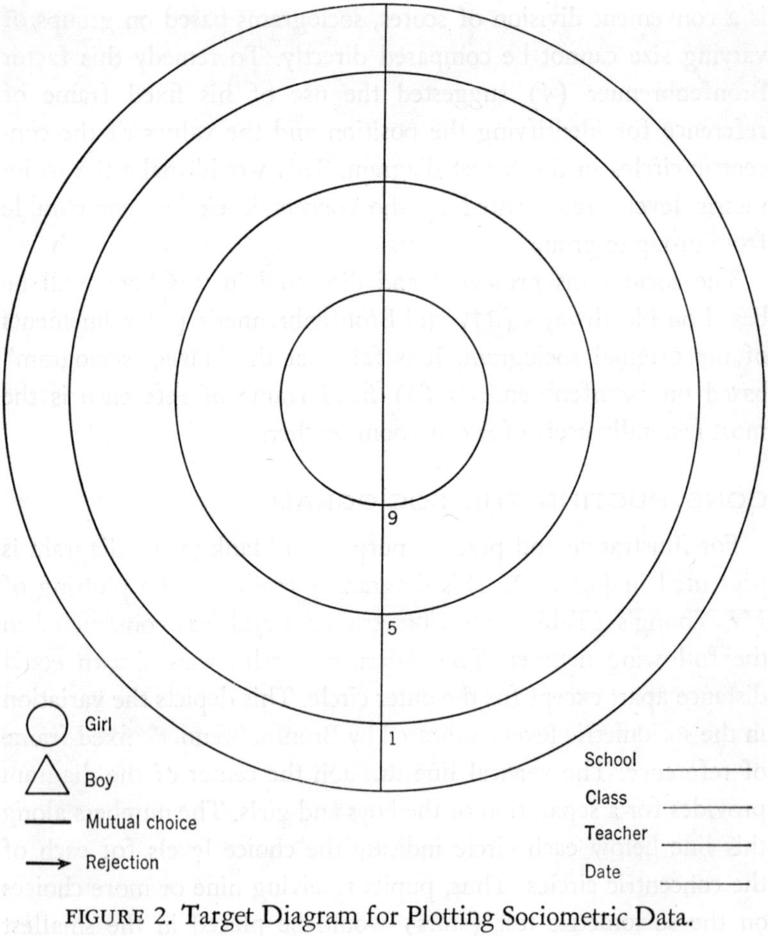

FIGURE 2. Target Diagram for Plotting Sociometric Data.

values in Table 3 for five choices and one sociometric criterion. For other sociometric situations, of course, the concentric circles would be given their corresponding values from Table 3.

After the diagram has been drawn as illustrated in Figure 2, the sociogram may be plotted by using the following steps. The reader may want to practice plotting a sociogram in Figure 2, using Mr. Young's sociometric data (presented in Table 2). Thus, these directions are adapted to Mr. Young's data.

1. From the matrix table (Table 2) select the boys having the largest number of mutual choices and place them in their proper position on the right half of the target diagram. Proper position means placing them in a relative position between the concentric circles corresponding to the number of choices they have received. For example, pupils 7, 8, and 10 all received seven choices so they would be placed near the center of the ring between the circles representing 5 and 9 choices in Figure 2. It should be noted that boys are represented by triangles and their corresponding matrix number is placed in the triangle for identification. When placing the boys in position on the diagram, attempt to put boys with mutual choices near each other. First attempts at placement should be done lightly in pencil since some rearrangement is usually necessary.

2. When the boys with the largest number of mutual choices have been placed in position, draw a solid line between those boys choosing each other. Some rearranging may be necessary at this time, to minimize the number of crossed lines (a good sociogram has a minimum of crossed lines). When shifting pupils around on a sociogram to get a better arrangement, be sure that they remain the same distance from the concentric circles, since this position indicates their sociometric status.

3. Next place the remaining boys in their proper position on the right half of the target diagram. Indicate the remaining mutual choices between boys, with solid lines. Again some rearrangement may be necessary to minimize crossed lines. Don't become dis-

couraged by the need for rearranging, since a certain amount of trial and error is necessary to obtain the best arrangement.

4. When all of the boys have been properly placed and the mutual choices among them indicated, follow the same procedure for girls using the left half of the target diagram. It should be noted that girls are represented by circles and their corresponding matrix number is placed in the circle for identification.

5. When the girls have all been plotted on the target diagram and their mutual choices indicated, draw a solid line between those boys and girls having mutual choices.

6. Rejection choices, from the matrix table (Table 2) may be indicated in the sociogram by a short arrow from the pupil giving the rejection (pointed toward the pupil being rejected).

The completed sociogram, based on Mr. Young's sociometric data in Table 2, is presented in Figure 3. The uncluttered appearance of this sociogram is due largely to the fact that only mutual choices are indicated. Some investigators plot all choices given by pupils. However, where as many as five choices are allotted to each pupil the sociogram becomes a maze of crossed lines that is difficult if not impossible to interpret. Plotting only mutual choices provides a clear picture of the underlying social structure of the group. Determining which pupils were selected by a specific individual, if desired, may be obtained directly from the matrix table.

INTERPRETING THE SOCIOGRAM

A glance at Figure 3 clearly reveals the advantage of the sociogram over the matrix table for presenting the social relations existing among group members. All of the mutual relations are presented at once, and the otherwise complex process of attraction and repulsion among group members becomes readily apparent. This particular sociogram, in Figure 3, illustrates the basic sociometric patterns found in group structure.

STARS. The two stars (numbers 6 and 12) appear in the

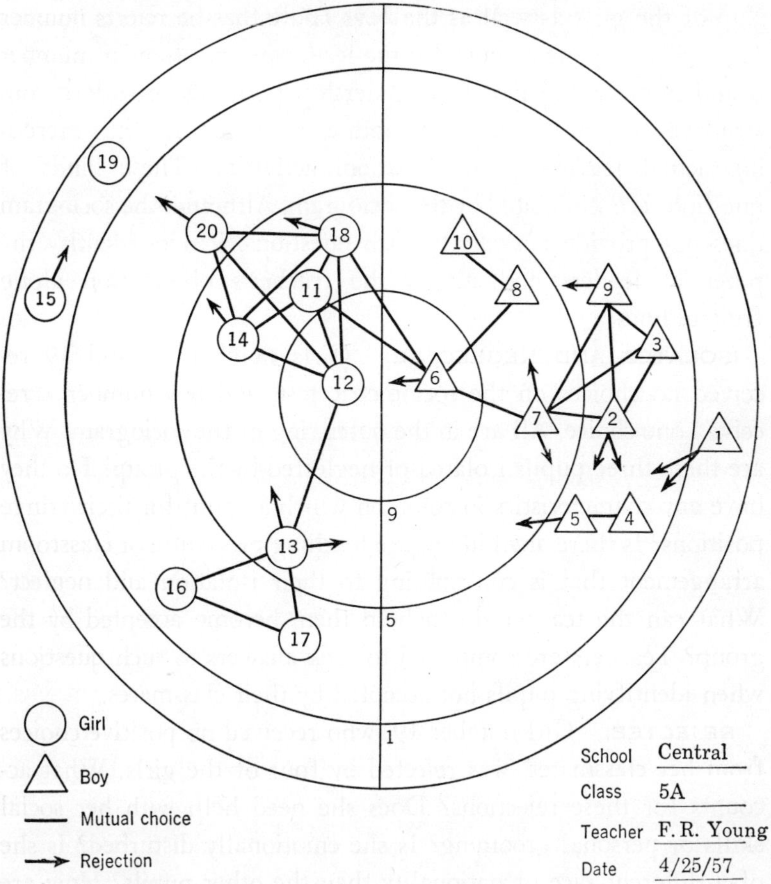

FIGURE 3. Sociogram of Choices and Rejections of Work Companions (Based on Data in Table 2).

center of the sociogram. The girl (number 12) has five mutual choices with other girls, which provides a chain of relationships with all but two of the girls. The boy (number 6) has only two mutual choices with other boys, but these choices attach him indirectly to six of the boys. His two mutual choices with girls provides him with a chain of contact with eight of the girls. Is he the real leader in the class? Is he vying with number 12 for the leadership of the girls as well as the boys (note that he rejects number 12)? What factors account for the leadership positions of number 6 and number 12? Do their leadership positions provide a constructive influence on the classroom as a whole? Are they exercising actual leadership in classroom activities? These kinds of questions are stimulated by the sociogram. Although the sociogram does not provide answers to such questions, it does identify the potential leaders and directs the teacher's observation along fruitful lines.

ISOLATES AND NEGLECTEE. Girls number 15 and 19 received no choices on the sociometric test, and boy number 1 received one choice. All are in the outer ring of the sociogram. Why are these three pupils isolated or neglected by the group? Do they have any characteristics in common which account for their fringe positions? Is there anything in the teaching procedure or classroom arrangement that is contributing to their isolation and neglect? What can the teacher do to help them become accepted by the group? Teachers are compelled to seek answers to such questions when identifying pupils not accepted by their classmates.

REJECTEE. Girl number 19, who received no positive choices from her classmates, was rejected by four of the girls. What accounts for these rejections? Does she need help with her social skills or personal grooming? Is she emotionally disturbed? Is she of a different race or nationality than the other pupils? How are her parents accepted in the community? Are they also rejected? Pupil number 19 needs help in her social relations, and the teacher is in one of the best positions to provide that help.

MUTUAL CHOICES. There are numerous mutual choices depicted in the sociogram. What factors might account for these various pairs of pupils choosing each other? Do they choose each other in actual work situations? How do these mutual friendships affect the classroom process? Which ones contribute to classroom harmony and which ones result in classroom disturbances?

Pupils number 4 and 5 form a separate *pair*. Although they have mutually chosen each other, they are below average in acceptance and are rejected by pupils number 1, 2, and 7. Why did they choose each other? Why are they rejected by several students? How do they differ from the other boys in class? What do they have in common? This pair warrants special observation from the teacher as a basis for integrating them into the larger group.

Pupils number 13, 16, and 17 form a *triangle* of mutual choices. How do they work with the other pupils in class? Do they exclude others from their little group? What do they have in common? Would it be desirable to integrate them into the larger group? Can the mutual choice between number 13 and number 12 be used to bring about a more integrated social structure?

Pupils number 10, 8, and 6 form a *chain* of mutual choices. What caused this structure to form? How do pupils number 10 and 6 get along in their personal relations? Does pupil number 8 have to divide his time between pupil number 10 and pupil number 6? If pupils number 10 and 6 are not compatible, how does number 8's in-between position affect his social relations and his personal adjustment? Such questions are not answered by the sociogram, but they direct the teacher's observation and guide him in the effective application of the sociometric results.

CLIQUES. There are two relatively large subgroups, or cliques, observable in the sociogram. Boys number 2, 3, 7, and 9 form one, and girls number 11, 12, 14, 18, and 20 form the other. What seems to account for the formation of these cliques? What characteristics do the members of each clique have in common? How do these cliques affect the harmony of the classroom and the attainment of classroom goals? What procedures will most effectively weaken these cliques and provide for a more general distribution of mutual choices? Cliques are not necessarily harmful, but they can lead to a disintegrated social structure which interferes with harmonious and purposeful relations in the classroom.

CLEAVAGES. Although minor cleavages are apparent between

small subgroups, the most obvious cleavage is between boys and girls. There are only two mutual choices between the sexes and both of these are with the same boy. This is a fairly common phenomenon in sociometric testing at the fifth-grade level. However, sociometric results from different schools show considerable variation in the amount of cleavage between the sexes. What factors might account for this rather extreme cleavage? Do the school procedures (i.e., separate playgrounds, boys vs. girls in games, etc.) contribute to this cleavage? To what extent can this cleavage be diminished? What classroom procedures will contribute to more harmonious boy-girl relations? Although it is normal for pupils of this age to prefer companions of the same sex, the cleavage between boys and girls can become so great that later heterosexual development is retarded.

As indicated by the questions in the above analysis, the sociogram merely presents the sociometric results in graphic form. It does not indicate why a particular social structure evolved, what influence a particular social structure has on the ongoing process of the classroom, nor what steps should be taken to modify the social structure. The sociogram is a useful starting point, but the judicious use of questions and the utilization of supplementary information is necessary if the sociogram is to be properly interpreted and the results effectively applied to educational problems.

COMMON ERRORS IN INTERPRETING THE SOCIOGRAM

The dramatic quality of the sociogram plus the apparent ease with which it can be understood has led to several misinterpretations. These errors in interpretation are generally due to a lack of familiarity with sociometric findings, rather than weaknesses in the sociogram technique itself. Avoiding such pitfalls will provide a more valid analysis of pupils' social relations in the classroom.

Although several authors (*11, 20, 23*) have pointed out the necessary cautions in interpreting the sociogram, the following errors of interpretation are common.

1. There is a tendency to consider the social relations depicted in the sociogram as actual relations among group members. Since the sociometric test measures the underlying social structure, this interpretation is neither desirable nor true. The sociogram presents a graphic picture of desired associations.

2. The sociogram is sometimes viewed as a complete picture of the social structure of the group. In addition to being limited to the internal structure of the group, it is also limited to the sociometric criteria used, the number of choices allotted, whether or not both positive and negative choices are used, and the procedures used in administering the test. Variations in any of these factors will modify the diagram of the social structure to some extent.

3. The network of choice patterns are frequently thought of as representing a fixed group structure rather than a picture of a changing social process. Although an individual's sociometric status in a group is relatively stable, the pattern of choices among individuals has less permanence. Friendships are made and broken; cliques are formed and dissolved; and cleavages are increased or reduced by particular classroom experiences. Periodic sociograms are as necessary in measuring the social development of the group members as periodic achievement tests are for the measurement of scholastic development. In either case, the results of one test merely indicate the present status of an ongoing process.

4. The social structure depicted in the sociogram will look slightly different when constructed by different individuals. This is sometimes viewed as an indication of the unreliability of the sociogram as a method of presenting sociometric data. However, this variation is due partly to the flexibility in organizing the sociogram and partly to the skill of the person constructing it. Using

standard procedures of construction, as suggested above, and obtaining practice in the construction of sociograms will minimize this difficulty.

As with any technique, a knowledge of the strengths and limitations of the sociogram is required for its proper use. Most of the errors of interpretation reflect attempts to oversimplify sociometric data. This is probably a reflection of our general tendency to seek simple solutions to complex problems. Although the sociogram presents a clear picture of sociometric results, an understanding of what these results mean in terms of social relations among group members is basic to the interpretation. Thus, a knowledge of sociometric theory and research is essential if all of the complexities of the sociometric choice process are to be clearly understood and sociograms are to be properly interpreted.

OTHER METHODS OF ANALYZING AND PRESENTING SOCIOMETRIC RESULTS

The use of the matrix table and the sociogram were described in some detail, since they are the most useful methods for most classroom purposes. The matrix table makes readily available information on the choices and rejections given and received, the mutual choices present, and the number of cross-sex choices. Sociometric data for each individual, or for the group as a whole, may be obtained directly from the matrix table. This information can be used in a descriptive manner or can be subjected to further analysis. The sociogram supplements the matrix table by presenting a graphic picture of the social relations of group members. If the target diagram and fixed reference points are used in the sociogram, as illustrated above, the sociometric status of individuals can also be depicted in the sociogram.

Other methods of analyzing and presenting sociometric results have been used for various purposes and with varying degrees of success.

INDEX METHOD

Early attempts to quantify the sociometric results presented in the matrix table led to a number of simple ratios or sociometric indices. For example, the *sociometric choice status* of individuals has been calculated by the following formula:

$$\text{sociometric choice status} = \frac{\text{number of choices received}}{\text{number of pupils in group} - 1}$$

Similar indices were calculated for the individual's *rejection status* and *emotional expansiveness,* with numerous variations among different investigators (*19*). In general, these indices were attempts to convert the sociometric results of individuals into comparable scores so that the sociometric status of individuals could be compared within groups and between groups. However, dividing the number of choices received, or given, by a constant ($N - 1$) does not change the relative position of individuals within groups and, therefore, makes no contribution to comparisons within groups. Comparisons between groups with such indices can be made only if the groups are somewhat similar in size. For example, an individual receiving five choices in a group of twenty would have a sociometric choice status of .26 (using the above formula), while an individual receiving five choices in a group of fifty would have a sociometric choice status of .10. Thus, with large variations in group size the results of such indices are distorted to such an extent that between-group comparisons are invalid. Indices based on the number of persons in a group generally assume that an individual in a larger group should receive more choices to have comparable status with an individual in a smaller group. This assumption lacks validity, since in the larger group there are also more individuals available to receive choices. For example, where five choices are allotted with one sociometric criterion, the average number of choices received will be five regardless of the size of the group. Consequently, the total number of choices received, or given, should be used directly for within group and between group comparisons. When comparing individuals between groups these raw scores may be categorized into Bronfenbrenner's (5) fixed frame of reference for comparable points of reference (i.e., comparing stars from one group with stars from other groups). Such between-group comparisons, of course, require that the same criteria and the same number of choices be used in all groups compared.

Sociometric indices have also been developed for analyzing the sociometric characteristics of groups. Although these indices are generally more useful than those developed for individuals, they also have their shortcomings. For example, the index for *group cohesion* assumes that the larger the number of mutual choices the higher the group cohesion. One formula for group cohesion is as follows:

$$\text{group cohesion} = \frac{\text{number of mutual choices}}{\text{number of possible mutual choices}}$$

In this index, the number of possible mutual choices equals the total number of choices given by all group members. In other words, it is possible for each group member to have all of his choices reciprocated. Applying this index to Mr. Young's class (Table 2), where there were 100 choices given (5 choices x 20 pupils) and, fifty of the choices were reciprocated, the index for group cohesion would be .50. Although this represents a relatively high ratio of mutual choices, a glance back at the sociogram in Figure 3 will reveal that the group structure is not very cohesive. Cliques, triangles, mutual pairs, and individual group members are generally separated from one another. With the same index of group cohesion a more integrated group structure or a less integrated group structure may result. For example, it would be possible with this index (.50) for all of the group members to have approximately half of their choices reciprocated or one-half of the group members to have all of their choices reciprocated.

Quite different levels of group cohesion would be present even though the index of group cohesion would be identical. Thus, this and similar indices of group cohesion (7) take into account only the number of mutual choices. The distribution of these choices, which is equally important, is neglected. Such indices should, therefore, be used with caution and a clear recognition of their limitations.

Numerous other indices have been developed for analyzing the social characteristics of groups. Indices of *group integration* (8), *group expansiveness* (27) and *subgroup preference* (10) are some of those more commonly used. A survey of such indices may be found in Proctor and Loomis (27). The rationale behind the use of such indices is discussed in some detail by Criswell (9). Although the index method of sociometric analysis can serve useful purposes in evaluating group structure, a careful consideration of the assumptions underlying its use is essential for proper application and interpretation.

MATRIX METHODS

Several investigators have attempted to combine the quantitative features of the matrix table with the graphic features of the sociogram. These attempts resulted in some modification or manipulation of the matrix table. Since these methods are new, or in the process of refinement, they will be discussed here briefly. More detailed information may be obtained from the references cited in the discussion.

SOCIOGRAPH. A recent modification of the matrix table has been presented by Bonney and Fessenden (3). They cut the matrix table in half along the main diagonal line and divided the squares for each person into halves. This triangular-shaped graph has the unique advantage of placing mutual choices in one square. Except for making mutual choices easily detectable, however, this method seems to have no special advantage over the square matrix table. A detailed description of the construction and use of this sociograph may be found in a manual (*3*) by the originators of the graph.

MATRIX ANALYSIS. Two major approaches have been used in manipulating the matrix table for the purpose of obtaining a more systematic analysis of sociometric data. Forsyth and Katz (*14, 17*) suggested a method of rearranging the order of the individuals in rows and columns so that subgroups or cliques would appear along the main diagonal. Similar procedures have been described by Clark (*6*) and Luebke (*22*). This method of rearranging the matrix table results in some of the graphic features of the sociogram. However, patterns of choice are not as clearly depicted as they are in the sociogram, and the process of rearranging pairs of rows and columns in the matrix table is extremely time consuming.

A second approach, suggested by Luce and Perry (*21*) and Festinger (*13*), is based on matrix algebra. Through the use of matrix multiplication the matrix is raised to various powers. This method is especially useful for identifying chains of communication and influence. Although the overall choice pattern depicted in the sociogram is not available with this method, it is especially adaptable to studies of rumor and other problems based on the network of relations among group members.

Matrix analysis is still in the process of development and may result in a standardized method of analyzing sociometric data. It can handle more complex sociometric data than the sociogram and it is subject to quantitative techniques. However, at its present stage of development matrix analysis is most useful in large-scale research studies. For this purpose the use of machine tabulation methods described by Beum and Criswell (*1*) and Katz (*18*) will diminish the time-consuming task of manipulating the matrix table.

RECORDING SOCIOMETRIC RESULTS IN PERMANENT RECORDS

One of the factors which has retarded the general usefulness of sociometric results in school settings is the difficulty of recording the results in permanent school records. Teachers frequently obtain considerable information about their pupils through sociometric measures, use the results for immediate diagnostic and remedial purposes, and then discard the matrix tables and sociograms. Since none of the information is recorded in the individual's cumulative records, this information is not available to other teachers or to guidance personnel who could benefit by such information.

The major difficulty in recording sociometric data in permanent school records is that of obtaining a method which reveals an individual's pattern of social relations as well as his sociometric status. It is a simple matter to record the number of choices an individual gives and receives, but to omit the identity of the group members with whom he relates and to leave out the pattern of relations reduces the usefulness of the information. Thus, a method of recording is needed which will retain the basic information presented in the matrix table and the sociogram but present it with respect to each individual. Recording methods suggested by Dunlap (*12*) and Northway (*25*) come closest to meeting this need. Both methods will be illustrated through the use of Mr. Young's sociometric data presented in Table 2 and Figure 3. Some modification will be made in the description of the methods, for this purpose.

DUNLAP METHOD

Although this method was designed for within-class use, it could be easily adapted to a permanent record system. Pupils may be identified by letters or numbers with this recording method. In the present description, numbers corresponding to the identification numbers of pupils in the matrix table, in Table 2, will be used. Boys will be identified by Arabic numbers and girls by Roman numerals. Different colors, of course, may also be used for this purpose. The recorded information for boy number 6 and girl number XIII is presented below:

Boy number 6 (work companion: 5 choices allotted)

Choices received from	1, 3, 4, 5, (7,) (8,) 9, 10, (XI,) XVI, (XVIII,) XX
Choices given to	(7,) (8) (XI,) XIV, (XVIII)
Rejections received from	
Rejections given to	XII

Girl number XIII (work companion: 5 choices allotted)

Choices received from	(XII,) XV, (XVI,) (XVII,) XIX, XX
Choices given to	(XII,) X, (XVI,) (XVII,) XVIII
Rejections received from	[5]
Rejections given to	[5,] XIV

It will be noted in this record that mutual choices are identified by circles and mutual rejections by rectangles. Other symbols (*12*) may be used where an individual chooses a person who rejects him or where he rejects a person who chooses him. The number of choices given and received is quickly determined, and the sex of the chooser and the chosen is also readily identified. Such a record must be accompanied by a list of the pupils' names and identification numbers, however, to identify the specific group members' choosing and being chosen by each individual.

Recording data with this method is simply a matter of transferring the information from the matrix table. The only change necessary is that of placing identical identification numbers in the same columns so that mutual choices and mutual rejections may be indicated.

NORTHWAY METHODS

After experimenting with different methods of recording data for a longitudinal study of children's sociometric patterns, Northway (*25*) developed two especially useful methods. One presents sociometric data in cumulative record form and the other presents the sociometric pattern for each individual. Modified versions of these two methods are discussed and illustrated with Mr. Young's data. Although other minor modifications are made, the main one is that of applying Bronfenbrenner's (5) fixed frame of reference to the sociometric categories.

CUMULATIVE RECORD FORM. This form of recording sociometric results eliminates the need for identification numbers used with the Dunlap Method. The recorded information for the same boy (number 6), used with the Dunlap Method, is presented below.

Score of Chooser	Chosen By	Choice Level	Pupil	Chooses	Choice Level	Score of Chosen
1	John A.	1		Lois C.	4	7
3	Jim B.	1	Bill H.			
2	Henry D.	2	(no. 6)			
4	Bob F.	2	9			
7	George L.	①		George L.	②	7
7	Dick N.	①		Dick N.	①	7
4	Dale P.	4	5			
7	Pete V.	2				
8	Mary A.	⑤		Mary A	③	8
2	Ann K.	3	1			
7	Sue R.	④		Sue R.	⑤	7
4	Carol W.	5				

NOTE: Criterion: *Work Companion*; choices allotted—5.

It will be noted in this record that the name of the pupil (Bill H.) is placed in the center column. This column is divided into four parts corresponding to Bronfenbrenner's (5) fixed frame of reference categories. The top section is that of star (nine or more choices). The remaining sections down the column in consecutive order are above average, below average, and neglect or isolation. Bill H.'s name was placed in the top section, since he received twelve choices. An individual receiving one or no choices would have his name placed in the bottom section. Those receiving between two and eight choices would have their names recorded in one of the two center sections depending on whether the number of choices they received was above or below average (five choices). Thus, the center column identifies the pupil and indicates his level of sociometric status.

The three columns to the left of center indicate which pupils have chosen Bill H., how many sociometric choices each chooser received, and whether each chooser gave Bill H. a first, second, third, fourth, or fifth choice. Knowing the sociometric status scores of the choosers aids in determining the types of individuals attracted to Bill H., and the choice level provides some indication of the strength of this attraction.

The three columns to the right of center indicate whom Bill H. chooses, the level of choice given to each, and the sociometric status scores of the pupils chosen. It will be noted that the names of the pupils chosen by Bill H., who have also chosen him, are placed on the same line so that mutual choices are readily identified. The numbers in the choice level columns may also be circled for this purpose, as illustrated.

Although rejection choices are not indicated in this record, this information may be included by merely adding appropriate columns. Choices on several criteria may also be included in the same record, by adding additional columns under choice level. For an illustration of the use of this recording form with three criteria see Northway (*25*).

SOCIOMETRIC PATTERN FORM. This method of recording sociometric data results in a graphic picture of the individual's sociometric pattern similar to the sociogram. In essence it is that part of the sociogram which is pertinent to the individual under consideration. The sociometric pattern for the same boy (number 6), discussed above, is presented in Figure 4.

This form for recording an individual's sociometric pattern is divided into four sections based on Bronfenbrenner's (*5*) fixed

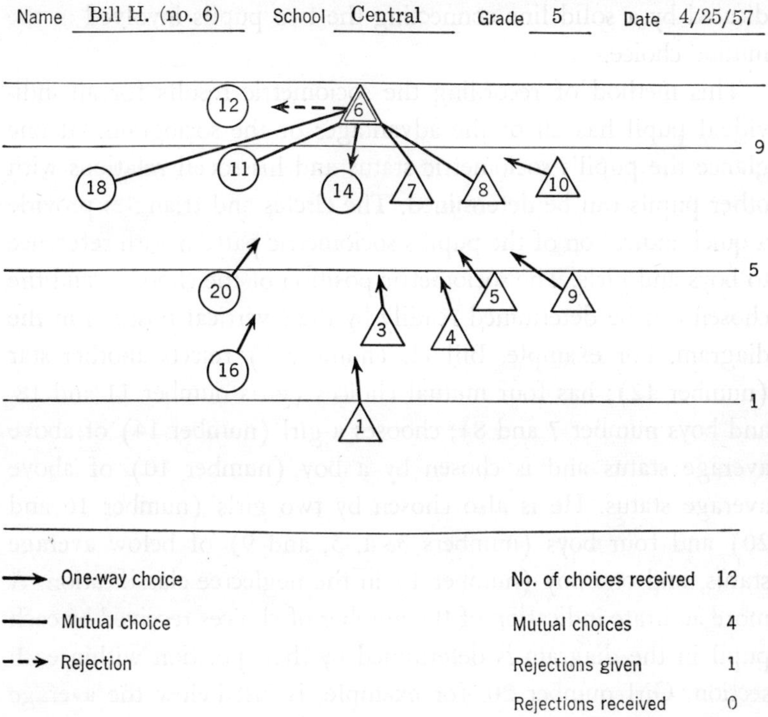

FIGURE 4. Sociometric Pattern of Choices and Rejections with Five Choices and One Sociometric Criterion (Work Companion).

frame of reference. These sections and reference points are identical to those used in the sociogram (Figure 3) and the cumulative record form above. Bill H. (number 6) was placed in the top section (star category) and indicated by a double triangle. All other group members choosing Bill H. and chosen by Bill H. were placed in a position on the diagram corresponding to the number of choices they received. As in the sociogram, girls were indicated by circles and boys by triangles with their identification numbers within the figures. Choices to and from Bill H. were indicated by a solid arrow and the single rejection choice, to pupil number 12, was indicated by a broken-line arrow. Mutual choices were indicated by a solid line connecting the two pupils involved in the mutual choice.

This method of recording the sociometric results for an individual pupil has all of the advantages of the sociogram. At one glance the pupil's sociometric status and his social relations with other pupils can be determined. The circles and triangles provide a quick indication of the pupil's sociometric pattern with reference to boys and girls. The sociometric position of the choosers and the chosen can be determined readily by their vertical position in the diagram. For example, Bill H. (number 6) rejects another star (number 12); has four mutual choices (girls number 11 and 18, and boys number 7 and 8); chooses a girl (number 14) of above average status and is chosen by a boy (number 10) of above average status. He is also chosen by two girls (number 16 and 20) and four boys (numbers 3, 4, 5, and 9) of below average status, and one boy (number 1) in the neglectee classification. A more accurate indication of the number of choices received by each pupil in the diagram is determined by their position within each section. Girl number 20, for example, is just below the average line, since she received four choices, while girl number 16, having received two choices, is in the lower part of the below average section. Thus, this method of recording yields most of the information presented in the cumulative record form plus a graphic picture of the individual's sociometric pattern. Although level of choice given by each individual pupil is not included in this illustrative form, it may be easily included by using different colors, or different types of lines, for each choice level. The numbers used to identify pupils may also be replaced by names, if the form is placed on a full-sized cumulative record sheet.

Although the advantages of this method of recording sociometric data for each individual are somewhat offset by the amount of work involved, the procedure is not as complicated as it first appears. In the illustration in Figure 4 the sociometric pattern is that of the most highly chosen boy. Since he had relations with approximately two-thirds of the pupils in class, his sociometric pattern is one of the most complex in the group. The majority of the pupils would have between five and seven group members in their sociometric patterns. Using a standardized mimeographed form, the information for most pupils could be recorded in a relatively few minutes.

In addition to using the sociometric pattern form as a method of recording sociometric data in permanent records, it is also useful for studying the social development of particular individuals within the classroom. When special efforts are directed toward improving the social adjustment of a certain pupil, constructing a separate sociometric pattern for that pupil helps to focus attention on his social relations with other group members. Such diagrams, based on periodic sociometric testing, will provide a more sensitive index of changes in his social relations than the more general sociogram or matrix table.

SUMMARY

In analyzing sociometric data the first step is usually the tabulation of the results in a matrix table. This is merely a twofold table for recording and summarizing the sociometric choices each individual has given and received. The construction and use of the matrix table is relatively simple and yields data which can be used in a descriptive manner or which can be subjected to further analysis. In determining the sociometric status of individuals in the matrix table each choice is given a value of one regardless of level of choice. This procedure is based on the lack of a sound rationale for weighting choices and the similarity in the reliability of weighted and unweighted sociometric choices. Interpretation of the matrix table can be simplified and sociometric data from different groups can be made comparable by classifying the data into Bronfenbrenner's (5) fixed reference groups.

For most classroom purposes the data in the matrix table are converted into a sociogram. This is a graphic presentation of the underlying social structure of a group. Plotting the social structure on a target diagram with fixed points of reference results in the most generally useful type of sociogram. Interpretations of the basic sociometric structures found in the sociogram depend on the judicious use of questions and supplementary information about the group members, as well as an understanding of sociometric theory and research.

Other methods of analyzing and presenting sociometric results include the index method, the sociograph, and matrix analysis. The latter method offers promising leads toward a standardized method of presenting sociometric results. However, matrix analysis is still in the process of development and is most useful in large-scale research studies.

Several methods of recording sociometric results in permanent records have been found useful. Both the Dunlap Method and the Northway Methods could be adapted for use with cumulative record systems in schools. The time invested in keeping such records would bring rich rewards, if used as a basis for improving the social development of individual pupils.

REFERENCES

1. Beum, C. O., and Criswell, J. H., "Application of Machine Tabulation Methods to Sociometric Data," *Sociometry,* 1947, *10:*227–232.
2. Bjerstedt, A., *Interpretations of Sociometric Choice Status,* Lund, Sweden, Gleerup, 1956.
3. Bonney, M. E., and Fessenden, S. A., *Manual, Bonney-Fessenden Sociograph,* Los Angeles, California Test Bureau, 1955.
4. Bronfenbrenner, U., "The Graphic Presentation of Sociometric Data," *Sociometry,* 1944, *7:*283–289.
5. Bronfenbrenner, U., "The Measurement of Sociometric Status, Structure and Development," *Sociometry Monographs,* No. 6, New York, Beacon House, 1945.

6. Clark, R. A., and McGuire, C., "Sociographic Analysis of Sociometric Valuations," *Child Development,* 1952, *23:*129–140.
7. Criswell, J. H., "Foundations of Sociometric Measurement," *Sociometry,* 1946, *9:*7–13.
8. Criswell, J. H., "The Measurement of Group Integration," *Sociometry,* 1947, *10:*259–267.
9. Criswell, J. H., "Sociometric Concepts in Personnel Administration," *Sociometry,* 1949, *12:*287–300.
10. Criswell, J. H., "Sociometric Methods of Measuring Group Preferences," *Sociometry,* 1943, *6:*398–408.
11. Dahlke, H. O., and Monahan, T. O., "Problems in the Application of Sociometry to Schools," *School Review,* 1949, *57:*223–234.
12. Dunlap, C., "Recording of Sociometric Data Made Concise and Continuous," *School Review,* 1952, *60:*225–229.
13. Festinger, L., "The Analysis of Sociograms Using Matrix Algebra," *Human Relations,* 1949, *2:*153–158.
14. Forsyth, E., and Katz, L., "A Matrix Approach to the Analysis of Sociometric Data: A Preliminary Report," *Sociometry,* 1946, *9:*340–347.
15. Gronlund, N. E., "The Relative Stability of Classroom Social Status with Unweighted and Weighted Sociometric Status Scores," *Journal of Educational Psychology,* 1955, *46:*345–354.
16. Jennings, H. H., "Structure of Leadership-Development and Sphere of Influence," *Sociometry,* 1937, *1:*99–143.
17. Katz, L., "On the Matrix Analysis of Sociometric Data," *Sociometry,* 1947, *10:*233–241.
18. Katz, L., "Punched Card Technique for the Analysis of Multiple Level Sociometric Data," *Sociometry,* 1950, *13:*108–122.
19. Lindzey, G., and Borgatta, E. F., "Sociometric Measurement," Chapter 11, in G. Lindzey (ed.), *Handbook of Social Psychology,* Cambridge, Massachusetts, Addison-Wesley Publishing Company, 1954.
20. Loomis, C. P., and Pepinsky, H. B., "Sociometry, 1937–1947; Theory and Methods," *Sociometry,* 1948, *11:*272–287.
21. Luce, D. R., and Perry, A. D., "A Method of Matrix Analysis of Group Structure," *Psychometrika,* 1949, *14:*95–116.

22. Luebke, P. T., "Charting Sociometric Data," *National Elementary Principal,* 1954, *34:*175–179.
23. Moreno, J. L., *Who Shall Survive?* New York, Beacon House, 1953.
24. Northway, M. L., "A Method for Depicting Social Relationships Obtained by Sociometric Testing," *Sociometry,* 1940, *3:*144–150.
25. Northway, M. L., "A Plan for Sociometric Studies in a Longitudinal Programme of Research in Child Development," *Sociometry,* 1954, *17:*272–281.
26. Northway, M. L., *A Primer of Sociometry,* Toronto, University of Toronto Press, 1952.
27. Proctor, C. H., and Loomis, C. P., "Analysis of Sociometric Data," Chapter 17, in M. Jahoda, M. Deutsch, and S. W. Cook (eds.), *Research Methods in Social Relations,* Part II, New York, Dryden Press, 1951.

CHAPTER 4

TYPICAL SOCIOMETRIC PATTERNS

Sociometric results obtained from different groups will vary according to the sociometric criteria used, the number of choices allotted, the directions used, and the level of socialization achieved by the various groups. Thus, it is not expected that the distribution of sociometric choices or the resulting social structures will be comparable from group to group. Some groups will contain a relatively large number of stars and isolates while others will contain few or none; some groups will have many mutual choices while others will have relatively few; and some groups will reflect a greater cleavage between subgroups than do others. Despite these variations, however, sociometric results from different groups have revealed some common patterns. Certain phenomena have occurred frequently enough in sociometric testing to be considered typical of sociometric findings.

This chapter will present some typical sociometric results for various grade levels. The basic data, presented in tabular form, were obtained from several school systems. Sociometric results for grades three through six were obtained from elementary schools in a large city located in the Midwest. The data for grades seven through twelve represent the total population of a junior and senior high school located in a small Midwestern city. The college classes were composed of seniors in a teacher-training curriculum. The sociometric data were gathered in all public school classrooms between six and eight months after the beginning of the school year. The college students had spent seven weeks together at the time of the sociometric testing. This involved class discussion in education classes that met daily. Similar directions were used with the sociometric test at all grade levels. In all groups the pupils were instructed to confine their choices to their classmates.

DISTRIBUTION OF SOCIOMETRIC CHOICES

One of the most common phenomena in sociometric testing is the uneven distribution of sociometric choices. A relatively small number of group members receive a large number of sociometric choices, while others receive few or none. When the total distribution of choices is analyzed, it is found to be positively skewed. That is, more group members appear at the lower sociometric status positions than appear at the higher sociometric status positions. This is brought out clearly in Table 4.

Table 4 presents the percentage of pupils above and below the expected value at various grade levels. Since five sociometric choices were allotted on one criterion, the expected value, or average number of choices received, would be five. With a normal distribution of choices 50 percent of the pupils would be above this expected value and 50 percent would be below. This assumes, of course, that those receiving exactly five choices would be evenly distributed between the above and below average groups. It will be noted in Table 4 that between 58 and 68 percent of the pupils received fewer choices than the expected value. In other words, almost two-thirds of the pupils were below average in sociometric status. This, of course, is a result of the undue proportion of choices going to pupils in the above average category. The percentage of pupils above and below the expected value is fairly consistent at all grade levels. Similarly consistent results were found by Bronfenbrenner (*2*) for pupils enrolled in classes from kindergarten through grade six. He found that approximately 60 percent of the pupils fell below the expected value in number of sociometric choices received. This tendency for the distribution of

TABLE 4. Percentage of Pupils Chosen Above and Below Expected Value, Using Five Sociometric Choices with One Sociometric Criterion

Grade Level	Number of Classrooms	Number of Pupils	Percentage of Pupils	
			Above Expected Value	Below Expected Value
3	9	270	40	60
4	10	277	41	59
5	10	268	40	60
6	10	284	39	61
7	6	171	38	62
8	6	146	41	59
9	8	173	42	58
10	6	135	38	62
11	6	105	35	65
12	5	105	32	68
College	5	144	38	62

NOTE: Criteria: *Work Companion* (grades 3–6), *Seating Companion* (grades 7–12), and *Teaching Companion* (college).

sociometric choices to be positively skewed has been designated a *sociodynamic law* by Moreno (*7*). He indicates that the uneven distribution of sociometric choices is similar to the uneven distribution of wealth in a society. Thus, few are "sociometrically wealthy" but many are "sociometrically poor."

A more detailed distribution of sociometric choices is presented in Table 5. Here the pupils are classified into the five sociometric categories based on Bronfenbrenner's fixed frame of reference (*2*). Thus, using five sociometric choices with one sociometric criterion the categories have the following values:

Star	9 or more choices
Above average	5–8 choices
Below average	2–5 choices
Neglectee	1 choice
Isolate	No choices

In calculating the two average groups, those pupils receiving exactly five choices were evenly divided between the above average and below average categories.

It will be noted that the percentage of pupils in each sociometric category remains fairly constant from grade three through grade ten. From grade eleven on, however, there is a consistently smaller percentage of pupils in the star and neglectee categories, with an increase in the percentage of pupils in the below average group. This shifting of pupils from the extreme sociometric positions toward the average may be due to the tendency to form more cliques and small subgroups at these grade levels. A larger number of groups at each grade level, however, would be necessary to verify such an assumption.

The extent to which distributions of sociometric choices are positively skewed is readily apparent in Table 5. At all grade levels, there are almost twice as many pupils in the below average category as there are in the above average group. The combined percentages in the neglectee and isolate categories also exceed those in the star category, at all grade levels except the fourth. Thus, there is a tendency for groups to contain more pupils with extremely low sociometric status than with high status. An analysis of the percentage of choices received by these extreme groups revealed that the 7 to 17 percent of the pupils in the star category captured between 17 and 41 percent of all of the choices given. In contrast, the pupils in the neglectee and isolate categories received less than 3 percent of the choices, although there were between 11 and 22 percent of the pupils in these groups.

Of special interest in Table 5 is the fact that isolates appear at all grade levels. It might be assumed that after attending school for a period of time every pupil would receive at least one choice as a desired associate. Apparently just being a member of a group does not assure acceptance by the group.

Although the percentage of isolates at the secondary school level is similar to that of the elementary school level, it must be

TABLE 5. Percentage of Pupils in Each Sociometric Category at Various-Grade Levels, Using Five Sociometric Choices with One Sociometric Criterion

Grade Level	Number of Class-rooms	Number of Pupils	Percentage in Each Sociometric Category: Star	Above Average	Below Average	Neglectee	Isolate
3	9	270	14	26	41	13	6
4	10	277	15	26	45	8	6
5	10	268	15	25	41	14	5
6	10	284	17	22	39	14	8
7	6	171	11	27	49	10	3
8	6	146	11	30	43	15	1
9	8	173	14	28	39	14	5
10	6	135	15	23	46	11	5
11	6	105	8	27	52	7	6
12	5	105	7	25	53	8	7
College	5	144	8	30	51	8	3

NOTE: Criteria: *Work Companion* (grades 3–6), *Seating Companion* (grades 7–12), and *Teaching Companion* (college).

taken into account that approximately 40 percent of the pupils drop out of school between grades nine and twelve. Since Kuhlen and Collister (*6*) have shown that drop-outs tend to have low social acceptance, fewer isolates would be expected at the secondary school level. Thus, it is possible that the percentage of isolates actually increases during the high school years and that this increase does not appear in Table 5 because of the disproportionate number of isolates dropping out of school. Nevertheless, the table does indicate that a certain percentage of pupils at all grade levels need help in improving their social relations. If the neglectees (those receiving only one choice) are included in this category, between 11 and 22 percent of the pupils could benefit from such help.

INFLUENCE OF CRITERIA ON CHOICE DISTRIBUTIONS

The typically uneven distribution of sociometric choices remains fairly consistent over different criteria, as well as over different age groups. A reanalysis of data (*3*) obtained from forty sixth-grade classrooms is presented in Table 6. It will be noted here that the percentage of pupils appearing in each sociometric category is similar for the criteria of seating companion, work companion, and play companion. The slightly smaller percentage of pupils in the star and neglectee categories on the play companion criterion indicates a more general distribution of choices. However, the positive skewness, discussed earlier, is clearly evident in all three distributions. Approximately 39 percent of the pupils had higher than average sociometric status with 61 percent falling somewhere below the average point.

TABLE 6. Percentage of Pupils in Each Sociometric Category on the Criteria of Seating Companion, Work Companion, and Play Companion in Forty Sixth-Grade Classrooms

Criteria (5 Choices Allotted on Each)	Percentage in Each Sociometric Category				
	Star	Above Average	Below Average	Neglectee	Isolate
Seating	15	24	42	11	8
Work	13	26	41	12	8
Play	11	29	45	8	7

NOTE: There was an average of 16 boys and 16 girls in each classroom.

Since the criteria of seating companion, work companion, and play companion cover the major activities in the pupils' school day, it is discouraging to note the consistency with which a certain percentage of neglectees and isolates appear in all three distributions. The hope that acceptance on the playground will make up for lack of acceptance in classroom activities becomes very unrealistic. To determine the extent to which pupils remained in the same relative position on the three sociometric criteria, their sociometric-status scores were correlated. For the forty classrooms, the mean correlation coefficients ranged from .76 to .89 between the various pairs of criteria (*4*). Thus, there was a tendency for pupils to remain in the same sociometric position on all three sociometric questions. Those with high sociometric status as seating companions tended also to have high status as work companions and play companions. Conversely, pupils least accepted as seating companions tended to remain in this position as work companions and play companions. This pervasiveness of the lack of acceptance on the part of some pupils should be of special concern to those interested in improving the social relations of pupils.

INFLUENCE OF THE PUPILS' SEX ON CHOICE DISTRIBUTIONS

Teachers frequently remark that girls are more accepted by their classmates than boys. Although their behavior may be more acceptable to the teacher, sociometric results show no difference in the degree of acceptance they experience among their peers. Table 7 presents a comparison of the relative percentage of boys and girls in the extreme sociometric categories. Although the average sociometric categories have been omitted from this table, they follow the same general distribution presented earlier with no distinction between boys and girls.

TABLE 7. Relative Percentage of Boys and Girls in the Star, Neglectee, and Isolate Categories on the Criteria of Seating Companion, Work Companion, and Play Companion in Forty Sixth-Grade Classrooms

Criteria (5 Choices Allotted on Each)	Percentage in Star Category		Percentage in Neglectee Category		Percentage in Isolate Category	
	Boys	Girls	Boys	Girls	Boys	Girls
Seating	13	17	11	11	7	8
Work	12	15	12	11	7	8
Play	12	10	8	9	8	6

NOTE: There was an average of 16 boys and 16 girls in each classroom.

The slightly larger percentage of girls in the star category on the seating companion and work companion criteria and the lower percentage on the play companion criterion can probably be accounted for by random variations in the data. For all practical purposes, an equal percentage of boys and girls are socially neglected or isolated among their classmates. The tendency of teachers to view girls as possessing more socially desirable characteristics than boys (*8*) needs to be overcome, if they are to be most helpful in improving the social relations of both boys and girls.

INFLUENCE OF THE NUMBER OF CHOICES ON CHOICE DISTRIBUTIONS

It might be assumed that increasing the number of choices allotted to a sociometric criterion would even out the distribution of choices among the pupils. However, it has been found in sociometric testing that when an increased number of choices is made available to a group, the pattern of distribution tends to remain the same. Highly chosen pupils receive an undue proportion of the new choices, and the majority of the isolates remain unchosen. The persistence of this uneven distribution of sociometric choices with varying numbers of choices allotted is illustrated in Table 8. This distribution of choices for a sixth-grade class indicates the number of choices each boy and girl received when three, four, and five choices were used with one sociometric criterion. It will be noted that the pupils remained in approximately the same relative position when an increased number of choices was available for distribution. In fact, a rank-order correlation of .92 was obtained between the sociometric status of these pupils based on the use of three choices and their sociometric status based on five choices. Similar correlations for eleven classrooms from the fourth to the sixth grades (*5*) ranged from .72 to .92. Thus, although nearly twice as many choices are available for distribution when five choices are allotted than when three are used, the distribution follows essentially the same pattern.

It will be noted in Table 8, however, that the number of stars increases slightly and the number of neglectees and isolates decreases slightly as the number of choices is increased. This partly accounts for the varying percentages of stars and isolates reported by different investigators (*2, 7*). The larger spread of scores with

TABLE 8. Relative Number of Choices Received by Boys and Girls in a Sixth-Grade Class, Using Three, Four, and Five Sociometric Choices on One Sociometric Criterion

	No. of Choices Received				No. of Choices Received		
Boys	3 Choices	4 Choices	5 Choices	Girls	3 Choices	4 Choices	5 Choices
1	12	12	13	1	11	12	13
2	10	12	12	2	6	7	12
3	4	9	11	3	6	8	11
4	4	6	7	4	5	11	12
5	4	5	5	5	4	6	8
6	2	3	3	6	4	4	6
7	1	1	3	7	3	4	5
8	1	1	2	8	2	3	4
9	0	1	2	9	2	2	2
10	0	0	0	10	1	2	2
11	0	0	0	11	1	1	1
12	0	0	0	12	1	1	1
13	0	0	0	13	0	1	3
				14	0	0	2
				15	0	0	0

NOTE: Criterion: *Work Companion.*

five sociometric choices would seem to favor their use. In fact, Bronfenbrenner's (*2*) table of critical raw status scores indicates that neglectees cannot be distinguished from isolates on one sociometric criterion unless five choices are allotted.

The persistent tendency for the uneven distribution of choices to remain as the number of sociometric choices is increased has been called *sociodynamic effect* by Moreno (*7*). It indicates that the largest number of choices will continue to go to the highly chosen group members, while other group members will be continually ignored in the choosing. Phrasing it in terms of the distribution of wealth, again, "the sociometrically rich get richer" and "the sociometrically poor remain poor."

In summary, the distribution of sociometric choices persistently reveals a larger percentage of pupils with low sociometric status than with high sociometric status. Since this uneven distribution of choices may be found at all age levels, over different sociometric criteria, among both boys and girls, and with varying numbers of choices, it may be considered typical of sociometric results. Although the relative percentage of pupils in each sociometric category will vary somewhat from one group to another, the positively skewed distribution of choices will remain.

CHOICES BETWEEN BOYS AND GIRLS

It has been noted in sociometric choosing among school children that there is a cleavage between the sexes. That is, boys tend to direct the majority of their choices toward boys, and girls confine the majority of their choices to girls. The extent to which this cleavage exists at various grade levels is shown in Table 9. The percentage of choices boys gave to girls varied between 11 and 18 percent up to the tenth grade where it increased slightly, reaching its peak at the college level. However, even at the college level less than a third of the boys' choices were given to the girls. Somewhat similar results are presented for girls, although no increase in cross-sex choices is apparent at the high school level. Except for the lower percentages at the sixth- and the tenth-grade levels, the percentage of choices girls gave to boys remained consistently

TABLE 9. Percentage of Choices Between Boys and Girls at Various Grade Levels, Using Five Sociometric Choices with One Sociometric Criterion

Grade Level	Number of Classrooms	Number of Pupils		Percentage of Choices	
		Boys	Girls	Boys Chose Girls	Girls Chose Boys
3	9	129	141	13	12
4	10	144	133	11	15
5	10	142	126	18	16
6	10	138	146	15	10
7	6	96	75	13	15
8	6	78	68	11	15
9	8	88	85	17	17
10	6	66	69	21	9
11	6	50	55	25	17
12	5	46	59	15	14
College	5	81	63	31	40

NOTE: Criteria: *Work Companion* (grades 3–6), *Seating Companion* (grades 7–12), and *Teaching Companion* (college).

between 12 and 17 percent for grades three through twelve. At the college level the percentage rose to 40 percent. Thus, it is apparent that a sex cleavage remains even at the college level, although it has lessened considerably by this time.

In terms of developmental trends among boys and girls, one would expect cross-sex choices to increase considerably during the junior and senior high school period. Although there was a slight trend in this direction among the boys, no such increase was apparent in the girls' choices. This may be due to selective factors in the data analyzed or to the restricted nature of the choosing situation. Since the junior and senior high school classrooms were located in a small community, it is possible that there was less opportunity for boy-girl interaction than would be found in a large city. Limiting the choices to classmates may also partly account for the lack of an increase in cross-sex choices, especially for the girls. They may have had an interest in associating with members of the opposite sex in other classrooms or at other grade levels but were compelled to choose among the members of their own classroom. This restriction on the choosing may have depressed the percentage of cross-sex choices given. Limiting the sociometric test to one criterion may also account for the lack of expected results, as will be noted later. Nevertheless, the tendency for boys and girls to confine the majority of their choices to members of their own sex indicates a sex cleavage that is typical of sociometric results at all grade levels.

INFLUENCE OF CRITERIA ON CROSS-SEX CHOICES

Observation of children's groups indicates the tendency for boys and girls to interact more readily in certain activities than in others. This would lead to the expectation that the degree to which a sex cleavage appeared in sociometric choosing would be partly dependent upon the nature of the sociometric criterion. To test this assumption, the percentage of cross-sex choices was determined for the criteria of seating companion, work companion, and play companion in forty sixth-grade classes (*3*). The results are presented in Table 10.

TABLE 10. Percentage of Choices Between Boys and Girls on the Criteria of Seating Companion, Work Companion, and Play Companion in Forty Sixth-Grade Classrooms

Criteria (Five Choices Allotted on Each)	Percentage of Choices			
	Boys Chose Girls		Girls Chose Boys	
	Total	Range	Total	Range
Seating	11	0–38	9	0–23
Work	8	0–29	6	0–16
Play	4	0–29	5	0–16

NOTE: There was an average of 16 boys and 16 girls in each classroom.

It will be noted that the percentage of sociometric choices boys and girls exchanged with each other shows a steady decline from the choice of seating companions to the choice of play companions. The relatively small percentage of cross-sex choices on the play companion criterion is readily understandable in terms of the distinction between play activities considered suitable for boys and girls in our culture. The terms "sissy" and "tomboy" are well-known labels for the boy and girl who dare venture into the play activities of members of the opposite sex.

The fact that the percentage of cross-sex choices does vary from one sociometric criterion to another limits the interpretations that can be made about boy-girl relations from one sociometric situation. Although a sex cleavage is apparent among school children, the extent of this cleavage cannot be determined except with reference to a particular activity. A large number of sociometric criteria would be necessary to obtain a true picture of boy-girl relations at various age levels.

Of particular interest in Table 10 is the *range* of cross-sex choices among the different classes. In some classrooms none of the boys chose girls, while in others as many as 38 percent of the choices went to girls. Similar results are indicated for the girls' choices of boys, although the range is smaller. This raised an interesting question concerning the degree to which the school influenced the presence or absence of cross-sex choices on the sociometric test. A reanalysis of the data provided at least a partial answer to this question.

INFLUENCE OF SCHOOL ON CROSS-SEX CHOICES

To determine the extent to which the percentage of cross-sex choices varied among different schools, the forty sixth-grade classrooms, discussed above, were arranged according to the fourteen elementary schools in which they were located. The percentage of cross-sex choices in each school is presented in Table 11. Since the percentage of boys choosing girls was so similar to the percentage of girls choosing boys, these were combined to provide one set of percentages indicating cross-sex choices.

TABLE 11. Percentage of Cross-Sex Choices on the Criteria of Seating Companion, Work Companion, and Play Companion in Forty Sixth-Grade Classrooms from Fourteen Different Elementary Schools

School	Number of Classrooms[a]	Percentage of Cross-Sex Choices[b]		
		Seating	Work	Play
1	3	21	15	7
2	2	17	11	8
3	3	13	12	8
4	2	12	6	5
5	3	11	8	6
6	4	10	9	5
7	3	9	7	5
8	2	9	6	8
9	4	8	7	4
10	3	8	5	4
11	3	8	7	2
12	2	8	3	2
13	3	7	4	2
14	3	6	4	2

[a] There was an average of 16 boys and 16 girls in each classroom.
[b] Based on five sociometric choices for each criterion.

A glance at Table 11 readily reveals the variation among schools in the percentage of cross-sex choices. Moving from school one down the table to school fourteen, it will be noticed that the percentage of cross-sex choices tends to drop consistently on all three sociometric criteria. This consistency from one criterion to another lends support to the hunch that the nature of the school influences the extent to which pupils express a desire to associate with members of the opposite sex for certain activities. Schools with a relatively small percentage of cross-sex choices, like the last several in the table, in all probability have separate playgrounds for boys and girls, encourage boy-girl competition in the classroom, and in other ways widen the cleavage between the sexes. In contrast, those schools with a relatively large percentage of cross-sex choices probably encourage and arrange for boy-girl interaction in school activities. Although we can only speculate concerning the probable causes of the differences between these schools, the fact that boy-girl relations can be modified is noteworthy.

The decline in the percentage of cross-sex choices, moving across the table, from the seating companion criterion to the play companion criterion is also clearly visible in Table 11. The fact that this decline is consistent among the various schools reinforces earlier statements that the percentage of cross-sex choices is influenced by the nature of the sociometric criterion. The relatively small percentage of cross-sex choices on the play companion criterion, in all fourteen schools, also substantiates the belief that the cleavage between boys and girls is greatest in the area of play activities.

Although the percentage of cross-sex choices in sociometric choosing varies with the grade level of the pupils, the nature of the sociometric criterion, and the school in which the test is administered, the fact that a sex cleavage continues to appear under all conditions should not be overlooked. Variations from one situation to another make it difficult to indicate what degree of sex cleavage is desirable or characteristic for a given age level. However, the preference boys and girls have shown for members of their own sex occurs so persistently in sociometric choosing that a sex cleavage can be considered typical of sociometric results at these age levels.

MUTUAL CHOICES

A mutual choice is indicated when two group members choose each other on the same sociometric criterion. Since mutual choices reflect a common desire to associate together, the number of mutual choices in a group is a general indication of the degree of socialization among the group members. Newly formed groups have relatively few mutual choices, and the number increases as the group members become better acquainted (*2, 7*). This variation in the number of mutual choices with the development of the group makes it difficult to indicate the percentage of mutual choices that might typically be expected in classroom groups at a particular time. However, data on mutual choices in groups where the choice process has become stabilized should provide some indication of the extent to which mutual choices might be expected.

Table 12 presents the percentage of boys and girls with mutual choices at various grade levels. It will be noted that a relatively large percentage of pupils have mutual choices at all grade levels. This is partly due to the fact that all of the class members, except those in the college group, had been together between six and eight months. Smaller percentages would be expected earlier in the school year. The pupils without mutual choices tend to be those in the low sociometric status categories. This is accounted for primarily by the fact that low status group members tend to choose high status group members and high status group members tend to choose each other (*1*). Since low status group members do not choose each other, their choices remain unreciprocated.

Although the percentage of pupils with mutual choices is relatively large at all grade levels, it is interesting to note that the percentage increases at the seventh-grade level and remains above

TABLE 12. Percentage of Pupils with Mutual Choices at Various Grade Levels, Using Five Sociometric Choices with One Sociometric Criterion

Grade Level	Number of Classrooms	Number of Pupils		Percentage With Mutual Choices	
		Boys	Girls	Boys	Girls
3	9	129	141	78	77
4	10	144	133	74	81
5	10	142	126	81	80
6	10	138	146	67	71
7	6	96	75	87	84
8	6	78	68	82	96
9	8	88	85	86	84
10	6	66	69	88	93
11	6	50	55	84	93
12	5	46	59	83	88
College	5	81	63	90	84

NOTE: Criteria: *Work Companion* (grades 3–6), *Seating Companion* (grades 7–12), and *Teaching Companion* (college).

82 percent throughout the high school and college levels. This is probably a reflection of the more complex social structures formed during this period (7). To check on this assumption the percentage of pupils with three or more mutual choices was calculated for each grade level. For grades three through six, between 19 and 31 percent of the pupils had three or more mutual choices. At grade seven the percentage rose to 45 and remained above 40 percent throughout the junior and senior high school period. The consistently larger percentage of pupils with three or more mutual choices, at these grade levels, indicates the formation of more complex sociometric patterns characteristic of a higher level of socialization.

DISTRIBUTION OF MUTUAL CHOICES BY SEX

The sex cleavage between boys and girls in sociometric choosing is strikingly apparent when mutual choices are considered. Although between one-third and one-half of the sociometric choices at various grade levels are mutual choices, a relatively small percentage of these mutual choices occur between members of the opposite sex. This tendency for mutual choices to be confined to members of the same sex is brought out clearly in Table 13. The percentage of mutual choices reported, within the same sex group and between the sexes, refers to the percentage based on the total number of choices given at each grade level. It will be noted that the percentage of mutual choices between boys and girls varies between 1 and 3 percent until the ninth grade. Here it rises to 6 percent and remains at this slightly higher level throughout the high school period. This increase in mutual choices between the sexes during the adolescent period would be expected in terms of the development of heterosexual interests. However, even a larger increase than that reported might be expected. The fact that the percentage of girls choosing boys did not increase during the high school period, as indicated earlier, probably accounts for the relatively small percentage of mutual choices between the sexes at these grade levels. It can only be surmised

TABLE 13. Percentage of Mutual Choices at Various Grade Levels, Using Five Sociometric Choices with One Sociometric Criterion

Grade Level	Number of Classrooms	Number of Pupils		Percentage of Mutuals		
				Within Sex		Between Sexes
		Boys	Girls	Boys	Girls	
3	9	129	141	34	38	2
4	10	144	133	36	35	2
5	10	142	126	35	37	3
6	10	138	146	31	35	1
7	6	96	75	40	41	2
8	6	78	68	42	48	2
9	8	88	85	41	49	6
10	6	66	69	38	48	4
11	6	50	55	34	39	7
12	5	46	59	33	38	5
College	5	81	63	33	22	12

NOTE: Criteria: *Work Companion* (grades 3–6), *Seating Companion* (grades 7–12), and *Teaching Companion* (college).

that more mutual choices between adolescent boys and girls would have occurred if the sociometric test had not restricted their choices to pupils in their own classroom.

There are a few interesting things to note concerning the percentage of mutual choices boys and girls exchanged with members of their own sex. First, the percentage of choices that were mutual is relatively high at all grade levels. It indicates that approximately two of the five choices given on the sociometric test were reciprocated by a mutual choice from a member of the same sex. In other words, the average boy and girl had approximately two mutual friends among their classmates.

The larger percentage of mutual choices from the seventh to the tenth grades indicates the increased socialization among adolescents, referred to earlier. The slight decline for boys from the eleventh grade on can probably be accounted for by the increased percentage of choices directed toward girls at these grade levels. The more noticeable drop in percentage for girls at the college level is also probably due to the relatively large percentage of cross-sex choices. It will be recalled that 40 percent of the college girls' choices went to members of the opposite sex.

Except for the fourth grade and the college level, girls had a consistently larger percentage of mutual choices than boys. This greater tendency of girls to form mutual pairs lends support to Moreno's (7) hypothesis that girls tend more toward socialization than boys. Since the largest differences between boys and girls occurred during grades eight to twelve, it appears that this tendency might be greatest during the adolescent period.

As with the other distributions of sociometric choices presented in this chapter, the data on mutual choices have been presented to indicate some typical sociometric results at various grade levels. However, the percentages reported here should not be considered a desirable goal or a set of norms by which to evaluate sociometric results from a specific classroom. So many factors enter into sociometric choosing that a specific set of standards or norms would be inappropriate for sociometric testing. Typically one can expect more mutual choices to appear as the level of socialization of the group members increases. The specific number of mutual choices obtained, however, must be evaluated in terms of the type of sociometric test used and the nature of the group being tested.

SUMMARY

Although sociometric results can be expected to vary from one group to another, certain phenomena occur with such persistence that they may be considered typical sociometric patterns. One of the most common findings in this regard is the positively skewed distribution of sociometric choices. This tendency for a larger percentage of the pupils to appear in the low sociometric status categories than in the high status categories has been shown to occur at all age levels, over different sociometric criteria, among both sexes, and with varying numbers of sociometric choices. The consistency with which this positive skewness has appeared in sociometric results has led to the formulation of Moreno's *sociodynamic law.* This law states that distributions of sociometric choices are positively skewed.

When an increased number of sociometric choices is made available to a group, there is a tendency for the largest number of choices to continue to go to the group members with high sociometric status while those with low sociometric status continue to receive a disproportionately small share of the choices. This tendency has been called *sociodynamic effect* by Moreno. Typical sociometric results, presented in this chapter, have illustrated the operation of the *sociodynamic law* and the *sociodynamic effect* among pupils at various grade levels in the public school.

The persistence with which socially neglected and socially isolated pupils appear in the classroom, at all grade levels, indicates their need for help in improving their social relations. Sociometric results at various grade levels indicated that between 11 and 22 percent of the pupils were neglected or ignored by their classmates.

Another common phenomenon appearing in sociometric results of children and adolescents is the sex cleavage. Boys and girls both show preference for members of their own sex in sociometric choosing. The extent of this cleavage, however, varies with the grade level of the pupils and the nature of the sociometric criterion. A slightly larger percentage of cross-sex choices has been shown to occur at the high school and college levels. The lowest percentage of cross-sex choices appeared on the play companion criterion, at all grade levels. It was also shown that the percentage of cross-sex choices varied from one school to another.

The extent to which mutual choices occur in sociometric choosing is a general indication of the socialization level of the group. Sociometric results at various grade levels have indicated an increase in mutual choices during the junior and senior high school periods. There was also a general tendency for girls to have more mutual choices than boys, indicating a possible trend toward greater socialization on the part of girls. The percentage of mutual choices between boys and girls was relatively low at all grade levels but showed a slight increase during the adolescent period. Although mutual choices can be typically expected in sociometric choosing, it was pointed out that the percentage of such choices will be influenced by the type of sociometric test used and the nature of the group being tested.

The sociometric results presented in this chapter were intended to illustrate some typical sociometric patterns among school children and adolescents. However, the percentages of pupils occurring in various distributions should not be considered as norms or standards for a given grade level. The complexity of factors entering into sociometric choosing makes norms and standards inappropriate for sociometric testing.

REFERENCES

1. Bonney, M. E., "A Study of the Sociometric Process Among Sixth-Grade Children," *Journal of Educational Psychology,* 1946, *37:*356–372.
2. Bronfenbrenner, U., "The Measurement of Sociometric Status, Structure and Development," *Sociometry Monographs,* No. 6, New York, Beacon House, 1945.
3. Gronlund, N. E., "The Accuracy of Teachers' Judgments Concerning the Sociometric Status of Sixth-Grade Pupils," *Sociometry Monographs,* No. 25, New York, Beacon House, 1951.
4. Gronlund, N. E., "Generality of Sociometric Status over Criteria in Measurement of Social Acceptability," *Elementary School Journal,* 1955, *56:*173–176.
5. Gronlund, N. E., "The Relative Stability of Classroom Social Status with Unweighted and Weighted Sociometric Choices," *Journal of Educational Psychology,* 1955, *46:*345–354.
6. Kuhlen, R. G., and Collister, E. G., "Sociometric Status of Sixth- and Ninth-Graders Who Fail to Finish High School," *Educational and Psychological Measurement,* 1952, *12:*632–637.
7. Moreno, J. L., *Who Shall Survive?* New York, Beacon House, 1953.
8. Tryon, C. M., "Evaluations of Adolescent Personality by Adolescents," *Monographs of the Society for Research in Child Development,* No. 4, Washington, D.C., National Research Council, 1939.

PART II

THE MEANING OF SOCIOMETRIC RESULTS

CHAPTER 5

THE RELIABILITY OF SOCIOMETRIC RESULTS

The extent to which sociometric results have any practical meaning is determined, in part, by the constancy of the sociometric scores. If the number of choices group members received on a sociometric test varied randomly from one test to another, sociometric results would be of little value in evaluating social adjustment, in analyzing group structure, in organizing classroom groups, or in diagnosing special school problems. Any such practical application assumes some constancy of the sociometric choices. On the other hand, perfect consistency from one test to another is neither expected nor desirable, owing to the dynamic nature of social relations. Revealing actual changes in social relations is as important a requirement of the sociometric test as providing results that are constant enough to have predictive value. These conflicting requirements—of revealing change and providing constancy of results—also occur with psychological measuring instruments. However, the greater variability in the area of social relations poses special problems in evaluating the reliability of sociometric results. Since special techniques have not been developed for coping with these problems, it has been necessary to utilize the traditional concepts of reliability developed in the area of psychometric measurement. Although there are recognized limitations in this procedure (*38*), it does provide evidence concerning the extent to which sociometric responses are constant under various conditions.

METHODS OF DETERMINING RELIABILITY

In general, reliability refers to the consistency with which a measuring instrument produces the same results. At least three types of consistency have been traditionally used in determining reliability.

1. Consistency within the test itself is determined by comparing the results on two halves of a test. The degree to which the scores on one-half of the test are related to the scores on the other half of the test serves as a measure of internal consistency. This is typically determined by correlating the two sets of scores, and the resulting correlation coefficient is called a *coefficient of internal consistency.* This coefficient merely indicates the degree to which different parts of the test are consistent in measuring the same thing. The general method for determining this type of reliability is commonly referred to as the *split-half method.*

2. Consistency of test results over two different administrations of the same test refers to the stability of the test. Typically the same test would be administered twice to a group, with a given time span between the two administrations, and the resulting test scores would be correlated. This correlation coefficient is called a *coefficient of stability* and indicates the degree to which the test results are stable over a given period of time. This general procedure is called the *test-retest method* of determining reliability.

3. Consistency over two different forms of the same test is also used as a measure of reliability. Two equivalent forms are administered at approximately the same time and their resulting scores are correlated. The *coefficient of equivalence* yielded by this procedure indicates the degree to which both forms of the test are

measuring the same thing. As might be expected this method of determining reliability is referred to as the *equivalent-forms method.*

All three of the above methods of determining reliability have been used in sociometric testing. Although these "borrowed" procedures have been directly applied to sociometric results, it should be pointed out that they have a different meaning in this new context. In the area of psychological testing, the various coefficients of reliability have been used to indicate the reliability of the test instruments themselves, whereas in sociometric testing they are more appropriately applied to the sociometric responses. Thus, when applied to sociometric testing, the various coefficients of reliability refer to the consistency of choice behavior, as reflected in the sociometric results, rather than to the characteristics of the test itself (*38*). In a very real sense, then, the question to be answered is, "How reliable are sociometric results?" rather than "How reliable is the sociometric technique?"

IMPORTANCE OF RELIABILITY OF SOCIOMETRIC RESULTS

The degree to which consistency of response in sociometric testing is desirable is determined to a large extent by the use to be made of the results. If the results are to be used solely for organizing temporary classroom groups, the consistency of the results are not an important consideration. The class members choose associates for some activity, the groups are formed on the basis of their choices, and the sociometric test has served its purpose. What their choices would be like three months later or for some other activity is of no concern to the purpose for which the test was used. Since sociometric results have been frequently limited to this use, the importance of reliability has been deëmphasized. For such limited use of the results, of course, consistency is not an important factor. However, for other uses of the sociometric data, and even for the organization of more permanent groups, consistency of sociometric results is of special concern.

When sociometric responses are used to evaluate the social adjustment of individuals or the social structure of groups, certain assumptions concerning the consistency of the responses become necessary. For example, the sociometric status of an individual would have few practical implications concerning his social acceptability or his leadership status, if the number of choices he received on a sociometric test varied considerably from day to day or from one choosing situation to another. Likewise, the identification of mutual choices, cliques, and cleavages would have little meaning for studying the social structure of groups, if these sociometric patterns were highly unstable. Thus, where a study of the status, structure, and development of groups is under consideration, a certain degree of constancy is required in sociometric results. The difficulty in evaluating the degree of constancy, of course, is in determining the extent to which variability in sociometric results reflects actual changes in sociometric preferences and the extent to which it indicates instability of the choice process. This is a complex problem that cannot be completely resolved. However, numerous research studies have shed light on the problem by indicating the extent to which sociometric results are constant under various conditions.

INTERNAL CONSISTENCY OF SOCIOMETRIC RESULTS

The split-half method, used to determine the internal consistency of sociometric data, has been applied in a relatively small number of sociometric studies. The usual procedure is to divide the group into two arbitrary halves and then to calculate the degree to which the sociometric status of individuals is comparable from one-half of the group to the other. The several studies in this area have reported rather high coefficients of internal consistency. At the sixth-grade level, Grossman and Wrighter (*22*) reported coefficients of internal consistency ranging from .93 to .97 for a variety of sociometric criteria, with three choices allotted to each one. Although only four sixth-grade classes were used in this study, similar correlation coefficients have been found by other investigators. Both Bass and White (*3*), and Ricciuti and French (*39*), reported correlation coefficients of .90 at the college level. Probably the most extensive use of the split-half method was by Ausubel, Schiff, and Gasser (*1*). They determined the internal consistency of sociometric ratings at the third-, fifth-, seventh-, eleventh-, and twelfth-grade levels. The resulting correlation coefficients ranged from .54 to .86 for the elementary and junior high school pupils and between .89 and .90 for the two high school groups.

Although the above studies indicate a relatively high degree of internal consistency in sociometric responses, the practical implications of these results are rather limited. The split-half method merely indicates how consistently an individual is chosen by different members of a particular group. Although this indicates the possible presence of a general social acceptability factor in the choosing, this method of determining reliability has no special significance for studying the status, structure, or development of groups. The stability of sociometric results over a period of time or from one situation to another cannot be assumed from measures of internal consistency. Thus, the restricted interpretations that can be made from coefficients of internal consistency in sociometric testing make them of little value as a general measure of the reliability of sociometric responses.

STABILITY OF SOCIOMETRIC RESULTS

The most frequently used method of determining the reliability of sociometric results is that of the test-retest method. Time intervals between the two administrations of the test have varied from one day to several years. Although a number of variables have been shown to influence the results, a significant degree of stability of sociometric responses has been reported in these investigations.

Studies in this area have usually been concerned with the stability of the number of sociometric choices received. The number of choices group members receive on one administration of the test is correlated with the number of choices they receive on a later administration of the test. The correlation coefficient, then, indicates the degree to which the sociometric status of individuals remains stable over a given period of time. It should be noted that the number of choices received by individuals may have a high degree of stability even though the choices given by the group members vary considerably. In fact, studies have shown a greater stability in the choices received than in the choices given. This merely indicates that the social relations among individuals is more variable than the ability of individuals to attract a certain degree of favorable or unfavorable response from others. Thus, friendships are made and broken but individuals tend to attract the same relative number of friends.

The stability of the number of sociometric choices received has direct implications for evaluating the social adjustment of individuals. If acceptance by peers is to be used as one indicator of social adjustment then this acceptance must have some degree of constancy. Unless highly chosen individuals tend to remain highly chosen and isolates and neglectees continue to receive relatively few choices, the predictive value of sociometric results is lessened considerably. Any inferences test results have for an individual's social adjustment are dependent to some degree on the stability of the behavior being measured. Thus, stability of sociometric status is expected and necessary when predictions concerning social adjustment are being considered.

STABILITY OF SOCIOMETRIC STATUS

The stability of sociometric status has been shown to vary from one age level to another. In general, the stability of the results is lowest at the nursery school and kindergarten levels and increases with the age of the subjects. The exact increase from one level to another is difficult to determine, however, owing to variations in the studies conducted at the various age levels. Variations in the time span between tests, the criteria used, the number of choices allotted, the length of acquaintance of the subjects, and similar factors, tend to confuse the results. Despite these variations, however, a significant degree of stability is reported in all studies, and a trend toward increased stability among older age groups can be detected.

NURSERY SCHOOL AND KINDERGARTEN LEVELS. There are relatively few studies concerned with the stability of sociometric status at this age level. A study under the direction of Northway (*36*) reported test-retest stability coefficients for a group of thirty-six children in a nursery school. Allotting three sociometric choices for three different classroom activities, correlation coefficients of .63 and .56 were obtained over a one-month and a three-month period. Bronfenbrenner (*11*) made a similar study of fourteen nursery school children and reported a stability coefficient of .27 over a seven-month period. Although less stability is to be expected over a longer period of time between test and retest, the relatively small number of subjects studied by Bronfenbrenner in all probability depressed the correlation coefficient obtained. In the same study he reported a coefficient of .67 for the stability of the sociometric status of twenty kindergarten pupils over a seven-month period. At both age levels he used three choices for each of three sociometric criteria (work, play, seating).

It is apparent from these few studies that even among young children the sociometric status of individuals is fairly stable over a period of months. Those that are highly chosen by the group tend to remain highly chosen and those with low group acceptance tend to remain in that category. Knowledge of the variability of the behavior of young children makes these reports of the stability of sociometric status all the more impressive.

ELEMENTARY SCHOOL LEVEL. The stability of sociometric results has received the greatest attention at the elementary school level. Studies have reported on the relative stability of sociometric status over a period of weeks, months, and years. Stability at various grade levels has been considered, and a few studies have been concerned with the stability of sociometric results in a camp setting. Even the stability of sociometric responses among retarded children has been given some attention.

Two studies reported on the stability of sociometric status over one-week, four-week and five-week internals, at the sixth-grade level. In both studies three choices each were allotted to four criteria pertaining to in-school and out-of-school activities. The composite sociometric status scores yielded stability coefficients ranging from .60 to .90 in one of the studies (*47*) and from .85 to .92 in the other (*43*). Both investigations included four sixth-grade classes. The largest correlation coefficients were obtained over the one-week interval and the smallest over the five-week interval. Similar results were found by Hunt and Solomon (*25*) in a summer camp for boys. Using a one-limit choice for best-liked camper, they obtained correlation coefficients ranging from .70 to .95 for a one-week interval. Stability coefficients for a two-week interval ranged from .42 to .84. There were twenty-three boys, aged five to eight years participating in the choosing. Another study in a camp setting reported an average correlation coefficient of .77 for choice of tent mates over a one-week interval (*35*). In this latter study five choices were allotted, and the subjects were thirty boys ranging in age from ten to thirteen years.

The size of the coefficients of stability tend to be retained, even when a period of months appears between the test and retest. Byrd (*12*) permitted twenty-seven fourth-grade pupils to choose classmates as fellow actors in a classroom play. Using an unlimited number of choices, he obtained a correlation coefficient of .89

when the test was repeated two months later. For nine elementary classrooms, ranging from the fourth to the sixth grade, Gronlund (*19*) reported an average stability coefficient of .75 over a four-month interval. This was based on one sociometric criterion (work companion) with five choices allotted to each pupil. In general, the largest coefficients were obtained at the higher grade levels. It is interesting to note that Bjerstedt (*5*) obtained similar results among Swedish school children. For three classrooms at the later elementary level, he reported an average correlation coefficient of .82 for pupils' sociometric status as work companions, over a four-month period. For a nine-month interval between tests, he reported an average stability coefficient of .72. Lower correlation coefficients were reported by Bronfenbrenner (*11*) for a five-month interval between tests. Using three choices each for the criteria of work, play, and seating, he obtained coefficients ranging from .28 to .59 for classrooms from the first to the sixth grade. It should be pointed out, however, that some of the classes contained as few as fourteen pupils, which would tend to reduce the size of the correlation coefficients.

The most extensive studies conducted on this problem have been those by Bonney (*6, 7*). He studied the stability of sociometric status scores over one-year intervals, for a four-year period. He first administered a sociometric test to a group of forty-eight second-grade pupils and then administered the same test to them as they passed through each successive grade level, up to the fifth grade. Sociometric status at each grade level was determined by combining the choices each pupil received on a number of criteria, based on classroom and social activities. The stability of this composite sociometric status score was evaluated by correlating the pupils' relative sociometric status between the various grade levels. Stability coefficients ranged from .67 to .84, for the one-year intervals between the successive grade levels. As a basis for comparison, intelligence tests and achievement tests were administered to the same pupils each year. Coefficients of stability for the intelligence test results ranged from .75 to .86 for the same one-year intervals, and for the achievement test results they ranged from .60 to .83. In brief, the sociometric status scores were as stable from one year to the next as were the intelligence test scores and the achievement test scores. Thus, Bonney has demonstrated that sociometric status, based on a number of sociometric criteria, has a relatively high degree of stability over a period of several years.

A study of the stability of sociometric results by Murray (*34*) is of special interest, since it was conducted with forty-three retarded children. The average IQ for the group was 70 and the children had an average age of eleven years, three months. Each child was interviewed individually by the investigator and asked to indicate his choices for best friends. There was no limit to the number of choices that could be made. Three tests, given approximately four months apart, yielded stability coefficients of .33 and .50. Although these correlation coefficients are not large, they do indicate that even among mentally retarded children sociometric status scores have a significant degree of stability.

The consistently high degree of stability, reported in the above studies, indicates that sociometric results can be used with reasonable confidence at the elementary school level. The sociometric status a pupil attains on one sociometric criterion is a fairly reliable index of his acceptance by the group for that particular activity. Where a number of sociometric criteria are used and a composite social acceptance score is calculated, the results are as stable as those of intelligence and achievement tests. In all probability, this composite social acceptance score is measuring the pupils' general social acceptability among his peers.

Although there is a tendency for sociometric status to be more stable over shorter periods of time and among older age groups, the degree of stability at lower grade levels and over relatively long periods of time is sufficient to warrant the use of sociometric testing in elementary classrooms at all grade levels. The greater variability at the lower grade levels, however, should alert teachers to the need for more frequent testing at these levels.

SECONDARY SCHOOL LEVEL. Although relatively few studies of the stability of sociometric status were conducted with high school classes, the stability coefficients reported tend to be as high or higher than those reported for the elementary school level. Studies among adolescents in out-of-school groups also tend to support the findings of studies conducted in school settings.

Northway (*37*) reported coefficients of stability of .90 over a one-week interval and .60 over a one-year interval for high school groups in Toronto. However, she did not indicate the nature of the choosing situation nor the size of the group tested. Bretsch (*10*) studied the stability of sociometric status among 150 ninth-grade pupils. Using two choices for each of six criteria he correlated the composite social acceptance score over a two-week interval. The resulting coefficients were .83 for boys and .76 for girls. Similar results were reported by Damrin (*14*) for 156 girls in grades nine through twelve. Using a composite score based on five criteria and three choices, a correlation coefficient of .86 was obtained over an eight-week interval between tests.

One of the original studies of the stability of sociometric status among adolescents was conducted by Jennings (*26*). Her study included 133 girls, ranging in age from twelve to sixteen years, who were residents in a New York training school. The girls were requested to choose those fellow residents they *most* preferred as work mates and roommates and those they *least* preferred for the same criteria. An unlimited number of choices was permitted. Correlation coefficients of .96 for positive choices and .93 for negative choices were obtained for a retest four days later. Coefficients of stability for an eight-month interval were .65 for positive choices and .66 for negative choices. Since this is one of the few studies reporting on the stability of negative choices, it is interesting to note that rejection status is as stable as acceptance status over varying periods of time. The tendency for the stability of sociometric status to decrease as the time between test and retest increases is clearly evident in Jennings' results. However, even after a period of eight months, a relatively high degree of stability is indicated.

A study concerned with the stability of sociometric status among adolescent boys was conducted by Newstetter, Feldstein, and Newcomb (*35*) at a summer camp. They had thirty fourteen-year-old boys make five choices each for tent mate at various times during the camping period. The correlation coefficient for a two-day interval between tests was .92. This coefficient decreased to .82 for a one-week interval, to .77 for a two-week interval, and to .71 for a three-week interval. This decline in stability with an increasing time interval between tests is in harmony with the results obtained by Jennings and others.

A recent study by Wertheimer (*45*) is of special significance, since it indicates the stability of sociometric status among high school pupils over varying periods of time, up to twenty months. He administered a sociometric test to approximately 100 boys and 100 girls who remained in the same homeroom classes over a two-year period. The sociometric test was based on three criteria for leisure-time activities and three choices were allotted to each criterion. The stability of the resulting sociometric status scores for an eight-month, twelve-month, and twenty-month period, were as follows:

	8 Months	*12 Months*	*20 Months*
Boys	.67	.56	.69
Girls	.72	.62	.62

It will be noticed that the coefficients of stability for the eight-month period are similar to those reported by Jennings for the same time interval. Of even greater interest is the fact that the stability coefficients do not seem to decline between the eight-month and the twenty-month interval. Apparently sociometric status scores are fairly stable among high school students, even over a period of almost two years.

Although it is difficult to compare these studies because of their diverse nature, they seem to be in substantial agreement concerning the stability of sociometric status among adolescents. In general, they suggest that stability coefficients of approximately .90 might be expected over time interals of less than a week. Coefficients in the vicinity of .80 are indicated for time intervals of several weeks, and coefficients of approximately .60 are indicated for time intervals ranging between eight and twenty months. Some deviation from these approximations can be expected to occur, however, due to variations in testing procedures and situational factors.

COLLEGE LEVEL. Studies of the stability of sociometric status at the college level report essentially the same findings as those obtained at the high school level. Zeleny (*48*) allotted five choices for work companion in a discussion group to three college classes ranging in size from fifteen to thirty-five. The results over a two-day interval correlated between .94 and .95. In a study of twenty-eight fraternity men, Newstetter, Feldstein, and Newcomb (*35*) reported stability coefficients of .88 for a one-week interval and .72 for a ten-week interval. Almost identical results were obtained by the same authors for sorority women. In this case, they obtained correlation coefficients of .88 for a one-week interval and .80 for a nine-week interval. In both studies, the students were allotted five choices each for roommate. A stability study over a longer period of time was reported by McIntyre (*31*). In this study, men in a college dormitory made five choices each for roommate and companion in recreation. The results over a six-month interval correlated .65.

The consistent drop in stability coefficients from over .90 for a two-day interval to .65 for a six-month interval is similar to the drop in coefficients reported for high school students. Even the correlation coefficients for the weekly intervals are similar in size to those at the high school level. The consistency of these results points to the possibility that the variability of sociometric results reflects real changes in sociometric preferences to a greater degree than it indicates random instability in the choice process. However, owing to the diverse procedures used in the various studies in this area, such a hypothesis must be viewed as highly tentative.

STABILITY OF HIGH AND LOW SOCIOMETRIC STATUS POSITIONS

The studies considered thus far have been concerned with the general stability of sociometric results. Although a relatively high degree of stability has been indicated, there is evidence that even greater stability occurs at the extreme sociometric status positions. In other words, stars, neglectees, and isolates tend to shift less in sociometric status than individuals in the average sociometric status categories. This is of special importance, since the positions of high and low status are of central concern to teachers and research workers alike. Developing the potential leadership abilities of highly chosen pupils and improving the acceptance of pupils with low status are common classroom endeavors. Likewise, research concerned with the personal and social correlates of sociometric status is generally directed toward the positions of leadership and isolation. Thus, the stability of high and low sociometric status positions has practical significance for both groups.

Thompson and Powell (*43*) studied the stability of stars and neglectees in four sixth-grade classes ranging in size from thirty-one to thirty-eight pupils. They reported that between 66 percent and 100 percent of the stars maintained the same sociometric position over one- and five-week intervals. The relative stability of the neglectees ranged from 59 percent to 90 percent for the same periods of time. In a similar study by Gronlund (*19*), the stability of high and low sociometric status positions was studied over a period of four months. Nine elementary school classrooms, from grades four through six, were included in the study. High and low sociometric status positions were based on five sociometric choices for work companion. The high status group included those pupils receiving nine or more choices (stars). The pupils in the low status group received one choice (neglectees) or none (isolates). The four-month stability was 60 percent for the high status group and 67 percent for the low status group. Further calculation indicated that an average of 80 percent of the pupils in both groups remained in the same sociometric category, or one choice removed from it, over the four-month interval. Apparently, shifts in sociometric status are relatively rare at the extreme sociometric status positions. This would tend to indicate that the high and low sociometric status positions are more stable than those in the average sociometric categories and thus can be used with greater confidence.

STABILITY OF SOCIOMETRIC STRUCTURE

Although it is difficult to obtain direct evidence on the stability of sociometric structure, an analysis of the stability of choices given by individuals and the stability of mutual choices between individuals provides some clues. The choices given determine the pattern of interaction, and mutual choices form the basis of sociometric structure. As indicated previously, the choices given to others might vary considerably even though the sociometric status of individuals is fairly constant. Likewise, mutual relations could change without changing the extent to which individuals were accepted by the group. In this section, then, we are concerned with the stability of the social relations of group members rather than with the stability of their degree of acceptance or rejection by the group.

CHOICES GIVEN. The stability of choices given by 238 pupils in grades one through six was reported by Criswell (*13*). She allotted two choices for seating companion and noted the variability of the choices given after a six-week interval. On the second test 59 percent of the choices given were the same as those given on the first test. She reported that 38 percent of the pupils made no changes in their choices, 42 percent made one change, and 20 percent changed both of their choices. Fewer changes occurred in the first choice than in the second. At that level 69 percent of the choices remained the same, while only 49 percent of the second choices were the same after six weeks. This decline in the stability of sociometric choices given, as the choice level decreases has also been noted in other studies (*5, 19, 32, 36*). Over a period of four months, the average stability of the various choice levels has been reported as follows, for two investigations at the elementary school level:

	Gronlund (19)	*Bjerstedt (5)*
First choice	72%	82%
Second choice	59%	72%
Third choice	52%	68%
Fourth choice	45%	50%
Fifth choice	38%	—

These findings indicate that the first several choices have a relatively high degree of stability. However, as the choice level decreases, the social relations become less stable. The stability of the social structure, then, is dependent to a large degree on the choice level. Mutual choices and clique formations based on first choices can be expected to endure over relatively long periods of time. In contrast, much greater variability in social structure should be expected where choices at a lower level are involved. It should be noted, however, that although the sociometric structure is more variable with fourth and fifth choices, the use of five choices provides more stable sociometric status scores than the use of fewer choices (*19*). This is due to the greater spread of scores with the use of five choices.

Two rather extensive studies by Horrocks and Thompson (*24, 42*) indicate the relative stability of the choice process at the high school level. They requested 905 rural children and 969 urban children, from the sixth to the twelfth grades, to indicate their three best friends. On the same test two weeks later, approximately 60 percent of both groups chose the same persons as best friend. An increase in stability with increased age was noted in the results. For ages fifteen to eighteen in the urban group, between 60 percent and 90 percent of the pupils chose the same persons as best friend. This seems to reflect greater stability in the social structure among the older age groups. It should also be noted, however, that the stability of choices reported in these studies is not much higher than those reported at the elementary school level. This can probably be accounted for by the fact that "near-sociometric" procedures were used. Choice of best friends does not indicate as clear and uniform a basis for choice as would more definite criteria. Variations in interpretations of the meaning of best friend would in all probability lower the stability of the results. Thus, they cannot be compared directly with the previous studies cited. Nevertheless, these studies do support the findings of other sociometric studies, by indicating a significant degree of stability in the choice process.

MUTUAL CHOICES. Bonney's (6) study of the stability of sociometric results over a three-year period included a study of the stability of mutual choices. For one-year intervals, from the second to the fifth grade, Bonney reported stability coefficients ranging between .41 and .49. Although these correlation coefficients indicate a significant degree of stability, they are considerably smaller than the coefficients of .67 to .84 which he reported for the stability of sociometric status. Thus, the social structure tended to be more variable than the social acceptance of individual group members. This is not surprising, in view of the observed variability in children's relations with each other. The surprising thing is, however, that even after a period of one year a significant number of the mutual relationships existed.

Variations in the social structure of children's groups can be accounted for in part by the variability of specific aspects during group development. For example, changes in boy-girl relations will contribute to variability in the choices given and will also reduce the stability of mutual relations among members of the same sex. In conjunction with this, choices between boys and girls are exploratory in nature and consequently tend to be very unstable. In one study at the elementary school level (*19*), it was reported that only 24 percent of the boys' choices of girls were the same after a four-month interval. The stability of girls' choices of boys was even lower, with only 14 percent of the choices remaining the same over the four-month interval. Such extreme variability in one aspect of the group structure contributes disproportionately to variability in the general pattern of social relations. Despite these shifts in social relations, however, considerable stability of social structure has been indicated.

In summary, sociometric status scores have a relatively high degree of stability over varying periods of time and at various age levels. The extremely high and low sociometric positions tend to be more stable than those in the average categories. When choices given and mutual choices are considered, it appears that the social structure of a group tends to be less stable than the sociometric status scores of its members. Thus, the degree of social acceptance an individual obtains in a group remains fairly constant, even though the source of the choices may vary somewhat. Whether considering sociometric status or sociometric structure, however, a significant degree of stability has been indicated in the numerous reliability studies.

CONSISTENCY OF SOCIOMETRIC RESULTS OVER DIFFERENT SITUATIONS

Adaptations of the equivalent-forms method of determining reliability have also been applied to sociometric results. In general, the procedures and purposes in applying this method to sociometric testing have varied somewhat from those traditionally used in psychological testing. Studies have investigated the extent to which sociometric status was consistent from one criterion to another, from one group to another, and from one method of making responses to another. The major purpose of these studies has been to determine the extent to which sociometric status serves as a reliable index of an individual's social acceptability, rather than to evaluate the general reliability of the technique itself. If an individual's sociometric position remained approximately the same for different sociometric criteria, from one group to another, and from one method of making responses to another, then it could be concluded that a general factor of social acceptability was being measured. In contrast, if considerable variation in sociometric position was found under these conditions, it would indicate that sociometric status was dependent on the form of sociometric test used and the situation in which it was administered. The implication for studying the social adjustment of individuals is quite obvious. A general social acceptability factor would make it possible to predict what an individual's social acceptance is likely to be in different situations.

The procedure for determining the consistency of sociometric status over different situations is similar in all studies. Two test forms are administered at approximately the same time and their results correlated. Where the results from different sociometric criteria are correlated, all other aspects of the test (i.e., directions, number of choices allotted, etc.) are kept equivalent. Where the results from different groups are correlated, the test form is usually identical for both groups. In comparing the different methods of making responses, the test forms are kept as equivalent as possible. This is usually difficult, since different types of responses require some modifications in the test form.

CONSISTENCY OF SOCIOMETRIC STATUS OVER CRITERIA

Several studies have indicated the extent to which the sociometric status of individuals on one criterion is related to their sociometric status on other criteria. In general, the results have shown a significant relationship between various pairs of criteria. Those individuals that are highly chosen on one criterion also tend to be highly chosen on other criteria. Likewise, those individuals that receive few or no sociometric choices on one criterion tend to maintain the same low sociometric status on other criteria. This tendency of individuals to maintain the same relative sociometric position from one criterion to another is greatest where general criteria are used and where the choice situations have some psychological similarity.

In a study of 632 boys and 626 girls at the sixth-grade level, Gronlund (*18*) determined the extent to which sociometric status was related on three sociometric criteria. Five sociometric choices were allotted for the choice of seating companions, work companions, and play companions, and the resulting sociometric status scores were correlated. The average correlation coefficients ranged from .76 to .86 for boys and from .76 to .89 for girls. The highest correlations were between the seating companion and work companion choices, for both sexes. The lowest correlations were between the play and work criteria. The relatively high degree of relationship indicated by these correlation coefficients points toward a general social acceptability factor operating in the choice process. It should be noted that five choices and general criteria were used in this study.

Loeb (*30*) investigated the same problem using a number of sociometric criteria. A composite sociometric status score based on four criteria was correlated with another composite sociometric status score based on four different criteria. The resulting correlation coefficients ranged from .65 to .85 for twelve classes from the fourth to the eighth grades. Although larger correlation coefficients might be expected where several criteria are combined, the size of the coefficients was probably reduced by the fact that only one choice was allotted to some criteria and three to others. Despite these variations, the results are in substantial agreement with the hypothesis that a general social acceptability factor is present in sociometric choosing.

A comprehensive study in this area was conducted among Swedish school children by Bjerstedt (*5*). He administered a sociometric test to thirty classrooms from the third to the eighth grades. Correlation coefficients between sociometric status as a "work mate" and as a "friend" ranged from .67 to .92 for grades three through five and from .49 to .89 for grades six through eight. The average correlation coefficients were .84 for the lower grades and .74 for the higher grades. This declining degree of relationship indicates a greater tendency on the part of older age groups to discriminate among criteria. Bronfenbrenner (*11*) noted a similar decline in relationship from fall to spring sociometric testing in elementary classrooms. The sociometric status of individuals tended to be more variable from one criterion to another during the spring testing. Apparently an increase in acquaintanceship, as well as increased age, leads to more discriminating sociometric responses. Thus, the influence of a general social acceptability factor in sociometric choosing would tend to be less pronounced in a mature group where the group members were well acquainted with each other. Even under these conditions, however, the sociometric status of individuals remains fairly consistent from one criterion to another.

In a girls dormitory, at the college level, Smucker (*40*) obtained a correlation of .64 between sociometric status based on choices of best friends and college representatives. Hackman and Moon (*23*) obtained similar results among college students for the choice of committee leader and fellow committee members. Correlations of sociometric status between the two criteria were .85 and .86 for two different classroom sections. Findings from similar studies of college students and adult groups were reviewed by Mouton, Blake, and Fruchter (*33*). The results were consistent in indicating that sociometric status on one sociometric criterion was significantly related to sociometric status on other sociometric criteria. These findings lend support to the belief that a general factor of social acceptability is present in sociometric choices at all age levels.

There is some evidence that specific criteria provide a less reliable index of social acceptability than general criteria. Kerr (*28*) administered a sociometric test, containing eight different criteria, to her fifth-grade class. Although no correlation coefficients were reported, an inspection of the distribution of choices on the various criteria indicate more variation in sociometric status among specific criteria than among general criteria. There was little variation in pupils' sociometric status between the criteria of seating companion and work companion. However, choices of companions for a cooking group provided quite different results.

The variability of sociometric status among specific criteria is brought out clearly in a study by Wardlow and Greene (*44*). They requested thirty-seven high school girls to choose three associates for each of the following activities—review for a quiz, go on a wiener roast, and play basketball. Correlation coefficients between the sociometric status scores on the various criteria ranged from .31 to .61. The lowest relationship was found between reviewing for a quiz and playing basketball. It seems likely that knowledge and skill entered into the sociometric choices on these two criteria to a larger extent than did the factor of social acceptability. Similar results were obtained by Bonney (*9*) for ninety-nine sixth-grade pupils. The results of choices of play companion and choices of fellow-participants on a quiz program correlated .42. The criterion based on the quiz program clearly indicated the need for knowledge for successful participation. Apparently where specific criteria indicate the need for knowledge or skill the social acceptability factor is suppressed somewhat, in the choosing, in favor of success in the activity. Thus, situational factors contribute to the variability of results from one specific criterion to another. Even on highly specific criteria, however, some overlap of sociometric status is present.

The consistency of sociometric status over criteria points toward the presence of a general social acceptability factor in the sociometric results. This factor seems to be greatest where general sociometric criteria are used and lowest where specific skills and knowledge enter into the sociometric responses. The consistency of sociometric status over criteria also seems to decline slightly with an increase in age level and an increase in acquaintanceship among group members. Despite these variations, a general social acceptability factor appears to be present, to some degree, in all sociometric choosing situations.

CONSISTENCY OF SOCIOMETRIC STATUS OVER GROUPS

Probably a more rigorous test of the extent to which sociometric status reflects a social acceptability factor is the degree to which it remains constant with changes in the membership of the group. If an individual's sociometric status remained fairly constant from one group to another, a general social acceptability factor would be indicated. The difficulty, of course, is in obtaining sociometric results from different groups that can be compared. This problem has been handled in different ways by different investigators. However, most studies have dealt with the constancy of sociometric status with variations in group membership rather than with the consistency of sociometric status from one group to another.

Using a modified form of sociometric test, Laughlin (*29*) measured the sociometric status of 525 sixth-grade pupils and then administered the same test again the following year. Since the pupils were regrouped in the seventh grade, all of the pupils had some new classmates. The proportion of new class members ranged from 30 percent to 95 percent for individual pupils. With this variation in group membership, a correlation coefficient of .55 was obtained between the two administrations of the test. It should be noted that in this study there was a one-year interval between the tests. Thus, the correlation coefficient reflects the stability of sociometric status over different grade levels as well as its consistency over different group members. This is a rather severe test of the constancy of sociometric status. Although a significant degree of relationship was indicated, there is little doubt that a larger correlation coefficient would have resulted if the interval between tests had been shorter.

A study by Gronlund and Whitney (*21*) compared pupils' sociometric status within the classroom with their sociometric status among the entire school population. They had a total student body of 340 junior high school pupils in twelve homeroom classes name the *5 classmates* they most preferred as seating companions. At the same time, the pupils were requested to name any five pupils *in the entire junior high school* that they most preferred as classmates the following year and as neighborhood play companions after school. On the first choosing situation, all choices went to pupils within the classrooms in which they were given. On the latter two choice situations, between 38 percent and 40 percent of the choices went to pupils outside of the classrooms in which they were given. Thus, choices on the latter two criteria permeated the entire junior high school. An average correlation coefficient of .72 was reported for the relation between pupils' sociometric status as seating companion (within the classroom) and future classmate (throughout the school). The relation between seating companion and neighborhood play companion was represented by an average correlation coefficient of .67. Thus, in both instances there was a significant relationship between pupils' social acceptance in the classroom and their social acceptance throughout the school.

A more detailed analysis of the sociometric results revealed that stars and neglectees in the classroom tended to maintain their same relative positions throughout the school. Pupils in the star category received an average of 11.3 choices as seating companion from their classmates. These same pupils received an average of

11.7 choices as future classmates and 9.5 choices as neighborhood play companions from the total school population. Approximately half of the choices on the latter two criteria came from pupils outside of class. Thus, although approximately 50 percent of the choices changed, the average sociometric status of the stars remained fairly constant. A similar constancy of status was noted among the classroom neglectees. They received an average of 0.8 of a choice in the classroom and an average of 1.8 choices as future classmates and 1.6 choices as neighborhood play companions in the school. Apparently their low sociometric status was general throughout the school and not restricted to the classroom situation. These findings indicate that sociometric status is a fairly reliable index of an individual's general social acceptability where general sociometric criteria are used and five choices are allotted to each criterion.

Studies at the college level also indicate constancy of sociometric status with variation in group membership. Northway (37) measured the sociometric status of nineteen college students in a group of eighty and the following year determined their sociometric status in a group of twenty-nine. When the rank order of the nineteen students appearing in both groups was correlated, a coefficient of .58 resulted. Thus, there was a tendency for the students to maintain the same relative degree of acceptance in different sized groups, despite the fact that there was a one-year interval between the tests. Similar findings were reported by Bonney (8), although his results were not reported in the form of correlation coefficients. He studied the constancy of sociometric ranks among college students, over successive semesters, for a two-year period. Classes ranged in size from twenty-one to thirty-six and an average of 88 percent of the students were new for the individuals studied. A total of seventy-two cases was studied during the two-year period. Over successive semesters, he noted average shifts in sociometric ranks ranging from 1.7 to 4.5. In general, then, the students tended to maintain their same relative sociometric positions from semester to semester, even though the majority of the group membership was new.

In a study by Bell and French (*4*) the variation in group membership was experimentally controlled. They had twenty-five male college students, who were not acquainted with each other previously, participate in six discussion groups of five men each. During each discussion session every student met with four different students. At the close of each discussion session, the students were requested to rank the other four group members in terms of their preference for a discussion leader for another meeting. Sociometric status was determined for each member, for each group meeting, by averaging the ranks received. Thus, a measure of sociometric status in six different groups of completely new membership was obtained for each student. When the sociometric status of individuals in each group was correlated with their average status in the other five groups in which they participated, an average correlation coefficient of .75 was obtained. In other words, the acceptance of individuals as leaders remained fairly constant over the various groups, despite a complete change in membership.

Studies in natural classroom settings as well as those under experimentally controlled conditions both demonstrate the consistency of sociometric status with variations in group membership. These findings indicate the general nature of sociometric status and lend support to the belief that a general social acceptability factor is present in sociometric responses.

CONSISTENCY OF SOCIOMETRIC STATUS OVER DIFFERENT METHODS OF MAKING RESPONSES

The traditional procedure for obtaining sociometric responses has been to request individuals to choose associates for some group activity or situation. The group members may be permitted an unlimited number of choices or they may be limited to a fixed number of choices. Where a limited number of choices has been used, they have generally varied from one to five in number with a three-limit choice being used most frequently. Several investigators have compared sociometric status scores based on these simple choice methods with those based on more complex procedures. The most common methods in this regard have been the paired-comparison method, the rank-order method, and the rating method. The main difference between these latter methods and the simple choice method is that they require individuals to respond to every group member rather than to a limited number of them.

In using the paired-comparison method, all possible combinations of group members are placed in pairs and each individual checks the group member in each pair that he most prefers for the activity stated in the sociometric criterion. The rank-order method requires each individual to rank all group members on the basis of his preference for them as associates in the designated activity. The rating method requests each individual to rate each of the other group members, on a three-, five-, or seven-point scale, in terms of degree of preference for associating with them in some activity. It can readily be seen that these latter methods have the disadvantage of being more time consuming in the administration of the test and in the analysis of the results. However, they have generally been shown to provide extremely stable results (*33, 46*). In addition, they provide a general measure of group acceptance, since an individual's sociometric status is based on an average of individual responses from all group members. Thus, each of these methods provides a good criterion against which the simple choice method may be evaluated.

Two studies reported on the intercorrelations among techniques where an unlimited number of choices was used with the simple choice method. A study at the elementary level, by Bjerstedt (*5*), indicated that sociometric status scores based on the simple choice method correlated .83 with the paired-comparison method, .85 with the rank-order method, and .79 and .87 with two different rating methods. Similar results were reported by Eng and French

(*15*) for college students. They obtained correlation coefficients of .90 between the simple choice method and the paired-comparison method, and .89 between the simple choice method and the rank-order method. It appears that where an unlimited number of choices is used, the simple choice method provides essentially the same results as the more complex methods of eliciting responses.

Several studies have been concerned with the intercorrelations among techniques where a limited number of choices has been used with the simple choice method. In four sixth-grade classes, Witryol and Thompson (*47*) obtained correlation coefficients ranging from .41 to .89 between a three-limit choice method and the paired-comparison method. Ausubel, Schiff, and Gasser (*1*) compared sociometric status scores based on a three-limit choice method and a five-point rating method. For classrooms from the third to the twelfth grade, they reported correlation coefficients ranging between .29 and .73. Thompson and Powell (*43*) reported similar results for the relation between a three-limit choice method and a seven-point rating method. Their correlation coefficients ranged from .47 to .71, for pupils in four sixth-grade classes. Although a fair degree of relationship is indicated in these studies, it should be noted that in each case the simple choice method limited the pupils to three choices. There is some evidence that a higher degree of relationship is obtained where a five-limit choice is used. Gronlund and Barnes (*20*) reported that correlations between the simple choice method and the rank-order method increased steadily as the choice limit was increased from two to five choices. At the two-choice limit a correlation of .77 was obtained while at the five-choice limit a correlation of .92 was obtained. Bjerstedt (*5*) noted a similar increase in relationship. He correlated sociometric status scores based on paired-comparison and rating scale results with those based on the simple choice method with varying choice limits. His correlation coefficients increased from .60 with a one-choice limit to .80 with a five-choice limit. The findings of Eng and French (*15*) also support the conclusion that a higher degree of relationship is obtained where a five-choice limit is used. They correlated sociometric results based on a two-choice limit and a five-choice limit with results based on the paired-comparison method and the rank-order method. Correlations of .54 and .55 were obtained with the two-choice limit and correlations of .73 and .74 were obtained with the five-choice limit. Thus, the simple choice method seems to provide results similar to those of the more complex methods, where at least five choices are allotted to each individual.

Two studies have indicated that consistent sociometric status scores are obtained with a three-choice limit if both positive and negative choices are used. In both studies individuals were requested to indicate the three group members they most preferred and the three group members they least preferred for the sociometric situation. Sociometric status scores were then calculated for each individual by subtracting the number of negative choices he received from the number of positive choices he received. Correlating these scores with the results of a five-point rating method, Justman and Wrightstone (*27*) obtained correlations ranging from .78 to .96 in five eighth-grade classes. Using the same three-choice limit for positive and negative choices Gronlund and Barnes (*20*) obtained an average correlation of .94 between these sociometric status scores and results based on the total rank-order method, in fourteen college groups. Consequently, the three-choice limit provides essentially the same results as the more complex methods, where both positive and negative choices are used.

The relatively high degree of relationship between sociometric status scores based on the simple choice method and those based on the more complex methods adds further support to the belief that a general social acceptability factor is present in the sociometric responses. The method of making responses appears to have little influence on the amount of social acceptance individuals attain in a group. Although some of the more complex methods of obtaining responses may serve useful purposes in research studies, the ease with which the simple choice method can be administered and scored would seem to favor its use in the classroom. Where a limited number of positive choices is used, research findings indicate that a five-choice limit will provide the most reliable sociometric status scores. However, if both positive and negative choices are used a three-choice limit will provide equally reliable sociometric results.

FACTORS INFLUENCING THE RELIABILITY OF SOCIOMETRIC RESULTS

In general, sociometric results have been shown to be reliable under a variety of conditions. Studies of internal consistency have indicated that an individual's sociometric status is essentially the same from one-half of the group to the other. A fairly high degree of stability over varying periods of time has also been noted for sociometric status scores. Although sociometric structure tends to be less stable than sociometric status, it has also been shown to be fairly constant. The consistency of sociometric status from one situation to another has added further support to the reliability of sociometric results.

Although the results of reliability studies are consistent in indicating the general reliability of sociometric results, variations in the degree of reliability reported may be noted. When these variations are analyzed from the viewpoint of factors influencing the reliability of sociometric results, several general factors stand out. Some of these factors appear as general trends over various time intervals and different age periods. Other factors are more specifically related to the testing procedures used. In addition to the factors evolving from an analysis of the reliability studies, several other factors which tend to influence the reliability of sociometric results may be identified. The neglect of these latter factors in most reliability studies probably also accounts for some of the variation in the reported results.

A consideration of the factors influencing the reliability of sociometric results should assist in evaluating reliability studies. Such consideration should also develop an understanding of the situations which provide the most reliable data. Equally important, these factors point toward the type of sociometric instrument which provides the most generally useful and reliable sociometric results.

INFLUENCE OF TIME SPAN

In general, the stability of sociometric results declines as the time span between tests is increased. Sociometric tests administered several days apart provide essentially the same results. After several weeks some shifts in sociometric status are noted and sociometric results obtained several months apart show even greater variability. Although a significant degree of stability has been indicated over various time intervals, including a period of years, the stability of sociometric results can be expected to decline as the time interval between tests increases.

INFLUENCE OF THE AGE OF GROUP MEMBERS

Sociometric results tend to be less stable at the nursery school and kindergarten levels, with an increase in stability as the grade level increases. The greatest stability appears to be at the high school and college levels. Some of the instability at the elementary school level can probably be accounted for by the exploratory nature of cross-sex choices among preadolescent pupils. The general trend, toward increased stability with increased age, is not as clear-cut as that for time span, because of the diverse procedures used by different investigators at different age levels. However, where the same testing procedures have been used at different grade levels, a general increase in reliability from the lower to the higher grade levels has been noted.

INFLUENCE OF SOCIOMETRIC CRITERION

The nature of the sociometric criterion has been shown to have a definite influence on the reliability of sociometric results. General criteria (i.e., seating companion) tend to provide the most stable results over various time intervals and are most closely related to other measures of social acceptability. The less stable and less general results obtained with specific criteria (i.e., someone to study arithmetic with) can probably be accounted for by the influence of specific skills and other situational factors on the choice process. Thus, where sociometric results are based on general criteria, a more reliable measure of pupils' social acceptability is obtained.

Reliability studies have also shown that a composite sociometric status score, based on the results of a number of sociometric criteria, tends to be more stable than one based on a single criterion. In fact, the stability of such scores has been compared favorably with the stability of intelligence and achievement test results.

INFLUENCE OF NUMBER OF SOCIOMETRIC CHOICES

The number of sociometric choices allotted also influences the reliability of sociometric results. The most reliable results have generally been obtained where an unlimited number of choices was used with each criterion. However, certain choice limits have also been shown to provide a high degree of reliability. Where only positive choices were used, the five-choice limit produced the most reliable sociometric results. Consistently lower reliability was noted where fewer than five positive choices were allotted. Where both positive and negative choices were used the three-choice limit provided results comparable to those based on five positive choices. The reliability of sociometric results based on an unlimited number of choices, on five positive choices, and on three positive and three negative choices is so similar that the selection of which procedure to use should be based on factors other than the slight variations in reliability. However, the use of fewer choices than these generally results in less reliable sociometric results.[1]

INFLUENCE OF ASPECT OF SOCIOMETRIC RESULTS STUDIED

Various aspects of the sociometric results have shown different degrees of stability. In general, the choices given by individuals and the mutual choices between individuals tend to be less stable than the choices received by individuals. Thus, the social structure of the group has greater variability than the sociometric status of the individual group members. Reliability studies have also indicated that the extreme sociometric status positions are more stable than those in the central positions. The positions of leadership and isolation have shown a high degree of stability over varying periods of time and a high degree of consistency from one situation to another.

INFLUENCE OF ACQUAINTANCE SPAN

Determining the influence of acquaintance span on the stability of sociometric results is difficult, since the extent of acquaintance is seldom indicated in studies of reliability. Although Barker (*2*) indicated that the sociometric choices of strangers had a three-month stability of .55, there is little doubt that some interaction among group members is necessary before the choice process stabilizes. Studies by Hunt and Solomon (*25*), and French (*16*) have indicated that this stabilizing process occurs during the fifth or sixth week after the group has been formed. The stability of sociometric results appears to increase up to this point and then to level off. Although individuals are not acquainted with all of the group members at the end of six weeks, acquaintance span seems

[1] The increase in reliability with an increase in the number of sociometric choices allotted, as well as the higher reliability for composites of several sociometric criteria, may be phenomena referrable to the Spearman-Brown Prophecy formula.

to be unrelated to sociometric status after this point (*17*). Apparently, individuals in a new group achieve their normal acquaintance span by this time, and this in turn contributes to the stability of their sociometric choices. Nevertheless, variations in stability reported in the numerous reliability studies can probably be accounted for, in part, by differences in the time that the sociometric test was administered to the group. Sociometric results obtained early in the formation of a group would be expected to have less stability than those obtained after individuals had attained their normal acquaintance span.

INFLUENCE OF CLASSROOM PROCEDURES

Another neglected factor in most reliability studies that would contribute to variation in the results is that of classroom procedures. Where group procedures are used and social adjustment is stressed, one would expect greater changes in the sociometric results than in the traditional, subject-centered classroom. This view is supported by the findings of Taylor (*41*). He compared the three-month stability of sociometric results obtained in a progressive classroom with those obtained in an arbitrarily selected classroom and a traditional classroom. The correlation coefficients were .66 for the progressive classroom, .89 for the arbitrarily selected classroom, and .90 for the traditional classroom. The progressive classroom was described as one where group procedures and group goals were dominant, and where special stress was placed on social adjustment. In such a progressive classroom, less stability would be expected in the sociometric results. This lower stability, however, would not necessarily indicate the unreliability of the sociometric technique. It would tend to indicate that the sociometric test was measuring the actual changes which the group procedures had brought about.

Since most reliability studies do not describe the classroom atmosphere in which the sociometric results were obtained, it is difficult to determine the specific influence this factor had on the reported results. However, it probably accounts for some of the variations in reliability reported by different investigators. For example, the comparatively low stability coefficients reported by Bronfenbrenner (*11*) were based on sociometric results obtained from a progressive laboratory school, where group work was stressed and special attempts were made to improve sociometric status and structure. In such a situation, stability coefficients more aptly indicate the extent to which sociometric results are resistant to efforts toward change than the extent to which the sociometric results are reliable.

SUMMARY

The reliability of sociometric results has generally been determined by applying the traditional procedures used in psychological testing. These procedures are used to determine the consistency of the results under various conditions. When applied to sociometric testing, the procedures include measures of the internal consistency of the results, measures of the stability of the results over varying periods of time, and measures of the consistency of the results over various situations. Perfect consistency in these areas is neither expected nor desirable in sociometric testing, owing to the dynamic nature of social relations. However, where sociometric results are used as a basis for studying the social adjustment of individuals and the social structure of groups, a certain degree of consistency of results is necessary. Thus, although the traditional methods of determining reliability have their limitations when applied to sociometric testing, they do provide valuable information concerning the degree of consistency that can be expected in sociometric results.

Studies of the internal consistency of sociometric results have reported generally high reliability coefficients. This indicates that an individual's sociometric status remains fairly consistent from one-half of the group to the other. Although this may provide some implications concerning an individual's general acceptance by the group, this method of measuring reliability has limited value for studying the status, structure, or development of groups.

Studies of the stability of sociometric results have indicated a significant degree of stability over varying periods of time, for all age levels from the nursery school through the college level. The lowest stability coefficients were reported at the nursery school level and where the time interval between test and retest was longest. However, the stability of sociometric status scores, for elementary school pupils, was reported to be similar to the stability of intelligence and achievement test results over a one-year interval.

In general, the choices given by individuals and the mutual choices between individuals tended to be less stable than the choices received by individuals. It was also noted that the extreme sociometric status positions were more stable than those of the average positions. Despite these variations, however, a significant degree of stability was indicated for all aspects of the sociometric results.

A relatively high degree of consistency of sociometric status was noted over different situations. In general, sociometric status on one criterion was closely related to sociometric status on other criteria; sociometric status tended to be consistent in groups of varying membership; and sociometric status remained fairly consistent from one measuring technique to another. The reported consistency of sociometric status over different situations points toward a general social acceptability factor operating in the choice process.

An analysis of the various reliability studies indicated a number of factors influencing the reliability of sociometric results. These may be stated in terms of the following generalizations.

1. The stability of sociometric results tends to decline as the time span between tests is increased.

2. There is a tendency for the stability of sociometric results to increase as the age of the group members increases.
3. Sociometric status scores based on general criteria tend to be more stable and more consistent over various situations than those based on specific criteria.
4. Composite sociometric status scores based on several sociometric criteria tend to be more stable than sociometric status scores based on a single sociometric criterion.
5. The use of an unlimited number of sociometric choices, five positive choices, and three positive and three negative choices tends to provide similar sociometric results. The use of fewer choices provides less reliable sociometric results.
6. The social structure of a group tends to be less stable than the sociometric status of the individual group members.
7. The sociometric positions of leadership and isolation tend to be more stable and more consistent over various situations than those in the average sociometric categories.

In addition to these general trends noted in the reliability studies, two other factors were discussed in terms of their possible influence on the reliability of sociometric results. One was that of acquaintance span and the other that of classroom procedures. In general it was indicated that less stable sociometric results would be obtained in newly formed groups and in classrooms where flexible group procedures were used. It was further pointed out that although these factors were neglected in most reliability studies, they probably account for some of the variation in the reported results.

REFERENCES

1. Ausubel, D. P., Schiff, H. M., and Gasser, E. B., "A Preliminary Study of Developmental Trends in Sociempathy: Accuracy of Perception of Own and Others' Sociometric Status," *Child Development,* 1952, *23:*111–128.
2. Barker, R. G., "The Social Interrelations of Strangers and Acquaintances," *Sociometry,* 1942, *5:*169–179.
3. Bass, B. M., and White, O. L., "Validity of Leaderless Group

Discussion Observer's Descriptive and Evaluative Ratings for the Assessment of Personality and Leadership Status," *American Psychologist,* 1950, *5:*311–312.

4. Bell, G. B., and French, R. L., "Consistency of Individual Leadership Position in Small Groups of Varying Membership," *Journal of Abnormal and Social Psychology,* 1950, *45:*764–767.
5. Bjerstedt, A., "The Interpretation of Sociometric Status Scores in the Classroom," *Nordisk Psykologi,* 1956, *1–2:*1–14.
6. Bonney, M. E., "The Constancy of Sociometric Scores and Their Relationship to Teacher Judgments of Social Success and to Personality Self Ratings," *Sociometry,* 1943, *6:*409–424.
7. Bonney, M. E., "The Relative Stability of Social, Intellectual, and Academic Status in Grades II to IV, and the Interrelationships Between These Various Forms of Growth," *Journal of Educational Psychology,* 1943, *34:*88–102.
8. Bonney, M. E., "A Study of Constancy of Sociometric Ranks Among College Students Over a Two-Year Period," *Sociometry,* 1955, *18:*275–286.
9. Bonney, M. E., "A Study of the Sociometric Process Among Sixth-Grade Children," *Journal of Educational Psychology,* 1946, *37:*359–371.
10. Bretsch, H. S., "Factors Associated with Social Acceptance at the Ninth Grade Level and an Analysis of Sex Differences in the Factors Investigated," Ph.D. Dissertation, Syracuse University, 1948.
11. Bronfenbrenner, U., "The Measurement of Sociometric Status, Structure and Development," *Sociometry Monographs,* No. 6, New York, Beacon House, 1945.
12. Byrd, E., "A Study of Validity and Constancy of Choices in a Sociometric Test," *Sociometry,* 1951, *14:*175–181.
13. Criswell, J. H., "Social Structure Revealed in a Sociometric Retest," *Sociometry,* 1939, *2:*69–75.
14. Damrin, D. E., "Family Size and Sibling Age, Sex, and Position as Related to Certain Aspects of Adjustment," *Journal of Social Psychology,* 1949, *29:*93–102.
15. Eng, E., and French, R. L., "The Determination of Sociometric Status," *Sociometry,* 1948, *11:*368–371.

16. French, R. L., "Sociometric Status and Individual Adjustment Among Naval Recruits," *Journal of Abnormal and Social Psychology,* 1951, *46:*64–72.
17. Gronlund, N. E., "Acquaintance Span and Sociometric Status," *Sociometry,* 1955, *18:*62–68.
18. Gronlund, N. E., "Generality of Sociometric Status over Criteria in the Measurement of Social Acceptability," *Elementary School Journal,* 1955, *56:*173–176.
19. Gronlund, N. E., "The Relative Stability of Classroom Social Status with Unweighted and Weighted Sociometric Status Scores," *Journal of Educational Psychology,* 1955, *46:*345–354.
20. Gronlund, N. E., and Barnes, F. P., "The Reliability of Social-Acceptability Scores Using Various Sociometric-Choice Limits," *Elementary School Journal,* 1956, *57:*153–157.
21. Gronlund, N. E., and Whitney, A. P., "Relation Between Pupils' Social Acceptability in the Classroom, in the School, and in the Neighborhood," *School Review,* 1956, *64:*267–271.
22. Grossman, B., and Wrighter, J., "The Relationship Between Selection-Rejection and Intelligence, Social Status, and Personality Amongst Sixth Grade Children," *Sociometry,* 1948, *11:*346–355.
23. Hackman, R. C., and Moon, R. G., "Are Leaders and Followers Identified by Similar Criteria?" *American Psychologist,* 1951, *5:*312.
24. Horrocks, J. E., and Thompson, G. G., "A Study of the Friendship Fluctuations of Rural Boys and Girls," *Journal of Genetic Psychology,* 1946, *69:*189–198.
25. Hunt, J. McV., and Solomon, R. L., "The Stability and Some Correlates of Group Status in a Summer Camp Group of Young Boys," *American Journal of Psychology,* 1942, *55:*33–45.
26. Jennings, H. H., *Leadership and Isolation,* New York, Longmans, Green and Company, 1950.
27. Justman, J., and Wrightstone, J. W., "A Comparison of Three Methods of Measuring Pupil Status in the Classroom," *Educational and Psychological Measurement,* 1951, *11:*362–367.
28. Kerr, M., "A Study of Social Acceptability," *Elementary School Journal,* 1945, *45:*257–265.

29. Laughlin, F., *The Peer Status of Sixth- and Seventh-Grade Children,* New York, Bureau of Publications, Teachers College, Columbia University, 1954.
30. Loeb, N., "The Educational and Psychological Significance of Social Acceptability and Its Appraisal in an Elementary School Setting," Ph.D. Dissertation, University of Toronto, 1941.
31. McIntyre, C. H., "Acceptance by Others and Its Relation to Acceptance of Self and Others," *Journal of Abnormal and Social Psychology,* 1952, *47:*624–625.
32. Moreno, J. L., *Who Shall Survive?* New York, Beacon House, 1953.
33. Mouton, J. S., Blake, R. R., and Fruchter, B., "The Reliability of Sociometric Measures," *Sociometry,* 1955, *18:*7–48.
34. Murray, H., "The Sociometric Stability of Personal Relations Among Retarded Children," *Sociometry,* 1953, *16:*113–141.
35. Newstetter, W. I., Feldstein, M. J., and Newcomb, T. M., *Group Adjustment: A Study in Experimental Sociology,* Cleveland, Western Reserve University, 1938.
36. Northway, M. L., "Social Relationships Among Preschool Children; Abstracts and Interpretations of Three Studies," *Sociometry,* 1943, *6:*429–433.
37. Northway, M. L., Frankel, E. B., and Potashin, R., "Personality and Sociometric Status," *Sociometry Monographs,* No. 11, New York, Beacon House, 1947.
38. Pepinsky, P. N., "The Meaning of 'Validity' and 'Reliability' as Applied to Sociometric Tests," *Educational and Psychological Measurement,* 1949, *9:*39–49.
39. Ricciuti, H. N., and French, J. W., "Analysis of Ratings of Leadership Potential at the U.S. Naval Academy," *American Psychologist,* 1951, *6:*392.
40. Smucker, O., "Near-Sociometric Analysis as a Basis for Guidance," *Sociometry,* 1949, *12:*326–340.
41. Taylor, E. A., "Some Factors Relating to Social Acceptance in Eighth-Grade Classrooms," *Journal of Educational Psychology,* 1952, *43:*257–272.
42. Thompson, G. G., and Horrocks, J. E., "A Study of the Friend-

ship Fluctuations of Urban Boys and Girls," *Journal of Genetic Psychology,* 1947, *70:*53–63.

43. Thompson, G. G., and Powell, M., "An Investigation of the Rating-Scale Approach to the Measurement of Social Status," *Educational and Psychological Measurements,* 1951, *11:*440–455.
44. Wardlow, M. E., and Greene, J. E., "An Exploratory Sociometric Study of Peer Status Among Adolescent Girls," *Sociometry,* 1952, *15:*311–316.
45. Wertheimer, R. R., "Consistency of Sociometric Status Position in Male and Female High School Students," *Journal of Educational Psychology,* 1957, *48:*385–390.
46. Witryol, S. L., and Thompson, G. G., "A Critical Review of the Stability of Social Acceptability Scores Obtained with the Partial-Rank-Order and Paired-Comparison Scales," *Genetic Psychology Monographs,* 1953, *48:*221–260.
47. Witryol, S. L., and Thompson, G. G., "An Experimental Comparison of the Stability of Social Acceptability Scores Obtained with the Partial-Rank-Order and the Paired-Comparison Scales," *Journal of Educational Psychology,* 1953, *44:*20–30.
48. Zeleny, L. D., "Sociometry of Morale," *American Sociological Review,* 1939, *4:*799–808.

CHAPTER 6

VALIDITY OF SOCIOMETRIC RESULTS

An evaluation of the validity of sociometric results is an extremely complex process. This is partly due to the fact that the traditional concept of validity is difficult to apply to sociometric testing. Traditionally, the validity of a measuring instrument refers to the degree to which it measures what it is supposed to measure. When this concept of validity is applied to intelligence and achievement testing, the characteristics to be measured can be explicitly defined and, at least generally, agreed upon. However, in the area of sociometric testing there is little agreement as to what the sociometric technique is supposed to measure. Some sociometrists hold the viewpoint that the sociometric test is supposed to measure choice behavior and, therefore, is valid by definition (*27, 44*). This concept of validity implies that the proper construction and administration of the sociometric test will assure valid responses and that further validation of the results is unnecessary. Although such a limited concept simplifies the problem of determining validity, it also restricts the interpretation of the results.

In contrast to this limited interpretation of validity, other investigators have evaluated the validity of sociometric results by relating them to a host of psychological and sociological variables

(*34, 38*). This concept of validity implies that the sociometric test should measure meaningful variables of psychological and sociological interest. Which variables should be related to sociometric results, however, has not been clearly determined. Therefore, any evaluation of the validity of sociometric results must be, more or less, arbitrarily restricted to those variables which appear to have some logical relevance.

For the purposes of this chapter the validity of sociometric results will be evaluated by comparing them with the observed behavior of individuals, with teachers' judgments of pupils' social acceptance, with other measures of social adjustment, and with measures of personal adjustment. These criteria of validity seem to have logical relevance for sociometric results, although their limitations are also apparent. For example, the desired associations of individuals should be reflected to some degree in their actual associations. Thus, observations of social relations and judgments of social acceptance should provide results somewhat similar to sociometric results. If the results were completely different, it would be necessary to conclude that sociometric choices were not valid measures of desired associations or that desired and actual associations were unrelated. In either case sociometric results would have little practical meaning. On the other hand, however, it is not expected that observations and judgments of actual behavior will be perfectly correlated with sociometric results. An individual's actual associations are influenced by environmental limitations, personal inhibitions, lack of reciprocal feeling on the part of desired associates, and other related factors, as much as they are by his preferences. Thus, actual associations can be expected to show some variation from the desired associations indicated in sociometric choices. An additional limitation, of course, is the fact that observations and judgments of individuals are not completely reliable measures of actual behavior.

Similar advantages and limitations can be noted for the criteria of social and personal adjustment. Although a relationship between sociometric results and these two variables can logically be expected, the traditional measures of social and personal adjustment are not themselves completely reliable and valid. In addition, it is not expected that a perfect relationship exists between various aspects of social and personal adjustment.

Despite these limitations, however, the relationship between sociometric results and these criteria should indicate the degree to which sociometric results are valid for evaluating the general social and personal effectiveness of individuals.

SOCIOMETRIC RESULTS AND OBSERVATIONS OF BEHAVIOR

A number of studies have been concerned with the relationship between the results of sociometric choosing and observations of the actual behavior of group members. Behavior observations were generally controlled and based on samples of behavior obtained at various times. Although the majority of these studies were conducted among elementary school children, a few of them were concerned with older age groups.

Biehler (*4*) conducted a unique study at the kindergarten level. The twenty-five children participating in this study indicated their preferences for play companions by selecting pictures of their friends' heads and placing them on stick men organized into play groups of five, three, and two. Each child was instructed to place his own picture on one of the stick men first, and then to place the pictures of the other children, who should be in the play groups, on the remaining stick men. Variations in the size of the groups of stick men, of course, enabled the investigator to determine the degree of preference toward selected play companions. Observations made during two play sessions were used to identify the most frequent play companions of each child in actual play situations. A comparison of the sociometric choices with the behavior observations indicated close agreement for the children's first choice. Between 72 percent and 76 percent (for the two sessions) of the children's chosen play companions were the same as their actual play companions, when only the first choice was considered. Lower levels of choice revealed no clear relationships. These findings are in harmony with the fact that children at this age level make little discrimination beyond the first choice.

In studies at the first- and second-grade level, Bonney and Powell (*8, 10*) systematically observed the behavior of children with high and low sociometric status. In both studies, the original subjects included five classrooms of pupils. Sociometric status was determined by using an unlimited number of choices for work companion and play companion. Pupils whose sociometric status was in the top fourth of the group on both criteria were placed in the high status group. Those in the lowest fourth of the group on both criteria were placed in the low status group. Each child in the high and low status groups was observed between eighteen and twenty times, for periods ranging from five to ten minutes. These behavior samples were systematically obtained by time-sampling methods. At the first-grade level, observations were obtained in both play and classroom situations. However, at the second-grade level observations were restricted to free play situations. At both grade levels, twenty-five different behavior categories were used to aid in the observations. These categories were limited to elements of social behavior that could be objectively observed. The purpose of both studies was to determine how the social behavior of sociometrically high and sociometrically low children differed.

At the first-grade level, there was a significant difference between children of high and low sociometric status in five areas of social behavior. Those children with high sociometric status more frequently conformed to classroom requirements, smiled more often, participated more frequently in coöperative group activity, made more voluntary contributions to the group, and associated with more children during free play and activity periods. In general, these findings indicate that the highly chosen children were more active and flexible in their social relations than were those children with low sociometric status.

Similar results were reported for the second-grade level, although specific social behaviors varied due to the restriction of observations to free play situations. Children with high sociometric status were observed to talk more frequently, to laugh and giggle more, to participate more frequently in coöperative group activity, and to play with other children more frequently. Thus, as with the first-grade children, those pupils with high sociometric status tended to be more socially active and to have more social relations with a larger number of children than those pupils with low sociometric status.

In a fourth-grade classroom, Byrd (*12*) structured a situation so that he could directly relate sociometric choices to "real life" choices. He had twenty-seven pupils in a classroom write down the classmates they most preferred as fellow-actors in a classroom play. Over a two-month period, following the sociometric test, he had each pupil openly choose several classmates and put on an unrehearsed play. Following the "real life" choices, which were put into actual practice, he again administered the same sociometric test. The number of choices pupils received on each sociometric test was correlated with the number of choices they received for the actual play situation. Correlation coefficients of .76 and .80 were obtained, indicating a relatively high degree of relationship between sociometric choices and "real life" choices.[1]

In a camp setting, Newstetter, Feldstein, and Newcomb (*39*) compared the sociometric choices of thirty adolescent boys with the behavior observations of six camp counselors. The boys' sociometric status, based on five choices for tent mate, correlated .76 with the counselors' ratings of the boys' camp acceptance. Al-

[1] The correlation coefficients reported in this and the following chapter are difficult to interpret precisely because they have not been corrected for the unreliability in the sets of measures correlated. The true correlations, determined by correcting for attenuation, would be higher than the obtained correlation coefficients reported here.

though the counselors' ratings were based on both observed and inferred instances of actual association, this correlation coefficient indicates substantial agreement between choice behavior and actual behavior.

At the college level, Gibb (*18*) investigated the relation between sociometric status and observations of actual leadership shown in groups. In ten groups of ten college students, sociometric status was determined on the basis of choices for future work companions, best friends in the group, and the most influential group members. When sociometric status on each of these criteria was correlated with leadership ratings by observers, coefficients ranging from .42 to .45 were obtained. Somewhat similar results reported in other studies, at the college and adult levels, were reviewed by Mouton, Blake and Fruchter (*38*). They generally indicated low positive relationships between sociometric status and leadership ratings. These results are not directly comparable to those studies relating choice behavior to actual behavior, since the behavior observations were limited to leadership characteristics. Nevertheless, the consistently low degree of relationship reported indicates that high sociometric status is not closely related to actual leadership performance at these age levels.

In general, and especially at the elementary school level, choice behavior has been shown to be significantly related to observed behavior. Thus, sociometric preferences have shown considerable overlap with actual associations, and pupils with high sociometric status have been distinguished from those with low sociometric status by significant social behaviors. These findings, although based on a limited number of subjects, tend to indicate that sociometric results do have meaning in terms of actual behavior. However, the differences between sociometric results and observed behavior indicate that these two methods are evaluating different aspects of social behavior and cannot be directly equated. Although the evidence is meager, there is also some indication that the relationship between choice behavior and actual behavior may be lower among older age groups.

SOCIOMETRIC RESULTS AND TEACHERS' JUDGMENTS

This method of evaluating the validity of sociometric results is somewhat similar to the previous method. However, important differences may be noted. Instead of using controlled observations of actual behavior, teachers are requested to predict the relative social acceptance of their pupils, and these judgments are then compared with the results of a sociometric test. The teachers, of course, make their judgments before they see any sociometric results on their pupils. Using teachers' judgments as a criterion of validity assumes that teachers have had ample opportunity to know their pupils, that the characteristics of pupils' social acceptance are observable, and that teachers' judgments are reasonably accurate. The first assumption is usually met by obtaining the teachers' judgments toward the end of the school semester or school year. However, the last two assumptions cause some difficulty. The external group structure, upon which the teachers base their judgments, is not expected to be directly comparable to the internal structure revealed by the sociometric results. This is the same problem mentioned in the previous section—choice behavior cannot be directly equated with actual behavior. The other limitation is the great variability among teachers in their ability to make such judgments accurately. Nevertheless, the degree to which teachers' judgments of pupils' social acceptance are related to the results of a sociometric test should indicate the extent to which the sociometric test is measuring aspects of social behavior which are meaningful to experienced observers.

Several rather extensive investigations have been conducted in this area. Probably the most extensive is one conducted by Gage, Leavitt, and Stone (*17*). They compared the judgments of 103 teachers, in fourth-, fifth-, and sixth-grade classes, with the results of a sociometric test administered to their pupils. In the sociometric test, the pupils were requested to choose the five children in their room whom they would most prefer as classmates if the class were divided into two groups. The teachers made their judgments by predicting which five children each pupil would choose. The relationship between the sociometric results and the teachers' judgments was determined, for each teacher, by correlating the number of choices each pupil received on the sociometric test with the number of choices the teacher predicted each pupil would receive. An average correlation coefficient of .48 was obtained for the 103 teachers. This finding shows a fair degree of relationship between teachers' judgments and pupils' choices, but allows for considerable variation between the two measures. It would seem that the teachers' task in this study was an especially difficult one, since they were asked to predict the exact choices each pupil would make.

In several other studies the teachers were requested to rank their pupils in the order in which they thought the pupils were accepted by their classmates, rather than to predict the exact responses of the pupils. In these studies, the relationship between the teachers' judgments and the sociometric results was determined by correlating the teachers' rank-order predictions of their pupils' acceptance with the pupils' actual rankings, based on the number of sociometric choices each pupil received. Using this procedure, Gronlund (*21*) obtained an average correlation coefficient of .60 for forty sixth-grade teachers' judgments on three different sociometric criteria. The accuracy of the teachers' judgments was found to be similar on all three of the criteria. Their judgments of the pupils' acceptance as seating companion correlated .62 with the sociometric results. For the criteria of work companion and play companion the correlations were .61 and .55, respectively. These correlation coefficients are fairly standard for the degree of relationship between teachers' judgments of pupils' social acceptance and the results of a sociometric test. Almost identical results were reported in several other studies (*22, 23, 25*). In all of these latter studies, the average correlation coefficients were approximately .60. In one of the studies (*25*), the degree of relationship between the teachers' judgments of pupils' social acceptance and the sociometric results was comparable to the relationship between the teachers' judgments of intelligence and the results of an intelligence test.

These findings, that there is fairly close agreement between teachers' judgments and pupils' choices on a sociometric test, indicate that the sociometric test is measuring significant aspects of social behavior that are at least partially apparent to the classroom teacher. However, the fact that there is some variation between the social relations perceived by the teacher and those measured by the sociometric test should caution the teacher against sole dependence on classroom observations. It has been noted that teachers tend to overrate those pupils whom they themselves most prefer, those pupils holding student leadership positions, and those pupils who conform most closely to the classroom routine. In contrast, they tend to underrate those pupils whom they least prefer and those pupils who do not adjust readily to classroom activities. Apparently the feelings and behavior expectations of teachers bias their judgments of pupils' social acceptance in the classroom. This would tend to suggest that teachers' judgments of pupils' social relations should be used as a supplement to sociometric results, rather than as a replacement for them.

SOCIOMETRIC RESULTS AND OTHER MEASURES OF SOCIAL ADJUSTMENT

The sociometric test is frequently used as a direct measure of social adjustment. When used for this purpose, social adjustment is defined as the extent to which individuals are accepted by their peers. Thus, an individual who is highly chosen on a sociometric test is considered to be well accepted by his peers and, therefore, to have good social adjustment. In contrast, an individual who receives few or no choices on a sociometric test is considered to have low acceptance among his peers and, therefore, to have poor social adjustment. Since it has been shown that an individual's sociometric status is fairly consistent from one sociometric criterion to another and from one group to another, this interpretation of sociometric results is valid within the limits to which generalization from one sociometric situation to another is possible and within the limits of the above definition. However, the extent to which the sociometric test provides a more general indication of social adjustment must be evaluated in terms of the relationship between sociometric results and other measures of social adjustment. For this purpose sociometric results have generally been compared with ratings of social adjustment by adults, measures of pupils' reputation among their peers, and evidence of problems of social adjustment.

ADULT RATINGS OF SOCIAL ADJUSTMENT

Studies using ratings of social adjustment by adults are difficult to equate, since different procedures were used in different studies and the aspects of social adjustment rated were not uniform from one study to another. In general, however, the studies are in substantial agreement concerning the relationship between the sociometric status of individuals' and adults' ratings of their social adjustment. Individuals who are highly selected on a sociometric test tend to be rated highly on socially effective behavior characteristics and have been noted to make more satisfactory adjustments to their social environment. In contrast, those individuals who are isolated or rejected by their peers have been generally characterized as possessing socially undesirable behavior characteristics and as exhibiting adjustment difficulties in the social sphere.

Olson (*43*) compared the behavior descriptions of teachers with pupils' sociometric status scores in ten classrooms at the elementary school level. Those children receiving the largest number of choices were described most frequently as being dependable, well adjusted, friendly, quiet, and good-natured; while those receiving the fewest choices were described as being shy, bossy, sulky, conduct problems, ill, or new to class. Although there was, naturally, some overlapping in the descriptions of pupils in the two groups, the characterizations of pupils with high and low sociometric status clearly indicated a difference in social adjustment.

In an intensive study of five pupils with high sociometric status and five pupils with low sociometric status, at the elementary school level, Bonney (7) obtained results somewhat similar to those reported by Olson. In general, the highly chosen pupils were characterized by greater conformity and group identification, greater emotional stability and control, more social aggressiveness, greater dependability, and more frequent behavior indicating attitudes of friendliness, coöperativeness, and good will toward others. As in Olson's study, however, considerable overlap in individual characteristics was noted. It was only when the total adjustment pattern was considered that the highly chosen pupils were clearly superior in adjustment to the pupils with low sociometric status.

A comprehensive study in this area, at the adolescent level, was conducted by Jennings (27). She analyzed the behavior descriptions house mothers made of 124 adolescent girls living in a New York training school for girls. When these behavior descriptions were compared with the results of a sociometric test, significant differences were noted between those girls who were highly chosen on the sociometric test and those girls who were under-chosen. The highly chosen girls were described most frequently as being coöperative, having an even disposition, displaying initiative, and exhibiting behavior which contributed to the harmony and effectiveness of group living. In contrast, the under-chosen girls were characterized by socially disagreeable behavior characteristics. The house mothers indicated that they most frequently exhibited quarrelsome, complaining, nervous, aggressive, domineering, and attention-seeking behavior. In addition, the under-chosen were most frequently described as interfering with the activities of the group. Thus, even in a training school for girls, individuals with high sociometric status can be distinguished from those with low sociometric status by the social behaviors they exhibit in their social relations. Since all of the girls were sent to the training school by the New York State Courts, behavior indicating lack of conformity might be expected to be more closely related to high peer acceptance. However, the behavior descriptions most characteristic of the highly chosen girls are generally considered to be social assets which contribute to effective social adjustment.

A rather unusual study by Schoeppe and Havighurst (*50*) indicated the extent to which acceptance by peers was related to the achievement of other developmental tasks. They made an intensive study of fifteen boys and fifteen girls, at the ages of ten, thirteen, and sixteen, with information based on thirty-two different measures of adjustment, including sociometric results. On the basis of these data, eight or more research staff members rated each subject on a ten-point scale in terms of the extent to which each subject was achieving various developmental tasks. The developmental tasks included: (1) learning an appropriate sex role; (2) achieving emotional independence of parents and other adults; (3) developing conscience, morality, and a set of values; (4) getting along with age mates; and (5) developing intellectual skills. The extent to which the subjects had established good peer relations was found to correlate significantly with adjustment on the other developmental tasks, at all age levels. The correlation coefficients for age ten ranged from .57 to .83; for age thirteen they ranged from .64 to .82; and for age sixteen they ranged from .63 to .78. These correlations between the establishment of good peer relations and adjustment on the other developmental tasks indicate a rather close relationship between peer acceptance and general social development. Although a limited number of subjects was included in the study, the intensity with which they were studied and the consistency of the results over the various age levels add significance to the findings.

Studies at the college level also indicate better social adjustment for those individuals who are highly chosen on a sociometric test. Bonney, Hoblit, and Dreyer (*9*) compared the sociometric status of men in a college dormitory with the behavior descriptions of resident counselors. Those with high sociometric status were described as having a sincere and objective interest in others, being considerate of others while they were studying, reflecting an attitude of self-respect and self-confidence in their social relations, and participating actively in the more mature and socially approved forms of group activities. In contrast, those men who were rejected on the sociometric test were characterized by ego-centric attitudes, attention-demanding and dominating behavior, disparaging attitudes toward the opposite sex, occasional excessive drinking, and adroitness in escaping responsibility for antisocial acts. These characteristics of the social rejects are similar to those reported by Kidd (*29*) in another dormitory study. He reported that the men who were rejected on a sociometric test were most frequently described as being domineering, belligerent, noisy, and exhibiting other types of attention-seeking and generally inconsiderate behavior.

At all age levels from the elementary school through college, individuals with high sociometric status have shown superior social adjustment on the basis of adults' ratings of their social behavior. It should be noted that specific traits such as aggressiveness and a high level of verbal response are not the important variables that determine whether or not a person achieves high status on a sociometric test. The important factor seems to be whether the behavior contributes to the harmony and effectiveness of social living or whether it interferes with social interaction. The socially approved behaviors, characteristic of highly chosen individuals, indicate a sensitivity to the feelings and needs of others, while the behavior of individuals with low sociometric status can generally be characterized as self-centered behavior which is inconsiderate of the feelings and needs of others.

It should also be noted that although highly chosen individuals are described most frequently as possessing social assets which contribute to social adjustment, the specific social behaviors of individuals show considerable variation. Any attempt to equate high sociometric status with specific social responses overlooks the general behavior pattern which elicits positive feelings of attraction from others. Thus, individuals with high and low sociometric status cannot be distinguished on the basis of specific social behaviors. However, when the total behavior pattern of individuals is considered, sociometric results provide an indication of the general level of social adjustment attained by them.

MEASURES OF PUPILS' REPUTATION AMONG THEIR PEERS

Another means of evaluating the social adjustment of individuals is that of determining the reputation they hold among their peers. If sociometric results have implications for social adjustment, it should be possible to distinguish between individuals with high and low sociometric status in terms of how they are perceived by their fellow group members. Reputation among peers is usually determined by a "guess who" test. This technique requires individuals to identify those group members who best fit each of a series of behavior descriptions. The behavior descriptions include both positive and negative characteristics. Thus, reputation is measured in terms of both social assets and social liabilities. The number of mentions an individual receives on each of the behavior descriptions serves as a measure of his reputation among his peers.

There are two common criticisms concerning the use of reputation measures as a means of evaluating adjustment. One is that reputation measures are based on the perceptions of others and, therefore, do not provide an objective measure of an individual's behavior characteristics. The other is that a "halo effect" operates in the responses on reputation measures. In other words, if an individual is rated high on one socially desirable characteristic, he tends to be rated high on other socially desirable characteristics. Although both of these criticisms have merit, the reputation an individual holds among his peers has direct implication for his social adjustment. If he is perceived as possessing certain socially desirable characteristics, his social adjustment will be enhanced, whether or not some independent measure indicates that these characteristics are actually present. Likewise, if a few socially desirable characteristics cause an individual to be viewed in a generally favorable light, this "halo effect" will contribute to his reputation and, thereby, to his social adjustment. Thus, although reputation measures have their shortcomings as objective measures of personality characteristics, they do provide information concerning the general level of social adjustment individuals have attained among their peers.

Sociometric results have been compared to the results of reputation measures at various grade levels. Although variations in the specific characteristics included in the "guess who" forms make it impossible to equate the results from one grade level to another, some similarity in descriptive characteristics will be noted. This is due to the fact that most "guess who" forms are modified versions of one originally used by Tryon (55) in her study of children's reputations among their peers.

Bonney (6) reported significant differences between fourth-grade pupils with high and low sociometric status on a number of behavior characteristics. Pupils with high sociometric status were found to be significantly superior on both personal and social behavior descriptions. They were characterized most frequently by their peers as being tidy, good-looking, happy, friendly, and cheerful. In their social relations they were described as being enthusiastic, daring, active in recitations, at ease with adults, welcomed by other class members, and as exhibiting leadership in groups. Thus, the pupils who were highly chosen on the sociometric test were perceived by their classmates as possessing socially admired qualities which contribute to effective social interaction.

Kuhlen and Lee (*32*) conducted a study, similar to Bonney's, at the sixth-, ninth-, and twelfth-grade levels and reported similar results. Although there was some change in characteristics from one grade level to another, those pupils with high sociometric status were characterized more frequently as being good-looking, popular, happy, friendly, cheerful, and enthusiastic. In addition, they were noted to enjoy jokes and to initiate games and other activities more frequently than pupils with low sociometric status. Using twenty-one classrooms at the sixth- and seventh-grade levels, Laughlin (*33*) correlated sociometric results with the behavior descriptions of peers and found the same behavior characteristics related to high sociometric status.

Gronlund and Anderson (*24*) compared the characteristics of socially accepted, socially rejected and socially neglected pupils in a junior high school population. The socially accepted pupils were those who received the largest number of acceptance choices on the sociometric test; the socially rejected were those who received the largest number of rejection choices; and the socially neglected were those who received the smallest number of both acceptance and rejection choices. There were twenty pupils in each category, out of a total population of 158.

When these three groups were compared on the basis of responses to a "guess who" form, important differences were noted. The socially accepted pupils were generally characterized as possessing socially desirable behavior characteristics similar to those reported in the above studies. Specific characteristics such as good looks, tidiness, friendliness, likeableness, enthusiasm, cheerfulness, initiative, and sense of humor stood high on the list. In contrast, the socially rejected pupils were not only overlooked on these positive characteristics, but they were also frequently described as possessing the opposite attributes. Thus, they were characterized by their peers as being *not* good-looking, untidy, *not* likeable, restless, and talkative. The socially neglected pupils tended to be overlooked on the "guess who" form, receiving relatively few mentions on either positive or negative characteristics. The few mentions they did receive indicated that they were quiet and *not* talkative. Apparently they were truly socially neglected by their peers.

Sociometric results appear to be in close agreement with the reputation an individual holds among his peers. In general, pupils who are highly chosen on a sociometric test are perceived by their peers as possessing a pleasant, cheerful, and friendly appearance as well as socially effective aggressive tendencies. On the other hand, pupils with low sociometric status are either overlooked by their peers (socially neglected) or are perceived by them as possessing an unpleasant appearance and socially ineffective aggressive tendencies (socially rejected). Thus, sociometric results provide significant clues concerning the extent to which pupils are adjusting to their peers.

PROBLEMS OF SOCIAL ADJUSTMENT

Several investigators have directed their attention toward the special problems of social adjustment encountered by individuals with low sociometric status. Although diverse aspects of adjustment have been considered in these studies, the results are interesting and generally pertinent to the validity of sociometric results.

Northway (*40*) made an intensive clinical study of the behavior of twenty fifth- and sixth-grade children who were least often chosen on a sociometric test. On the basis of their behavior patterns, she classified them into three distinct groups. First there were the *recessive children* who were described as being listless, with no inner drive or interest in their environment. They appeared to merely exist and exerted little or no effort toward social adjustment. Second, there were the *socially uninterested children* who were quiet and retiring. Although they had individual interests, they showed little or no interest in social interaction. The last group consisted of *socially ineffective children* who were described as being noisy, boastful, arrogant, rebellious, and delinquent in classroom activities. They appeared to be aggressively striving for acceptance by peers, but they used socially ineffective means for attaining it. These behavior patterns are similar to those of the socially neglected and socially rejected pupils discussed in the previous section. They highlight the fact that, although pupils with low sociometric status are generally characterized by inadequate adjustment to their social environment, the specific problems of social adjustment vary considerably from one individual to another.

In a study at the second-grade level, Fuller and Baune (*16*) compared the problem tendencies and the number of injuries received by pupils with high and low sociometric status. Problem tendencies were determined by means of a rating scale, and the number of injuries was obtained from first aid referrals. The results indicated that pupils with low sociometric status had more problem tendencies and sustained more injuries than those with high status. The injuries of those pupils with low sociometric status tended to be due to accidents with other children. Although a limited number of subjects was used in this study, the findings are in general agreement with the results of similar studies conducted among adults. Speroff and Kerr (*52*) reported that steel mill workers with low sociometric status had more industrial accidents than those with high sociometric status. French (*15*), in a study of over 900 naval recruits, found that individuals with low sociometric status needed medical service more frequently and had more disciplinary offenses than those with high sociometric status. These studies suggest that sociometric results are related to accident proneness, health problems, and disciplinary problems.

However, further studies are needed to verify these findings among school children.

In a follow-up study of pupils whose sociometric status was determined in the sixth and ninth grades, Kuhlen and Collister (*31*) reported that pupils with low sociometric status tended to drop out of school more frequently than those with high sociometric status. Similar results were reported by Ullmann (*57*), in a follow-up study of ninth-grade pupils. Although there are numerous reasons why pupils drop out of school, the tendency for pupils with low sociometric status to drop out more frequently indicates that sociometric status scores obtained at the sixth- and ninth-grade levels are predictive of later adjustment in high school.

In summary, sociometric results have shown substantial agreement with other measures of social adjustment. Both adults' ratings and peer evaluations indicate more satisfactory social adjustment on the part of pupils with high sociometric status. In addition, both clinical and follow-up studies have indicated that pupils with low sociometric status make less satisfactory adjustments to their peers and to their school environment than do pupils with high sociometric status. Thus, sociometric results provide teachers and counselors with valuable evidence concerning the general level of social adjustment being attained by pupils.

SOCIOMETRIC RESULTS AND MEASURES OF PERSONAL ADJUSTMENT

Since individuals with high sociometric status are generally better adjusted socially than those with low sociometric status, they also might logically be expected to have better personal adjustment. Their higher status should provide more opportunity for satisfying their psychological needs for security, social approval, and self-respect, resulting in greater personal satisfaction and freedom from tension. Thus, sociometric results should show some relationship to measures of personal adjustment. A high degree of relationship is not expected, however, since the various measures of personal adjustment themselves have questionable or unknown validity.

In addition, personal and social adjustment may show considerable variation in any one individual. It is possible for an individual to exhibit socially approved behavior while feeling inwardly tense and insecure. In fact, an exaggerated need for security and social approval could result in behavior which conformed to the values of the group and, thereby, contributed to greater peer acceptance. Likewise, it is possible for an individual to achieve satisfaction of his psychological needs at the expense of his social relations. The need for security, social approval, and self-respect could be satisfied through individual accomplishments which remove the individual from extensive social contact, resulting in lower peer acceptance. A gifted pupil with many individual constructive interests would be characteristic of this type of person. Personal and social adjustment are not necessarily antithetical, but it is possible to achieve satisfactory adjustment in one area without achieving comparable adjustment in the other. Nevertheless, studies in this area should indicate the extent to which sociometric status is related to evidence of personal adjustment.

RESULTS OF SELF-REPORT TECHNIQUES

Evidence concerning personal adjustment has frequently been obtained from the pupils themselves, through the use of adjustment questionnaires, problem check lists, and self-ratings. Although such self-report techniques have numerous limitations as measures of personal adjustment, they do reflect how the pupil feels about himself and the problems of adjustment he faces. Thus, the relationship between sociometric results and the results of self-report techniques provides an indication of how a pupil's feelings toward himself compare with the feelings of other pupils toward him.

A number of studies have related sociometric results to personal adjustment as measured by personality and mental health questionnaires. Where the total scores on various adjustment questionnaires were correlated with pupils' sociometric status scores, low positive relationships were obtained (*6, 13, 19, 20, 35, 36, 46, 47, 54*) or a complete lack of relationship was indicated (*9, 14, 42, 51*). However, where the questionnaire responses of pupils with high sociometric status were compared with those of pupils with low sociometric status, differences in personal adjustment were noted. Grossman and Wrighter (*26*) reported that sixth-grade pupils who were highly chosen on a sociometric test had significantly higher adjustment scores on the California Test of Personality than those pupils who were rejected on the sociometric test. Using the same adjustment questionnaire, Scandrette (*48*) reported that eighth-grade pupils with high sociometric status had better personal adjustment than pupils with low sociometric status. In a more detailed analysis of the results (*49*), he noted that pupils with low sociometric status tended to feel insecure in their school relations. They also felt that both teachers and other pupils had little personal interest in them and treated them in an unfair and unkind manner. Similar results were noted by Bjerstedt (*5*) for Swedish school children.

Two rather extensive investigations compared the mental health characteristics of pupils with high and low sociometric status. In both studies the mental health characteristics were determined by the pupils' responses to Thorpe, Clark, and Tiegs' adjustment questionnaire, entitled Mental Health Analysis. Sociometric status was based on a variety of criteria concerned with classroom activities. In one of the studies, Bedoian (*3*) reported that pupils with high sociometric status had significantly higher mental health scores than pupils with low sociometric status, in twenty-one of the twenty-two sixth-grade classrooms included in the study. Similar findings were reported by Baron (*1, 2*), for pupils in eleven fifth- and sixth-grade classrooms. He noted that the high status pupils tended to feel more self-confident, more physically adequate, more secure in their school relationships, and gave indications of greater emotional stability than low status pupils. The results were similar for boys and girls, with the exception that low status girls indicated the presence of nervous symptoms which did not appear among low status boys.

Kuhlen and Bretsch (*30*) compared the personal problems felt by pupils with high and low sociometric status. They requested approximately 700 ninth-grade pupils to check the items on the Mooney Problem Check List which bothered them never, sometimes, or often. Although there was little difference between the total number of problems checked by the high and low status pupils, those pupils with low sociometric status checked more personal problems "often" than the pupils with high sociometric status. Those personal problems checked "often" by the low status pupils revealed concern with social skills, unhappiness, lack of status, family problems, and dislike of school. In a similar study by Keislar (*28*), the personal problems checked by 332 tenth-grade pupils were compared with sociometric results. He reported that the pupils with high and low sociometric status both checked approximately the same number of problems. Although the high status pupils tended to check more specific problems, there was little difference between the two groups. Since there was no indication that the pupils were requested to indicate the frequency with which thy experienced the problems, these results are difficult to compare to the previous study. It may be that pupils with high and low sociometric status both experience common problems of adjustment, but low status pupils experience these problems more frequently, as indicated by the findings of Kuhlen and Bretsch.

In a study of 696 ninth-grade pupils, Bretsch (*11*) compared the self-ratings of pupils with high and low sociometric status on eight different social skills. High status pupils rated themselves higher on the social skills than did the low status pupils. This finding seems to indicate that high status pupils are more confident of their ability to perform social skills.

These findings indicate that where complete groups are used, there tends to be a low positive relationship between sociometric status scores and the various measures of personal adjustment. However, where the more sensitive method of comparing extreme sociometric status groups is used, pupils with low sociometric status have consistently lower adjustment scores than pupils with high sociometric status. Pupils in the low status group tend to feel insecure, discriminated against, inadequate physically and socially, and show signs of emotional instability. They also compare themselves unfavorably with others and show concern with lack of social skills. In contrast, the responses of high status pupils generally reflect feelings of security, self-confidence, and other evidences of good personal adjustment. Thus, high and low status pupils tend to view themselves quite differently on self-report techniques.

RESULTS OF PROJECTIVE TECHNIQUES

In order to avoid some of the shortcomings of self-report techniques, projective techniques have been commonly used to measure personal adjustment. The unique feature of projective techniques is that they present unstructured and ambiguous situations to the individual, and he is permitted to respond in terms of his own perception of the situations. Since the situations are ambiguous, he projects his own feelings and interpretations in his responses. These can then be interpreted in terms of personality structure and dimensions of personal adjustment. The most widely used projective techniques are the Rorschach Inkblot Test and the Thematic Apperception Test. In the former test the individual responds to a series of inkblots, and in the latter test he responds to a series of ambiguous pictures. Both tests are complex and require special clinical training to administer and interpret. This, plus the time involved in administering the tests, probably accounts for the relatively few studies comparing sociometric results with these measures of personal adjustment.

Tindall (*54*) correlated sociometric status scores with responses to the Rorschach Inkblot Test and obtained a correlation coefficient of .32. However, Nowell (*42*) and Pepinsky (*45*) found no relationship between the same two measures. Northway and Wigdor (*41*) compared the Rorschach patterns of eighth-grade pupils with high, average, and low sociometric status. The high status pupils were characterized by greater sensitivity to their social environment. The low status pupils revealed less ability to control their emotions and tended to be more ego-centric, moody, and impulsive. However, it was reported that there were more seriously disturbed pupils in both the high and low status groups than there were in the average status group. Mill (*37*) reported similar results among college students. A comparison of the sociometrically high and sociometrically low students, on the basis of their responses to the Rorschach Inkblot Test and the Thematic Apperception Test, indicated that neither group was optimally adjusted. Although students with low status showed trends toward greater anxiety and deviate patterns of adjustment, some of the students with high status also reflected neurotic tendencies.

The findings of these studies, comparing sociometric results with the results of projective techniques, are somewhat similar to those obtained with self-report techniques. Correlations between sociometric status scores and personal adjustment scores indicated little or no relationship. However, when high and low status groups were compared, pupils with low sociometric status were characterized by more severe patterns of maladjustment. A significant factor, not brought out by the self-report techniques, is the fact that some pupils with high sociometric status also have rather severe problems of adjustment. Thus, low sociometric status seems to be related to tendencies toward maladjustment, but high sociometric status cannot be equated with good personal adjustment in individual cases.

In general, sociometric results are much more closely related to other measures of social adjustment than they are to measures of personal adjustment. As indicated previously, this is partly due to the fact that social and personal adjustment are not themselves closely related. Several studies (*53, 54, 56*) have reported relatively high intercorrelations among various measures of personal adjustment and among various measures of social adjustment, but relatively low relationships between measures in the two different areas. Consequently, the relatively low relationship between sociometric status and the various measures of personal adjustment should not be interpreted to mean that sociometric results are invalid. Rather it confirms the fact that the sociometric test and the various measures of personal adjustment are measuring two different types of adjustment and that the two types of adjustment are not necessarily closely related.

This should caution teachers and counselors against depending solely on the sociometric technique, or on any other single technique, as a measure of pupil adjustment. To fully understand the adjustment patterns of individual pupils, information from a variety of sources should be obtained. When used in this setting, sociometric results provide unique and valuable evidence concerning the social adjustment of pupils. Through the identification of pupils who are isolated and rejected by their peers, sociometric results can also be used to locate those pupils who are most likely to have personal problems of adjustment.

SUMMARY

Validity is traditionally defined as the extent to which a test measures what it is supposed to measure. When applied to sociometric testing, difficulties arise from the fact that there is little agreement as to what the sociometric test is supposed to measure. If the sociometric test is limited to the measurement of choice behavior, it is valid by definition. However, a more general use of sociometric results requires that they be validated by relating them to significant psychological and sociological variables. Although there are inherent difficulties in this procedure, numerous studies have reflected on the extent to which sociometric results provide a valid indication of educationally significant behavior.

In general, studies have shown that sociometric results are significantly related to the actual behavior of pupils, to teachers' judgments of pupils' social acceptance, to adults' ratings of pupils' social adjustment, to the reputations pupils hold among their peers, to specific problems of social adjustment, and, within limits, to problems of personal adjustment. Pupils with high sociometric status are generally characterized by feelings and behaviors which are indicative of good personal-social adjustment. In contrast, pupils with low sociometric status tend to have socially ineffective behavior characteristics, and tend to exhibit evidence of poor personal-social adjustment.

A more detailed analysis of the research findings indicates that sociometric results are more closely related to measures of social adjustment than they are to measures of personal adjustment. The observations and ratings of both adults and peers show consistently close agreement between sociometric results and other evidence of social adjustment. However, measures of personal adjustment show little relationship to sociometric results until the more sensitive method of comparing extreme sociometric status groups is used. When this is done, the pupils with high sociometric status are generally noted to have better patterns of adjustment than those with low sociometric status, although some high status pupils have also been noted to have problems of adjustment.

The evidence indicates that sociometric results can provide teachers and counselors with valuable clues concerning the social and personal adjustments of pupils. However, a comprehensive understanding of the adjustment patterns of individual pupils would also require the use of supplementary measures of social and personal adjustment.

REFERENCES

1. Baron, D., "Mental Health Characteristics and Classroom Social Status," *Education,* 1949, *69:*306–310.
2. Baron, D., "Personal-Social Characteristics and Classroom Social Status: A Sociometric Study of Fifth- and Sixth-Grade Girls," *Sociometry,* 1951, *14:*32–42.
3. Bedoian, V. H., "Mental Health Analysis of Socially Over-Accepted, Socially Under-Accepted, Overage and Underage Pupils in the Sixth Grade," *Journal of Educational Psychology,* 1953, *44:*366–371.
4. Biehler, R. F., "Companion Choice Behavior in the Kindergarten," *Child Development,* 1954, *25:*45–50.
5. Bjerstedt, A., "The Interpretation of Sociometric Status Scores in the Classroom," *Nordisk Psychologi,* 1956, *8:*1–14.
6. Bonney, M. E., "Personality Traits of Socially Successful and Socially Unsuccessful Children," *Journal of Educational Psychology,* 1943, *34:*449–472.
7. Bonney, M. E., "Popular and Unpopular Children, A Sociometric Study," *Sociometry Monographs,* No. 9, New York, Beacon House, 1947.
8. Bonney, M. E., "Social Behavior Differences Between Second Grade Children of High and Low Sociometric Status," *Journal of Educational Research,* 1955, *48:*481–495.
9. Bonney, M. E., Hoblit, R. E., and Dreyer, A. H., "A Study of Some Factors Related to Sociometric Status in a Men's Dormitory," *Sociometry,* 1953, *16:*287–301.
10. Bonney, M. E., and Powell, J., "Differences in Social Behavior Between Sociometrically High and Sociometrically Low Children," *Journal of Educational Research,* 1953, *46:*481–495.
11. Bretsch, H. S., "Social Skills and Activities of Socially Accepted and Unaccepted Adolescents," *Journal of Educational Psychology,* 1952, *43:*449–504.
12. Byrd, E., "A Study of Validity and Constancy of Choice in a Sociometric Test," *Sociometry,* 1951, *14:*175–181.
13. Forlano, G., and Wrightstone, J. W., "Sociometric and Self-

Descriptive Techniques in Appraisal of Pupil Adjustment," *Sociometry,* 1951, *14:*340–350.

14. Fox, W. H., and Segel, D., "Validity of the Choice of Friends, Method of Measuring Social Adjustment," *Journal of Educational Research,* 1954, *47:*389–394.
15. French, R. L., "Sociometric Status and Individual Adjustment Among Naval Recruits," *Journal of Abnormal and Social Psychology,* 1951, *46:*64–72.
16. Fuller, E. M., and Baune, H. A., "Injury-Proneness and Adjustment in a Second-Grade," *Sociometry,* 1951, *14:*210–225.
17. Gage, N. L., Leavitt, G. L., and Stone, G. C., "Teachers' Understanding of Their Pupils and Pupils' Ratings of Their Teachers," *Psychological Monographs,* No. 21, American Psychological Association, Washington, D.C., 1955.
18. Gibb, C. A., "The Sociometry of Leadership in Temporary Groups," *Sociometry,* 1950, *13:*226–243.
19. Greenblatt, E. L., "Relationship of Mental Health and Social Status," *Journal of Educational Research,* 1950, *44:*193–204.
20. Greenblatt, E. L., "Two Additional Studies in the Dynamics of School Social Structure of Classroom Seating and School Dances," *Journal of Educational Research,* 1953, *47:*261–270.
21. Gronlund, N. E., "The Accuracy of Teachers' Judgments Concerning the Sociometric Status of Sixth-Grade Pupils," *Sociometry Monographs,* No. 25, New York, Beacon House, 1951.
22. Gronlund, N. E., "The General Ability to Judge Sociometric Status: Elementary Student Teachers' Sociometric Perceptions of Classmates and Pupils," *Journal of Educational Psychology,* 1956, *47:*147–157.
23. Gronlund, N. E., "The Relative Ability of Homeroom Teachers and Special Subject Teachers to Judge the Social Acceptability of Pre-Adolescent Pupils," *Journal of Educational Research,* 1955, *48:*381–391.
24. Gronlund, N. E., and Anderson, L., "Personality Characteristics of Socially Accepted, Socially Neglected, and Socially Rejected Junior High School Pupils," *Educational Administration and Supervision,* 1957, *43:*329–338.

25. Gronlund, N. E., and Whitney, A. P., "The Relation Between Teachers' Judgments of Pupils' Sociometric Status and Intelligence," *Elementary School Journal,* 1958, *59:*264–268.
26. Grossman, B., and Wrighter, J., "The Relationship Between Selection-Rejection and Intelligence, Social Status, and Personality Amongst Sixth-Grade Children," *Sociometry,* 1948, *11:*346–355.
27. Jennings, H. H., *Leadership and Isolation,* New York, Longmans, Green, and Company, 1950.
28. Keislar, E. R., "Peer Group Judgments as Validity Criteria for the SRA Youth Inventory," *California Journal of Educational Research,* 1954, *5:*77–79.
29. Kidd, J. W., "An Analysis of Social Rejection in a College Men's Residence Hall," *Sociometry,* 1951, *14:*226–234.
30. Kuhlen, R. G., and Bretsch, H. S., "Sociometric Status and Personal Problems of Adolescents," *Sociometry,* 1947, *10:*122–132.
31. Kuhlen, R. G., and Collister, E. G., "Sociometric Status of Sixth- and Ninth-Graders Who Fail to Finish High School," *Educational and Psychological Measurement,* 1952, *12:*632–637.
32. Kuhlen, R. G., and Lee, B. J., "Personality Characteristics and Social Acceptability in Adolescence," *Journal of Educational Psychology,* 1943, *34:*321–340.
33. Laughlin, F., *The Peer Status of Sixth- and Seventh-Grade Children,* New York, Bureau of Publications, Teachers College, Columbia University, 1954.
34. Lindzey, G., and Borgatta, E. F., "Sociometric Measurement," Chapter 11, in G. Lindzey (ed.), *Handbook of Social Psychology,* Cambridge, Massachusetts, Addison-Wesley Publishing Company, 1954.
35. Lindzey, G., and Urdan, J. A., "Personality and Social Choice," *Sociometry,* 1954, *17:*47–63.
36. Lodge, W. J., "A Validity Study of Personality Questionnaires at the Upper Elementary Grade Level," *Journal of Educational Psychology,* 1951, *42:*21–30.
37. Mill, C. R., "Personality Patterns of Sociometrically Selected and Sociometrically Rejected Male College Students," *Sociometry,* 1953, *16:*151–167.

38. Mouton, J. S., Blake, R. R., and Fruchter, B., "The Validity of Sociometric Responses," *Sociometry,* 1955, *18:*181–206.

39. Newstetter, W. I., Feldstein, M. J., and Newcomb, T. M., *Group Adjustment: A Study in Experimental Sociology,* Cleveland, Western Reserve University, 1938.

40. Northway, M. L., "Outsiders: A Study of the Personality Patterns of Children Least Acceptable to Their Age Mates," *Sociometry,* 1944, *7:*10–25.

41. Northway, M. L., and Wigdor, B. T., "Rorschach Patterns Related to the Sociometric Status of School Children," *Sociometry,* 1947, *10:*186–199.

42. Nowell, A., "Peer Status as Related to Measures of Personality," *California Journal of Educational Research,* 1953, *4:*37–41.

43. Olson, W. C., *Child Development,* Boston, D. C. Heath and Company, 1949.

44. Pepinsky, P. N., "The Meaning of 'Validity' and 'Reliability' as Applied to Sociometric Tests," *Educational and Psychological Measurement,* 1949, *9:*39–49.

45. Pepinsky, H. B., Siegel, L., and Vanatta, E. L., "The Criterion in Counseling: A Group Participation Scale," *Journal of Abnormal and Social Psychology,* 1952, *47:*415–419.

46. Powell, M. G., "Comparisons of Self-Ratings, Peer-Ratings, and Expert's Ratings of Personality Adjustment," *Educational and Psychological Measurement,* 1948, *8:*225–234.

47. Satterlee, R. L., "Sociometric Analysis and Personality Adjustment," *California Journal of Educational Research,* 1955, *6:*181–184.

48. Scandrette, O. C., "Classroom Choice Status Related to Scores on Components of the California Test of Personality," *Journal of Educational Research,* 1953, *46:*291–296.

49. Scandrette, O. C., "School Through the Eyes of the Underchosen," *Clearing House,* 1952, *27:*35–37.

50. Schoeppe, A., and Havighurst, R. J., "A Validation of Development and Adjustment Hypotheses of Adolescence," *Journal of Educational Psychology,* 1952, *43:*339–353.

51. Singer, A., "Certain Aspects of Personality and Their Relation

to Certain Group Modes, and Constancy of Friendship Choices," *Journal of Educational Research,* 1951, *45:*33–42.

52. Speroff, B., and Kerr, W., "Steel Mill 'Hot Strip' Accidents and Interpersonal Desirability Values," *Journal of Clinical Psychology,* 1952, *8:*89–91.
53. Stier, L. D., "A Comparison of Self-Evaluation, Peer Evaluation, Teacher Evaluation and Standardized Tests on Personality and Achievement Factors in the Fifth and Eighth Grades," Unpublished Ph.D. Dissertation, Berkeley, University of California, 1948.
54. Tindall, R. H., "Relationships Among Indices of Adjustment Status," *Educational and Psychological Measurement,* 1955, *15:*152–162.
55. Tryon, C. M., "Evaluations of Adolescent Personality by Adolescents," *Monographs of the Society for Research in Child Development,* No. 4, Washington, D.C., National Research Council, 1939.
56. Ullmann, C. A., *Identification of Maladjusted School Children,* Public Health Monograph No. 7, Washington, D.C., Government Printing Office, 1952.
57. Ullmann, C. A., "Teachers, Peers and Tests as Predictors of Adjustment," *Journal of Educational Psychology,* 1957, *48:*257–267.

CHAPTER 7

PERSONAL AND SOCIAL FACTORS RELATED TO SOCIOMETRIC RESULTS

In the preceding chapter the main concern was with the relationship between sociometric results and factors most directly pertinent to the validity of sociometric responses. In addition to those factors, there are numerous personal and social variables that have been shown to be related to sociometric results. Although some of them also reflect on the validity of the sociometric technique, their significance from a validity standpoint is mainly indirect. A consideration of these personal and social variables related to sociometric results, however, does provide an understanding of the factors which influence sociometric responses. Such an understanding is necessary if the basis of sociometric choice is to be clearly understood and the sociometric results are to be accurately interpreted. The personal and social factors related to sociometric results also have some implications for the use of the sociometric technique in educational practice.

PERSONAL FACTORS

There is considerable interest in the relationship between sociometric results and the personal characteristics of the person choosing or being chosen on a sociometric test. In the last chapter those characteristics which indicated personal and social adjustment were considered. From an educational standpoint it is equally important to consider the relationship of sociometric results to such factors as intelligence, achievement, the possession of skills, and other educationally significant variables. Although cause and effect are not always clear, this investigation should provide some insight into the personal factors which influence children's sociometric responses.

INTELLIGENCE AND SOCIOMETRIC RESULTS

A number of studies have been concerned with the relationship between intelligence and sociometric results. Where the sociometric status of individuals has been correlated with their intelligence test scores, low positive correlations have been generally obtained. Some typical correlation coefficients for various grade levels are indicated here:

Study	*Grade*	*N*	*Correlation (r)*
Bonney (10)	2	48	.32
Bonney (9)	3	48	.34
Bonney (9)	4	81	.31
Bonney (9)	5	100	.45
Laughlin (42)	6	525	.31
Laughlin (42)	7	525	.27

These relatively small correlation coefficients indicate that there is little direct relationship between intelligence and the degree of acceptance by peers. This does not imply, however, that intelligence is not an important factor in sociometric choosing. When pupils with extremely low and extremely high intelligence are compared, distinct differences in sociometric status may be noted.

In studies of the social acceptance of mentally handicapped

pupils in the regular elementary grades, Johnson (*38*), and Johnson and Kirk (*39*) reported that approximately two-thirds of the mentally handicapped pupils were rejected on the basis of sociometric results. A further analysis in one of the studies indicated that, within the mentally handicapped group of pupils, the lower the intelligence the greater the percentage of isolates and rejectees.

A study of the social acceptance of pupils at the other end of the intelligence scale was conducted by Gallagher and Crowder (*31*). They investigated the sociometric status of thirty gifted pupils in the regular elementary grades. All pupils had obtained a Stanford Binet IQ of 150 or higher. Over 80 percent of the gifted pupils had above average sociometric status, with 53 percent of them being placed in the top quartile of their classroom groups. These results indicate that, as a group, gifted pupils are distinctly superior in terms of social acceptance by their peers. It should be noted, however, that 20 percent of the gifted pupils had below average sociometric status and that 7 percent of them were in the bottom fourth. This indicates that although high intelligence is closely related to high sociometric status, some gifted pupils are not well accepted by their peers.

Studies conducted in classrooms with a normal range of intelligence tend to support the above findings. Bonney and Powell (*15*) compared the IQ's of first-grade pupils with high and low sociometric status. The high status pupils had a median IQ of 113 and the low status pupils had a median IQ of 97. Another study by Bonney (*11*) produced essentially the same results among second-grade children. It is interesting to note in this latter study that pupils with high sociometric status had a range in IQ from 111 to 135, whereas low status pupils had a range from 89 to 129. As suggested by Bonney, this indicates a greater tendency for a pupil of high intelligence to have low sociometric status than for a pupil of low intelligence to have high sociometric status. This view is also supported by the findings of Grossman and Wrighter (*35*). They studied the relationship between intelligence and sociometric status among sixth-grade children and reported that the two variables were related up to a point, but that high intelligence did not assure high sociometric status.

Apparently the relationship between intelligence and sociometric status is similar to that between intelligence and achievement. For example, low intelligence is predictive of low achievement, but high intelligence does not assure high achievement, since so many factors (i.e., motivation, study habits, etc.) other than intelligence enter into achievement. Likewise, low intelligence may interfere with acceptance by peers, but high intelligence is not a sufficient condition for high peer acceptance. Other qualities and characteristics must also be present. This probably accounts for the relatively low correlation coefficients reported between intelligence and sociometric status where an entire group has been considered.

There is also some evidence that intelligence enters into mutual relationships among school children. Those children who choose each other on a sociometric test tend to be more alike in intelligence than the children who do not choose each other. Potashin (*56*) and Bonney (*13*) both reported this tendency, based on studies of mutual choices among elementary school children. Thus, the extent to which intelligence influences sociometric choices depends on the level of intelligence of the chooser as well as that of the chosen. This is brought out clearly in a study by Barbe (*3*). He analyzed the choice process of 244 elementary school children with IQ's ranging from 65 to 140. His results indicated that although there was a general tendency to choose children of higher intelligence as friends, the slow-learning children tended to choose pupils of below average intelligence, whereas the bright children tended to choose pupils of above average intelligence. Approximately 62 percent of the slow-learning children chose friends from the below average group. None of them chose pupils with IQ's over 120 as friends. In contrast, 80 percent of the bright children chose friends with above average intelligence.

The results of these studies indicate that pupils tend to choose companions who are similar to themselves in intelligence. Although pupils with higher intelligence are in the most favorable position for receiving sociometric choices, too great a deviation from the group in either direction will most likely result in low sociometric status. Thus, a mentally retarded child would tend to experience isolation and lack of mutual friendships when placed in a group of children with above average intelligence. Likewise a gifted pupil would tend to have low sociometric status and few, if any, mutual friendships if placed in a group of children with below average intelligence. This does not conflict with the study by Gallagher and Crowder (*31*). The relatively high sociometric status of their gifted pupils can be partly accounted for by the fact that they were selected from classrooms where the pupils tended to have above average intelligence. Since pupils tend to choose associates with slightly higher intelligence, the pupils with high intelligence tended to have higher sociometric status. However, the level of sociometric status achieved by a pupil seems to depend as much on the degree of intelligence possessed by the other group members as it does on his own level of intelligence. Too great a deviation from that of the group results in low sociometric status and lack of mutual relationships.

These findings would seem to indicate that ability grouping, as commonly used in the public schools, is in greater harmony with pupils' preferences than is commonly believed. If the stigma usually attached to low ability groups could be removed, such grouping may contribute to improved group relations as well as to more effective group instruction.

ACHIEVEMENT AND SOCIOMETRIC RESULTS

The relationship between the sociometric status of pupils and their academic achievement is similar to that reported for intelligence, as might be expected. Where achievement test scores are correlated with sociometric status scores, a low positive relationship is generally indicated. Studies by Bonney (*10*) and Laughlin (*42*) reported correlation coefficients ranging from .14 to .36 between achievement in various school subjects and sociometric status, for grades two through seven. Lindzey and Urdan (*43*) reported no relationship between sociometric status and achievement among college students. However, they did point out that there was a limited range of achievement in the group.

Where the more sensitive method of comparing high and low sociometric status groups has been used, significant differences in achievement have been noted. Grossman and Wrighter (*35*) reported that sixth-grade pupils with high sociometric status had significantly higher scores on a standardized reading test than those pupils with low sociometric status. Buswell (*20*), in an extensive study of fifth- and sixth-grade pupils, reported that those pupils who were highly chosen on a sociometric test had significantly higher achievement in the basic subject skills than those pupils who were least accepted. Differences in scholastic averages between pupils with high and low sociometric status were reported by Brown (*18*) for the high school level. He compared the achievement of the 200 most accepted and the 200 least accepted students in a total population of 1600 high school students. The most accepted students had higher scholastic averages than those in the least accepted group. Feinberg (*28*) reported the same results for a study of 2000 adolescent boys, and Ohlsen and Dennis (*54*) reported similar results for college students.

The relationship between sociometric status and achievement tends to follow the pattern reported for intelligence. It seems likely that achievement is related to social acceptance up to a point. Beyond that, other factors determine whether or not an individual is highly accepted by his peers. A unique study by Keislar (*40*) casts some light on this interpretation. He obtained measures of prestige and sociometric status for 165 boys and 188 girls at the tenth-grade level. The prestige of each pupil was determined by means of a "guess who" test and sociometric status was based on the choice of best friends and classroom companions. The correlations between prestige and sociometric status ranged between .42 and .47, which indicates that they were measuring somewhat different characteristics. The finding most pertinent to our present discussion is the fact that an individual's prestige was more closely related to his school achievement than was his sociometric status. In other words, pupils with high achievement were respected by their classmates even though they were not necessarily highly chosen by them as friends and classroom associates. Thus, school achievement may attract recognition and respect from other students which places the individual in a favorable position to be chosen on a sociometric test. Whether he actually is chosen would depend on other factors operating in the choice process.

Another possibility, of course, is that being accepted by peers contributes to school achievement. When a child feels accepted and secure in his social relationships, he is better able to concentrate on his school work and he has greater motivation to maintain a reasonable level of scholastic achievement. This social pressure to achieve and to maintain status is a common phenomenon in group work. Its influence would seem to be greatest among pupils with high sociometric status, since they have the largest number of relations with other group members and consequently a greater source of social pressure.

We can only speculate as to whether achievement contributes to social acceptance or social acceptance contributes to achievement. Classroom observations would seem to indicate that both directions of influence are possible and that improvement in one area is likely to result in improvement in the other area. However, the complexity of the factors entering into both school achievement and social acceptance should make the teacher wary of simple generalizations concerning cause and effect.

School achievement is probably most closely related to sociometric status where such achievement is highly valued by the group. As with intelligence, however, too great a deviation in achievement from that of the other group members is likely to interfere with peer acceptance. Bonney (*13*) and Smith (*62*) have reported that both elementary and secondary school pupils tend to choose associates who are similar to themselves in achievement. Thus, when the relation between school achievement and sociometric position is being considered, the level of achievement of the choosers as well as that of the chosen must be considered.

AGE AND SOCIOMETRIC RESULTS

Several rather extensive investigations have been concerned with the extent to which underage and overage pupils, at particular grade levels, are accepted on a sociometric test. Bedoian (*5*) studied the influence of age on sociometric choices among 743 sixth-grade pupils from twenty-two different classes. Sociometric status was determined on four sociometric criteria based on classroom activities. Rejection choices were also obtained on one of the sociometric questions. The results indicated that pupils who were overage (nine months above class average) had the lowest sociometric status and tended to be rejected more frequently by their classmates. The underage pupils (nine months below class average) had the highest sociometric status and also had the largest percentage of stars in class. However, the underage pupils who were between twelve and fourteen months below the class average had lower sociometric status than those pupils who were only nine months under age. These results probably reflect, in part, the influence of intelligence and achievement on sociometric choosing. The overage pupils are generally the slow learners who have been retained, while the underage pupils tend to be those with higher ability. The tendency for pupils to choose companions of similar age, however, is noted in the declining sociometric status of those underage pupils who deviated most from the average age of the other pupils in the group.

Two similar studies were reported by Morrison and Perry (*51*), although they confined their interest to overage pupils. Their studies included 745 children in grades four through eight. Both studies indicated a consistent tendency for overage children in grades four through six to have lower sociometric status. In grades seven and eight there was no difference in the sociometric status of the overage and the average-age children. This latter finding was accounted for by the authors in terms of the increased number of choices overage children received from members of the opposite sex and the greater athletic ability of the overage boys. Apparently age differences become less important in sociometric choosing beyond the sixth-grade level due to the greater prestige attached to physical maturity by members of the opposite sex. This is especially noticeable in the preferences of junior high school girls. Since they mature earlier than boys, they tend to choose boys older than themselves when selecting companions of the opposite sex.

SKILL AND SOCIOMETRIC RESULTS

Both social and physical skills have been shown to be related to sociometric status at various age levels. Investigators have used self-ratings, peer ratings, adult ratings, and actual performance as criteria of skill. Regardless of the method of determining skill, those with greater skill in activities tended to be chosen more frequently on a sociometric test.

Bretsch (*17*) had 325 boys and 325 girls at the ninth-grade level rate their own ability on eight social skills. These included dancing, singing, swimming, tennis, skating or skiing, playing cards, playing an instrument, and carrying on a conversation. The pupils were also asked to choose associates on six sociometric criteria concerning work, play, and social activities. The boys and girls who were most highly chosen (top 25 percent) on the sociometric test rated themselves higher on the social skills than the boys and girls who were poorly accepted (bottom 25 percent). The highly chosen pupils also indicated that they participated more frequently in social activities than the poorly accepted group.

In a summer camp Polansky, Lippitt, and Redl (*55*) compared peer ratings of sixty-four boys and forty girls with the results of a near-sociometric test. The children's ages ranged from ten to fifteen. Those children who were best liked as camp companions were rated most frequently by their peers as being the best athletes and being good at doing things. Another study in a camp setting (*37*) indicated that youngsters who were highly chosen on a sociometric test were rated by their counselors as possessing the greatest athletic ability. It should be noted that the sociometric tests used in these studies included choices for eating companion, sleeping companion, and best-liked campers. None of the choosing situations pertained to activities specifically requiring skill. Apparently the prestige associated with athletic ability has a general influence on sociometric responses.

A rather extensive study by Breck (*16*), at the college level, also used peer ratings as a measure of skill. She compared the peer ratings of 586 college women in beginning classes in swimming, volleyball, and dance with their friendship choices. The correlations between friendship choices and peer ratings of skill in the three activities ranged from .43 to .57. Those women who were most frequently chosen as friends tended to be rated as most skillful in the activities.

Although the above studies are consistent in indicating a relationship between skill in activities and sociometric status, there are obvious shortcomings in using ratings as a measure of skill. Self-ratings may reflect the confidence an individual has in himself rather than the actual possession of the skills. Ratings by peers and adults tend to be influenced by the "halo effect." That is, individuals who are well liked by others tend to be rated higher on all desirable characteristics. To overcome these deficiencies of the rating method, two investigations included measures of actual performance as an index of skill in activities. Both were concerned with the relationship between athletic performance and sociometric status.

McCrow and Tolbert (*49*) compared athletic ability, based on performance in running and jumping, with the results of a near-sociometric test of 438 junior high school boys. Sociometric status was based on the number of choices received from peers on the criterion of being "liked best." The results indicated a significant positive relationship between athletic ability and sociometric status. They also found that boys who were "liked best" participated more frequently in athletic activities and were rated by their peers as being the best athletes. A similar study was conducted by Biddulph (*6*) among high school students, but his sociometric test included choices for specific activities. He asked 461 pupils in high school physical education classes to choose companions for work, play, and social situations. He also determined the athletic ability of each pupil by testing their strength and speed in various physical education activities. A comparison of the fifty pupils with highest athletic ability and the fifty pupils with lowest athletic ability indicated significantly higher sociometric status scores for the group with greater athletic ability.

Both social and physical skills appear to be related to the number of choices received on a sociometric test. These and other studies (*18, 28*) have also indicated that frequency of participation in sports and extracurricular activities is related to greater acceptance by peers. As with school achievement, these findings indicate the prestige value generally associated with social skills, athletic ability, and participation in various school activities. The frequent suggestion that isolated pupils can be helped with their social relations through the development of skills and by more active participation in sports and social activities is supported by this research. A caution should be noted here, however. Although the possession of skills and active participation in activities attracts favorable attention from peers, there is no assurance that the individual will be accepted as a companion for close interpersonal relationships. The value a particular group places on the activity in which the skill is demonstrated, as well as the extent to which the individual possesses those personality characteristics that count most in interpersonal contacts, will also influence the degree to which he is accepted.

PHYSICAL APPEARANCE AND SOCIOMETRIC RESULTS

Although physical attractiveness is frequently overemphasized as a factor influencing an individual's acceptance by others, there is considerable evidence to indicate that it is significantly related to sociometric status. Studies among school children at various grade levels (*1, 8, 41, 66*) have consistently indicated that pupils who are highly chosen on a sociometric test are characterized as being "good looking," "neat in appearance," and "physically attractive." Those pupils who are rejected most frequently by their peers are characterized as being physically unattractive and unkempt in appearance (*33*). There appears to be a closer relationship between physical appearance and sociometric status at the junior and senior high school levels, and the relationship tends to be more pronounced in the case of girls. However, physical appearance shows some relationship to sociometric status at all age levels and among both sexes.

The prestige value associated with physical attractiveness is probably a reflection of the emphasis our society places on physical beauty and personal neatness. Commercial advertising places so much stress on appearance that individuals are frequently led to believe that physical attractiveness is a sufficient condition for acceptance by others. Although it may contribute to desirable "first impressions," it is by no means a sufficient condition for peer acceptance. It should also be recognized, of course, that being accepted by others tends to motivate individuals to improve their appearance. This could partly account for the relationship between sociometric status and appearance. Thus, although physical attractiveness has considerable prestige value in peer relations, its importance in developing close interpersonal relations can be easily overemphasized.

INTERESTS, VALUES, AND SOCIOMETRIC RESULTS

The interests and values of individuals seem to play a significant role in sociometric choosing. Studies have shown that highly accepted boys and girls have different interests than do boys and girls who are least accepted on a sociometric test. In addition, research in this area reflects a general tendency for individuals to choose associates who have interests and values similar to their own.

Marks (*47*) compared the interests of highly accepted and least accepted boys and girls at the high school level. Interest was based on an interest record, and social acceptance was based on friendship choices. There were sixty-eight boys and eighty-three girls in each social acceptability group. Those in the highly accepted group received three or more choices as friend, and those in the least accepted group received one choice or none. The highly accepted pupils showed more social and heterosexual interests than those least accepted as friends. Highly accepted girls had fewer intellectual-cultural interests than the least accepted girls, and highly accepted boys had fewer mechanical-constructive interests than the least accepted boys. It was suggested by the author that the intellectual interests of isolated girls and the mechanical interests of isolated boys may act both as a cause of their isolation and as a compensation for it.

The greater interest in intellectual and mechanical activities by isolated pupils appears logical in that these interests can be pursued in isolation. However, there is a danger in overgeneralizing from such data, since the interests of the group members making the sociometric choices must also be considered. In a classroom of gifted pupils, intellectual interests might contribute to group acceptance rather than to isolation. Likewise, in a course in physics, mechanical interests might have considerable prestige value. Thus, although there may be a general tendency for intellectual and mechanical interests to be associated with lower social acceptance, caution is necessary in applying such generalizations to specific groups.

The tendency for high school students to choose associates with similar interests has been noted by Bonney (*13*). He compared the interest scores, obtained with the Kuder Preference Record, of mutual friends and reported a significant relation between their interests. Since he also found that pupils who chose each other were similar in intelligence, socioeconomic background, and personality, it is difficult to identify the specific role interests played in the choice process. Nevertheless, his results indicated that mutual friends tended to have common interests.

A rather extensive study by Precker (*57*) revealed that there is also a tendency for students to choose associates whose values are similar to their own. He asked 242 college students and forty-two faculty members to rank thirty-nine value statements in the order of their importance. Each student was also requested to indicate the three students he would most like to keep in touch with after college and the faculty members he would most prefer as faculty adviser. An analysis of the results indicated that the students tended to choose fellow-students and faculty members whose values were similar to their own. Values among students were most similar where students had chosen each other.

As with other factors related to the choice process, it is difficult to determine whether individuals consciously choose associates with similar interests and values. However, extensive studies at both the elementary school level (*1*) and the secondary school level (*18*) have reported that an analysis of pupils' reasons for their sociometric preferences includes a relatively large number of statements pertaining to similarity of interests and values. "We like to do the same things," "we have the same interests," "we have similar beliefs," "we have common ideals," and similar statements, frequently appear in pupils' lists of reasons for choosing certain companions. Thus, similarity of interests and values seems to be of considerable importance to pupils in their choice of associates. The extent to which their chosen associates actually are similar in these characteristics, of course, depends largely on the accuracy with which they are able to perceive the interests and values of others.

PERSONALITY CHARACTERISTICS AND SOCIOMETRIC RESULTS

The personality characteristics related to sociometric status were reviewed in the last chapter. However, some mention of them should be made here, since they are probably the most important personal factors influencing sociometric choices. In fact, when pupils at both the elementary and the secondary school levels are asked to give reasons for their sociometric choices, the majority of their reasons refer to the personality characteristics of the individuals chosen. Characteristics such as kindness, coöperativeness, generosity, loyalty, agreeableness, sincerity, helpfulness, considerateness, and friendliness are frequently mentioned (*1, 18, 37, 61*). The great stress individuals place on such characteristics seems to indicate that they tend to choose associates who most adequately satisfy their own psychological and social needs. Within this frame of reference, the pupil who is most highly chosen on a sociometric test is the one who is perceived by the largest number of persons as possessing need-satisfying personality characteristics.

Evidence for the theory that personality characteristics which imply greatest need-satisfaction to others influence sociometric choices may be derived from a variety of sources. Studies of adolescent friendships have indicated that pupils with high sociometric status are more sensitive to the feelings of others (*44*) and exhibit behavior which satisfies the needs of others (*59*). In a study of junior high school girls' ratings of each other (*53*), it was reported that the girls rated their chosen associates higher than themselves on ten personality characteristics related to need-satisfying behavior. In addition, they rated the girls whom they did not choose on the sociometric test lower than themselves on the same personality characteristics. This obvious distortion of the perception of their friends' characteristics indicates that they perceive their chosen associates in terms of their own psychological needs. Although such findings cast doubt on the validity of students' stated reasons for their sociometric choices, they do indicate the importance of personal need-satisfaction to the chooser.

There is also some evidence that individuals choose companions who are similar to themselves in personality characteristics. Bonney (*8, 13*) reported that mutual friends tended to be similar in personality traits. Greenblatt (*32*) also noted that friends tended to be similar in mental health status. However, the actual similarity between friends is probably not as significant in sociometric choice as the extent to which individuals perceive their friends as being similar. Studies by Davitz (*26*) and Fiedler, Blaisdell, and Warrington (*29*) have shown that individuals tend to perceive their preferred associates as being more similar to themselves than they actually are. Here again, this distortion of similarity probably indicates the choosers' desire to satisfy his own needs. If he perceives his friends as being similar to himself, he will feel a greater opportunity to satisfy his own needs in association with them and he will tend to feel more secure in his interpersonal relations.

EVALUTION OF PERSONAL FACTORS IN SOCIOMETRIC CHOICE

It is difficult to determine the specific influence that any single personal factor has on sociometric results. All personal factors show some relation to sociometric status. However, no single trait or characteristic can account for the high degree of acceptance some pupils have among their peers. Some personal factors such as intelligence, achievement, physical maturity, social skill, physical ability, physical attractiveness, and socially aggressive personality characteristics have general prestige value among children and adolescents. Because of their prestige value, the possession of such factors tends to attract favorable attention from peers. The extent to which such factors contribute to an individual's peer acceptance in a specific group, however, depends on a number of other conditions.

NATURE OF THE GROUP. The value a group places on certain personal characteristics seems to be an important determiner of status within the group. Although some personal characteristics have general prestige value, as indicated above, the amount of prestige associated with any specific characteristic varies with the composition of the group. The value placed on intelligence or school achievement, for example, would be quite different in a class of gifted pupils, in a social club and in a street-corner gang. One would expect the value attached to any single personal characteristic to vary with the purpose of the group, the age of the group members, and the nature of the interpersonal relationships within the group.

A closely related factor is the extent to which the group members possess the personal characteristics being considered. Since group members tend to choose associates who are similar to themselves, the individual whose personal characteristics are most similar to those of the other group members would be in the most favorable position for receiving sociometric choices. The highly chosen individual tends to be slightly higher on the personal characteristics valued by the group, but too great a deviation from that of the group members results in lower sociometric status.

PATTERN OF PERSONAL CHARACTERISTICS. Although lack of acceptance among peers may be due to the absence of a single highly valued personal characteristic, high status among peers depends on the entire pattern of personal characteristics possessed by an individual. Thus, lack of social skill may result in low sociometric status among peers, but a high degree of social skill will not lead to high acceptance among peers unless other personal characteristics are present. The importance of the total pattern of personal characteristics for achieving high peer acceptance makes it exceedingly difficult to evaluate the influence of any specific factor. However, an analysis of the choice process seems to suggest the operation of two types of personal characteristics in sociometric choosing.

Prestige factors such as intelligence, achievement, skill, and physical attractiveness seem to attract the attention of peers and thus place the individual in a favorable position to be chosen on a sociometric test. The extent to which these prestige factors contribute to peer acceptance depends, in part, on the extent to which they are accompanied by need-satisfying behaviors, which seem to be most important in close interpersonal relationships. Personal factors such as kindness, helpfulness, considerateness, and friendliness are frequently stated reasons for choosing associates. They suggest that the chooser tends to choose as companions those individuals with whom he feels comfortable and secure. In short, he tends to choose those who most satisfactorily meet his own psychological needs.

Thus, individuals highly chosen on a sociometric test seem to have a pattern of personal characteristics which include both prestige factors and need-satisfying behaviors. Prestige factors contribute to respect among peers, but behavior which contributes to harmonious interpersonal relationships is also necessary if this respect is to result in acceptance by peers.

SOCIAL FACTORS

Although the personal attributes an individual possesses are probably the main determiners of the degree to which he is accepted by his peers, social factors also have some influence on sociometric choices. Socioeconomic status, family background, residential proximity in the community, and various social cleavages have all shown some relationship to sociometric results. These factors seem to limit and modify the sociometric choices of children in accordance with the social pattern of the community. Thus, when the sociometric status and structure of children's groups are being analyzed, the possible influence of social factors must also be considered.

SOCIOECONOMIC STATUS AND SOCIOMETRIC RESULTS

The socioeconomic status a family holds in a community, as determined by occupation, income, type of house, and other objective and subjective criteria has been shown to influence sociometric results. In general, there appears to be a tendency for children to choose associates with a similar socioeconomic background or one slightly higher than their own. In accordance with this choice pattern, children from homes with a high socioeconomic position tend to attain higher sociometric status among their peers than children from homes with a low socioeconomic position. This relationship between socioeconomic status and sociometric results is not consistently found in all sociometric studies, but appears to be the dominant trend reported.

CHOICE PATTERN. In a small New England community, Stendler (*63*) studied the sociometric choice pattern of elementary school children from various socioeconomic class levels and noted a general tendency for pupils to choose companions from their own socioeconomic level. A finding of special significance in this study was the fact that the nature of the sociometric criterion influenced the degree to which socioeconomic class affected the choice pattern. When the children were asked to choose classroom seating companions, their choices were generally distributed among the class members, with only a very slight tendency to choose those of the same socioeconomic class. However, when the same children were asked to choose companions for out-of-school activities, the majority of their choices were confined to members of their own socioeconomic class. Apparently children's choices of out-of-school associates are influenced to a greater extent by the expectations and restrictions of "class-conscious" parents. This finding emphasizes the importance of selecting the proper sociometric criterion where there is a desire to minimize the influence of socioeconomic status on the sociometric results.

Sociometric studies by Bonney (*13*), Smith (*62*), and Lundberg and Beazley (*46*) have consistently shown that students at the elementary, secondary, and college levels tend to choose associates who have a socioeconomic status similar to their own. An analysis of friendship patterns among an entire high school population, by Hollingshead (*36*), revealed similar results. He reported that both friendship choices and observations of friendship patterns indicated that adolescent cliques tended to follow socioeconomic class lines.

Similar findings were reported by Neugarten (*52*) and Cook (*21*), although they noted a greater tendency for students to choose associates from a higher socioeconomic level than that of their own. Neugarten studied the choice patterns of students in grades five, six, ten, and eleven. She reported that sociometric choices tended to be directed toward students whose socioeconomic class level was the same or higher than that of the chooser. The tendency to choose companions of a higher socioeconomic status seemed to be more pronounced in grades five and six than in grades ten and eleven. Cook, in a study of tenth-grade students, also noted that the trend in sociometric choosing was upward, with regard to socioeconomic class level. The most frequent exceptions to this trend occurred in boy-girl choices.

It is difficult to determine the extent to which various factors cause children to choose companions with similar or higher socioeconomic status than their own. It could be argued that children from homes with a higher socioeconomic position tend to be more intelligent, to be more socially skillful, to be better groomed, and to possess other personal characteristics which contribute to their desirability as companions. On the other hand, the subtle influences of the community class structure, the middle class values emphasized in the school, and the pressure of parents "to associate with the right children," probably all have their effect on children's sociometric choices.

CHOICE STATUS. Studies by Brown (*18*), Stendler (*63*), Cook (*21*), Neugarten (*52*), and Grossman and Wrighter (*35*) have shown a consistent tendency for children from homes with a higher socioeconomic position to have higher sociometric choice status. Where rejection choices were included (*52, 63*), it was also reported that children from homes with the lowest socioeconomic position tended to be rejected most frequently on the sociometric test. Although studies by Bonney (*9*) supported these general findings, he noted numerous exceptions when individual cases were analyzed. Some children from homes of relatively low socioeconomic status were highly chosen on the sociometric test, because they possessed physical skills, pleasing personal traits, or other social assets. Thus, the group trend reported in most studies can be easily overemphasized when considering individual cases.

A number of sociometric studies do not support the above results. Davis (*25*), Dahlke (*23*), and Young and Cooper (*66*) reported no relationship between children's sociometric status and the socioeconomic level of their parents. Brown and Bond (*19*) reported no relationship for boys, but a high degree of relationship for girls (correlation of .82). Although this would seem to suggest that girls are more influenced by socioeconomic status when choosing associates, other studies indicate that this is not the case. Stendler (*63*), for example, has shown that boys and girls tend to make similar choices with regard to the socioeconomic level of the children chosen.

The somewhat contradictory results concerning the relationship between sociometric status and socioeconomic level can probably be partly accounted for by the varying degree of social stratification found in the different communities. In communities where the socioeconomic class lines are more sharply drawn and where the residents are more "class conscious," one would expect socioeconomic status to be reflected to a greater degree in children's sociometric choices. In communities with a less firmly established social structure and where there is less awareness of socioeconomic class differences, a child's sociometric status would be likely to be more influenced by his own personal and social assets and less by his family's socioeconomic position in the community.

FAMILY FACTORS AND SOCIOMETRIC RESULTS

Since the family plays a significant role in the personality development of a child, one might expect certain aspects of family background to be related to sociometric results. Various investigators have considered this problem. In general, little or no relationship has been reported between sociometric status and objective factors such as size of family, position in family, and whether the child came from a broken home. The important factors seem to be the sociability of the parents and the type of parent-child relationship that exists in the home.

FAMILY SIZE. Bonney (*9, 14*) studied the relationship between family size and sociometric results at both the elementary school level and the college level and reported a tendency for highly chosen pupils to come from smaller family units. In harmony with these findings he noted that "only children" tended to have higher sociometric status than children with siblings. Although Damrin (*24*) also reported a slight tendency for high school girls from smaller families to have higher sociometric status, a number of other studies have indicated no relationship between family size and sociometric results.

Young and Cooper (*66*) compared pupils with high and low sociometric status, from grades five through eight, and found no differences in the number of siblings they had. They also reported no difference in the number of "only children" in each status group. Similar results were reported by Thorpe (*65*) and Brown

(*18*) at the high school level, and Loomis, Baker, and Proctor (*45*) at the college level.

The inconsistent findings reported in these studies are probably due to factors which counteract each other. It would be expected that an individual with a larger number of siblings would be better able to establish peer relations, as a result of the experience gained from interaction with his brothers and sisters. However, since larger family units tend to be in the lower socioeconomic classes, their socioeconomic position would tend to depress the sociometric status scores. Thus, the influence of increased socialization in the larger family unit is counteracted by the influence of lower socioeconomic status. The slight tendency for pupils from smaller family units to have higher sociometric status, reported by Bonney and Damrin, probably reflects the influence of socioeconomic factors rather than the psychological benefits of having few siblings or of being an "only child."

POSITION IN FAMILY. The relationship between the position a child holds in his family and his sociometric status has been of interest to several investigators. Thorpe (*65*) related these two factors in thirty-four school classes and reported a slight tendency for the younger members of families to have higher sociometric status. However, the correlation coefficients were consistently low in all classes, and the opposite relationship occurred in nine of the thirty-four classes. A similar study among high school girls by Damrin (*24*) showed no relationship between position in family and sociometric status. Damrin also reported that the age and sex of the siblings were not related to sociometric status. In an extensive study by Brown (*18*), 200 high school pupils with high sociometric status were compared with 200 high school pupils with low sociometric status and no difference was found with regard to position in the family. Although girls with brothers but no sisters were reported to have higher acceptance among peers, no other factors regarding role in the family were found to be significant.

These studies are difficult to evaluate since socioeconomic class differences, parent-child relationships, personality characteristics, and numerous other factors have not been controlled. However, the findings seem to indicate that position in the family is of little significance in the attainment of effective peer relations as measured by the sociometric test.

BROKEN HOMES. It is generally accepted that broken homes have an adverse effect on the personality development, and consequently on the social adjustment, of children. Thus, investigators have logically expected that children from broken homes would have less effective relations with their peers. Fairly extensive studies at the elementary school level (*66*) and the high school level (*18*), however, have shown that pupils from broken homes achieve high sociometric status as frequently as other pupils. As with the influence of the position in the family, lack of controls in these studies may have influenced the results. Since divorces are more common at the higher socioeconomic class levels, this factor may have inflated the sociometric status scores of the group of pupils from broken homes. Nevertheless, these studies indicate the caution necessary in generalizing about the adverse effects of broken homes on a child's peer relationships.

FAMILY MOBILITY. There are at least two possible influences of family mobility on children's peer relationships. Frequent changing of schools, resulting from family mobility, may broaden a child's interpersonal contacts and thereby improve his ability to interact with different types of age mates. On the other hand, too frequent moving on the part of the family may also result in feelings of insecurity on the part of the child which interfere with his peer relations. Studies in this area are inconsistent, but they suggest that those pupils who change schools most frequently tend to have lower social acceptance among their classmates.

Matlin (*48*) analyzed the sociometric status scores of 199 fifth- and sixth-grade children and reported that the most permanent pupils had the highest sociometric status. Pupils who remained in the school for a short period of time tended to have both lower sociometric status and less adequate social adjustment as measured by a personality questionnaire. Young and Cooper (*66*), investigating the same problem, reported no relationship between sociometric status and the number of different schools attended. It should be noted, however, that Young and Cooper eliminated from their study those pupils who were new in class. This undoubtedly removed some of the more transient pupils. Of course, leaving them in the study, as Matlin apparently did, poses new problems, since new pupils in class tend to have lower sociometric status due to their lack of acquaintance among classmates.

Another factor that contaminates the relationship between family mobility and children's sociometric status is that of socioeconomic status. Since families from lower socioeconomic classes tend to move more frequently, transient children might be expected to have lower sociometric status scores. This lower social acceptance among peers could be a reflection of their families' lower social position rather than the psychologically harmful effects of frequent moving. There is some evidence that pupils tend to retain their level of peer acceptance when they transfer from one school to another (*42*).

FAMILY EXPERIENCES. Probably the most significant family factors, as far as the peer relations of children are concerned, are the types of family experiences provided in the home. Studies have shown that the parents of pupils with high sociometric status tend to be interested in sports and social activities (*28*), to participate in social activities more frequently (*18*), and to not show favoritism among their children (*28*). There is also some evidence that pupils who are rejected by their parents tend to be rejected by their peers (*2*).

The relationship between the sociability of the parents and the sociometric status of their children could be partly influenced by the socioeconomic status of the family. However, Feinberg (*28*) reported that the greater interest in sports and social activities on the part of the parents of highly accepted pupils occurred at all socioeconomic levels. Thus, the parents' interest in social activities may be a reflection of a personality pattern and a social aggressiveness which influences the social development of their children. Parents who are more active socially (provided they include their children) may also provide more opportunity for their children to obtain experience in interpersonal relations with others.

The fact that the parents of highly accepted pupils do not show favoritism toward any of their children and that parental rejection tends to result in peer rejection suggests the significance of the parent-child relationship for developing children's ability to establish satisfying relationships with their peers. This is neither new nor surprising, since numerous studies (*64*) have shown the influence of the parent-child relationship on the social development of children. However, it is surprising that so many sociometric studies neglected this important area and were concerned with family size, position in family, and other objective, but relatively unimportant, factors. Future research in this area should throw light on the extent to which various types of parent-child relationships influence children's sociometric choice patterns.

RESIDENTIAL PROXIMITY AND SOCIOMETRIC RESULTS

Children would be expected to develop friendships more frequently with those children living near them than with children living a greater distance away. Both the influence of socioeconomic status on friendship patterns and the greater availability of contacts would favor the development of friendships among children living in close proximity. The extent to which this residential proximity in the community is related to sociometric choices in the classroom has been studied by a number of investigators. In general, residential proximity has been shown to have some influence on sociometric results, especially among elementary school children.

Segoe (*60*) compared the distance between the homes of mutual friends and the homes of unselected pupils among 823 children in grades three through eight. The average distance between the homes of mutual friends was .26 mile while the average distance between the homes of unselected pupils was .96 mile. In a more recent study, Gallagher (*30*) related residential proximity and the friendship choices of 355 children in grades two through five. He compared the average geographical distance between each child and his chosen friends with the average distance between each child and all of his classmates. Approximately 77 percent of the children chose friends who lived nearer to them than the average geographical distance between them and their other classmates. No indication was given, however, concerning the actual distance between the homes of friends and nonfriends.

It should be noted that in both of the above studies the children were asked to name their actual friends rather than their desired associates. It would seem that such "near-sociometric" procedures would result in a closer relationship between residential proximity and friendship choices than might occur where desired associates were being chosen. A child's actual friends are limited by parental restrictions regarding both the socioeconomic status of companions and the distance a child can go from home in search of playmates.

Where investigators have asked children to indicate their desired associates for classroom activities, the influence of residential proximity on the sociometric choices has been less marked. Potashin (*56*) administered a sociometric test to children in grades five, six and seven, and compared the percentage of mutual friends and nonfriends living in the same section of the community. Approximately 62 percent of the mutual friends lived near each other in the community. However, 52 percent of the nonfriends also lived close to each other. Although these findings indicate that more mutual friends lived near each other, the difference is so small that residential proximity can be considered a minor factor in the sociometric choosing.

DeVault (*27*) also studied the influence of residential proximity on sociometric choosing, but his interest was limited to the distance between the homes of mutual friends. He administered six sociometric tests to 370 pupils in grades one through twelve, over a period of three months. For all pupils that chose each other, he tabulated the total number of choices exchanged between them. Since six sociometric tests were used, it was possible for each mutual pair to exchange a maximum of twelve choices. The minimum number of choices they could exchange, of course, was two, since they would have to choose each other at least once to form a mutual pair. A comparison of the frequency with which the mutual pairs chose each other and the distance between their homes revealed no relationship. In other words, mutual pairs who lived closer together did not choose each other more frequently on the sociometric test. This would seem to suggest that the degree of mutual attraction between children is not increased by closer residential proximity in the community, even though the possibility of a mutual relationship developing may be increased slightly.

In analyzing the actual geographical distance between mutual pairs on the sociometric test, DeVault noted a consistent tendency for the distance to increase as the grade level increased. At the early elementary school level, the average distance between the homes of mutual pairs was 1.2 miles. This distance increased to 1.6 miles at the later elementary school level to 2.2 miles at the junior high school level, and 2.4 miles at the high school level. This trend is consistent with the fact that older pupils have fewer parental restrictions and greater mobility in the community. It indicates that residential proximity has its greatest influence on the sociometric results of young children and that it may be relatively unimportant at the junior and senior high school level. This is indirectly supported by other research studies. Gronlund and Whitney (*34*) reported that junior high school pupils who were least accepted on a sociometric test had as many neighborhood play companions of junior high school age as those pupils who were most accepted on the test. Brown (*18*), in a study of 1600 high school students, noted that there was no relationship between the number of choices received on a sociometric test and the location of the students' residence in the community.

Thus, it appears that residential proximity has the greatest influence on friendship patterns at the elementary school level and that actual friendships are more influenced than are sociometric measures of desired associations. Residential proximity limits the range of children with whom an individual can associate. His actual friends, then, are determined only partly by his desire to associate with them. Environmental restrictions force him to develop friendships with those children who are most frequently available to him. When given the opportunity to choose desired associates for classroom activities, he has a wider range of choice and the influence of residential proximity diminishes.

SOCIAL CLEAVAGES AND SOCIOMETRIC RESULTS

Sociometric choice patterns reflect social cleavages existing in a community. As pointed out previously, children's choices tend to follow social class lines indicating a social cleavage between the various socioeconomic class levels. Other social cleavages along rural-urban, racial, and religious lines will also appear in sociometric results where such cleavages exist in a community. It should be noted that these cleavages are not inherent in the sociometric technique but that sociometric results merely reflect the existing attitudes in a particular situation.

Several studies were concerned with the sociometric choices of rural and urban students in consolidated high schools. Bonney (*12*) analyzed the sociometric choice patterns of students in three consolidated high schools and reported that urban students had higher sociometric status than rural students. In one of the schools, which had been consolidated for only a short time, a definite cleavage was noted between the students coming from four different communities. In a similar study. Blanchard (*7*) compared the sociometric scores of 109 urban students and 103 rural students attending the same high school. He noted a tendency for the rural and urban students to choose friends from their own group more frequently than from the other group. However, the cleavage was slight and the rural and urban students had similar sociometric scores. Becker and Loomis (*4*), studying the same problem, reported that their sociometric results revealed a good integration of rural and urban students in a consolidated high school. This was attributed to the fact that special efforts were made to integrate the students when the school was consolidated.

Similar results are reported for interracial school groups. Where racial cleavages exist in a community, these cleavages are reflected in children's sociometric choices. However, where racial integration has been in effect for some time, children's sociometric choices freely cross race lines. Older studies, by Moreno (*50*) and Criswell (*22*), have shown distinct cleavages between white and Negro children, with the members of both groups most frequently choosing companions from among their own racial group. Both studies were conducted in a large metropolitan area where segregation was common. More recent studies have shown that where racial integration has been in effect for a period of years, racial cleavages are not as apparent in sociometric results.

Raths and Schweikart (*58*) studied the social acceptance scores of fifty-eight fifth-grade pupils and sixty sixth-grade pupils. Approximately half of the pupils in each group were Negro and the remainder were white. The results indicated that both groups experienced the same degree of social acceptance among their classmates. Although the white pupils' acceptance of Negro pupils tended to be slightly higher than the Negro pupils' acceptance of white pupils, the members of both racial groups chose members of the other racial group to approximately the same extent that they chose members of their own racial group. Similar results were noted in sociometric testing by the author in eight fourth-grade classrooms. Approximately 27 percent of the pupils in each classroom were Negro and the remainder were white. Both racial groups reflected a slight tendency to choose members of their own racial group more frequently, but the sociometric results indicated that the pupils' choices freely crossed racial lines in both directions and that the Negro and white pupils were similar in the degree of social acceptance accorded them by their classmates.

A study by Bonney (*14*) has shown that social cleavages among religious groups may also appear in sociometric results. He analyzed the sociometric choices of seven groups of college students and noted that in six of the groups students chose members of their own religious group more frequently than could be expected by chance alone. The fact that such cleavages need not appear is indicated by the lack of religious in-group preferences in one of the groups. As with other sociometric cleavages, the extent to which religious group membership influences sociometric results is probably determined by the extent to which mutual feelings of acceptance occur between the various religious groups. The sociometric results merely reflect an existing condition.

These studies have several implications for sociometric testing. First, since existing social cleavages do appear in sociometric results, they must be considered when interpreting the sociometric status of an individual or the social structure of a group. Second, social cleavages between rural-urban, racial, and religious groups can be overcome where special efforts are directed toward social integration and the sociometric technique is a good instrument for measuring the effects of these efforts. Third, no individual or group should be reluctant to use sociometry merely because it does reveal social discrimination where social discrimination exists. This would be like refusing to be examined by a doctor because he might find cancer. When used properly, the sociometric technique can be used to diagnose the extent to which social discrimination does exist, can be used to arrange groups so that social cleavages are diminished, and can be used again later to determine the extent to which social integration is being achieved.

EVALUATION OF SOCIAL FACTORS IN SOCIOMETRIC CHOICE

The social structure of the community, the family experiences provided in the home, the residential proximity of children's homes in the community, and social cleavages between rural-urban, racial, and religious groups, all seem to have some influence on children's sociometric choices. The exact influence of any of these factors is difficult to evaluate because of the diverse populations studied, the lack of sufficient controls in most of the studies, the interrelatedness of the various factors, and the contradictory results reported by the various investigators. Despite these limitations, several generalizations appear warranted.

Sociometric results obtained in the classroom seem to reflect the attitudes and values of the members of the community. Where socioeconomic class lines are clearly drawn, where neighborhood groups are socially cohesive, and where cleavages exist between various social, ethnic, and religious groups, one can expect these social pressures to limit and modify children's sociometric choices. Thus, both the sociometric status of an individual pupil and his position in the classroom social structure will be affected by his family's social position in the community and their various group affiliations. However, where social class lines are not marked, and where social integration exists among the various social, ethnic, and religious groups, sociometric status and structure will be determined to a greater extent by the personal characteristics of the individual pupils. Variations in the social structure and the amount of social integration from one community to another may partly account for the contradictory results concerning the relationship between the various social factors and sociometric results.

Social factors in the community seem to have the greatest influence on sociometric results when children are asked to name their *actual* friends (near-sociometric test). Less influence seems to occur when they are given an opportunity to choose *desired* associates for some activity. If the choice of desired associates is for some classroom activity (i.e., seating, work, etc.) the influence of social factors is reduced to a minimum. Apparently the expectations of parents, the availability of contact in the neighborhood, and the general social pressures of the community place environmental limitations on the range of children with whom a child can develop actual friendships. Thus, when attempting to measure the underlying social structure of a group, it is necessary to ask children to indicate their preferred companions and to ask them to choose them on the basis of sociometric criteria least influenced by these extraneous environmental factors.

Since sociometric results do reflect the social structure of a community to some degree, any interpretation of sociometric results must take into account the possible influence of social factors. The interpretation of sociometric status or clique formations strictly in terms of the personal attributes of the group members would be grossly inaccurate where social factors are limiting and modifying the sociometric choice pattern.

SUMMARY

A number of personal and social factors have been shown to be related to sociometric results. An understanding of such factors should contribute to more accurate interpretations of sociometric data and should provide implications for the use of the sociometric technique in educational settings.

Personal factors such as intelligence, achievement, age, skill, physical appearance, interests, values, and personality characteristics have all shown some relationship to children's sociometric responses. In general, children who are highly chosen by their peers on a sociometric test tend to be more intelligent, to have higher scholastic achievement, to be younger in age, to have greater social and athletic skill, to participate more frequently in sports and social activities, to have a more pleasing physical appearance, to have more social and heterosexual interests, and to have more need-satisfying personality characteristics than children who receive few or no sociometric choices from their peers. Sociometric choice patterns also indicate that children tend to choose as associates those children whose ability, skill, and interests are similar to their own or are slightly higher. Too great a deviation from the other group members on any personal characteristic seems to contribute to lower sociometric status on the part of the deviant.

The numerous exceptions to the above trends and the complexity and interrelatedness of the factors which influence sociometric results should caution against attributing too much significance to any single personal characteristic. Although certain personal characteristics have general prestige value, an individual child's sociometric status and his position in the social structure of a particular group is influenced by the *total pattern* of personal characteristics he possesses as well as by the values held by the group members. Thus, the general trends reported in these studies provide valuable clues for the analysis and interpretation of sociometric data, but they do not replace the need for individual diagnosis in specific situations.

Various social factors have also shown some relationship to sociometric results. Children's sociometric responses seem to be limited and modified by the community social structure, the family experiences they have had, their residential proximity to other children, and social cleavages existing in the community. The inconsistent results in some of these areas suggest that the sociometric results reflect the social pattern in the community. Where socioeconomic class lines are firmly established, children tend to choose associates from their own socioeconomic class level or from one higher than their own. Where rural-urban, racial, or religious cleavages exist, children tend to choose associates from the group with which they are affiliated. However, where social integration is present in the community, socioeconomic status and social, ethnic, and religious group membership appear to have little influence on sociometric results. Both the family experiences of the child and the existing attitudes in the community probably determine the extent to which social discrimination appears in children's sociometric choices.

Residential proximity in the community has the greatest influence on children's *actual* friendships. When children are asked to choose their *desired* associates, the influence of residential proximity is minimized. As might be expected, this also holds true for socioeconomic class differences and other social factors.

The fact that children's sociometric results do reflect the social pattern existing in a community indicates that the possible influence of social factors must be considered when analyzing sociometric data. The sociometric status scores of individuals and the sociometric structure of a group can be interpreted most accurately when both the social and the personal factors operating in the choice process are identified. An understanding of these factors will also aid in the selection of procedures for improving individual status and group structure.

REFERENCES

1. Austin, M. C., and Thompson, G. G., "Children's Friendships: A Study of the Bases on Which Children Select and Reject Their Best Friends," *Journal of Educational Psychology,* 1948, *39:*101–116.
2. Ausubel, D. P., *Theory and Problems of Adolescent Development,* New York, Grune and Stratton, 1954.
3. Barbe, W. B., "Peer Relationships of Children of Different Intelligence Levels," *School and Society,* 1954, *80:*60–62.
4. Becker, M. G., and Loomis, C. P., "Measuring Rural-Urban and

Farm and Non-Farm Cleavages in a Rural Consolidated School," *Sociometry,* 1948, *11:*246–261.

5. Bedoian, V. H., "Social Acceptability and Social Rejection of the Underage, At-Age, and Overage Pupils in the Sixth Grade," *Journal of Educational Research,* 1954, *47:*513–520.
6. Biddulph, L. G., "Athletic Achievement and the Personal and Social Adjustment of High School Boys," *Research Quarterly,* 1954, *25:*1–7.
7. Blanchard, B. E., "A Social Acceptance Study of Transported and Non-Transported Pupils in a Rural Secondary School," *Journal of Experimental Education,* 1947, *15:*291–303.
8. Bonney, M. E., "Personality Traits of Socially Successful and Socially Unsuccessful Children," *Journal of Educational Psychology,* 1943, *34:*449–472.
9. Bonney, M. E., "Relationships Between Social Success, Family Size, Socio-Economic Home Background and Intelligence Among School Children in Grades III to V," *Sociometry,* 1944, *7:*26–39.
10. Bonney, M. E., "The Relative Stability of Social, Intellectual, and Academic Status in Grades II to V, and Inter-Relationships Between These Various Forms of Growth," *Journal of Educational Psychology,* 1943, *34:*88–102.
11. Bonney, M. E., "Social Behavior Differences Between Second Grade Children of High and Low Sociometric Status," *Journal of Educational Research,* 1955, *48:*481–495.
12. Bonney, M. E., "A Sociometric Study of the Peer Acceptance of Rural Students in Three Consolidated High Schools," *Educational Administration and Supervision,* 1951, *37:*234–240.
13. Bonney, M. E., "A Sociometric Study of the Relationship of Some Factors to Mutual Friendships on the Elementary, Secondary and College Levels," *Sociometry,* 1946, *9:*21–47.
14. Bonney, M. E., "A Study of Friendship Choices in College in Relation to Church Affiliation, In-Church Preferences, Family Size, and Length of Enrollment in College," *Journal of Social Psychology,* 1949, *29:*153–166.
15. Bonney, M. E., and Powell, J., "Differences in Social Behavior Between Sociometrically High and Sociometrically Low Children," *Journal of Educational Research,* 1953, *46:*481–495.

16. Breck, S. J., "A Sociometric Measurement of Status in Physical Education Classes," *Research Quarterly,* 1950, *21:*75–82.
17. Bretsch, H. S., "Social Skills and Activities of Socially Accepted and Unaccepted Adolescents," *Journal of Educational Psychology,* 1952, *43:*449–504.
18. Brown, D., "Factors Affecting Social Acceptance of High-School Students," *School Review,* 1954, *42:*151–155.
19. Brown, W. H., and Bond, L., "Social Stratification in a Sixth Grade Class," *Journal of Educational Research,* 1955, *48:*539–543.
20. Buswell, M. M., "The Relationship Between the Social Structure of the Classroom and the Academic Success of the Pupils," *Journal of Experimental Education,* 1953, *22:*37–52.
21. Cook, L. A., "An Experimental Sociographic Study of a Stratified Tenth Grade Class," *American Sociological Review,* 1945, *10:*250–261.
22. Criswell, J. H., "A Sociometric Study of Race Cleavage in the Classroom," *Archives of Psychology,* No. 235, 1939.
23. Dahlke, H. O., "Determinants of Sociometric Relations Among Children in the Elementary School," *Sociometry,* 1953, *16:*327–338.
24. Damrin, D. E., "Family Size and Sibling Age, Sex, and Position as Related to Certain Aspects of Adjustment," *Journal of Social Psychology,* 1949, *29:*93–102.
25. Davis, J. A., "Correlates of Sociometric Status Among Peers," *Journal of Educational Research,* 1957, *50:*561–569.
26. Davitz, J. R., "Social Perception and Sociometric Choice of Children," *Journal of Abnormal and Social Psychology,* 1955, *50:*173–176.
27. DeVault, M. V., "Classroom Sociometric Mutual Pairs and Residential Proximity," *Journal of Educational Research,* 1957, *50:*605–610.
28. Feinberg, M. R., "Relation of Background Experience to Social Acceptance," *Journal of Abnormal and Social Psychology,* 1953, *48:*206–214.
29. Fiedler, F. E., Blaisdell, F. J., and Warrington, W. G., "Unconscious Attitudes and the Dynamics of Sociometric Choice in

a Social Group," *Journal of Abnormal and Social Psychology,* 1952, *47:*790–796.

30. Gallagher, J. J., "Social Status of Children Related to Intelligence, Propinquity, and Social Perception," *Elementary School Journal,* 1958, *59:*225–231.
31. Gallagher, J. J., and Crowder, T., "The Adjustment of Gifted Children in the Regular Classroom," *Exceptional Children,* 1957, *23:*306–312, 317–319.
32. Greenblatt, E. L., "Relationship of Mental Health and Social Status," *Journal of Educational Research,* 1950, *44:*193–204.
33. Gronlund, N. E., and Anderson, L., "Personality Characteristics of Socially Accepted, Socially Neglected, and Socially Rejected Junior High School Pupils," *Educational Administration and Supervision,* 1957, *43:*329–338.
34. Gronlund, N. E., and Whitney, A. P., "Relation Between Pupils' Social Acceptability in the Classroom, in the School, and in the Neighborhood," *School Review,* 1956, *64:*267–271.
35. Grossman, B., and Wrighter, J., "The Relationship Between Selection-Rejection and Intelligence, Social Status, and Personality Amongst Sixth Grade Children," *Sociometry,* 1948, *11:*346–355.
36. Hollingshead, A. B., *Elmtown's Youth,* New York. John Wiley, 1949.
37. Hunt, J. McV., and Solomon, R. L., "The Stability and Some Correlates of Group-Status in a Summer-Camp Group of Young Boys," *American Journal of Psychology,* 1942, *55:*33–45.
38. Johnson, G. O., "A Study of the Social Position of Mentally-Handicapped Children in the Regular Grades," *American Journal of Mental Deficiency,* 1950, *55:*60–89.
39. Johnson, G. O., and Kirk, S. A., "Are Mentally-Handicapped Children Segregated in the Regular Grades?" *Journal of Exceptional Children,* 1950, *17:*65–68.
40. Keislar, E. R., "Distinction Between Social Acceptance and Prestige Among Adolescents," *Child Development,* 1953, *24:*275–283.
41. Kuhlen, R. G., and Lee, B. J., "Personality Characteristics and

Social Acceptability in Adolescence," *Journal of Educational Psychology,* 1943, *34:*321–340.

42. Laughlin, F., *The Peer Status of Sixth- and Seventh-Grade Children,* New York, Bureau of Publications, Teachers College, Columbia University, 1954.
43. Lindzey, G., and Urdan, J. A., "Personality and Social Choice," *Sociometry,* 1954, *17:*47–63.
44. Loban, W., "A Study of Social Sensitivity (Sympathy) Among Adolescents," *Journal of Educational Psychology,* 1953, *44:*102–112.
45. Loomis, C. P., Baker, W. B., and Proctor, C., "The Size of the Family as Related to Social Success of Children," *Sociometry,* 1949, *12:*313–320.
46. Lundberg, G. A., and Beazley, V., "Consciousness of Kind in a College Population," *Sociometry,* 1948, *11:*59–74.
47. Marks, J. B., "Interests, Leadership and Sociometric Status Among Adolescents," *Sociometry,* 1954, *17:*340–349.
48. Matlin, J. P., "The Social Acceptance and Adjustment of Fifth- and Sixth-Grade Children Analyzed on the Basis of Transiency in the School," *California Journal of Educational Research,* 1955, *6:*129.
49. McCrow, L. W., and Tolbert, J. W., "Sociometric Status and Athletic Ability of Junior High School Boys," *Research Quarterly,* 1953, *24:*72–80.
50. Moreno, J. L., *Who Shall Survive?* Washington, D.C., Nervous and Mental Disease Publishing Company, 1934.
51. Morrison, I. A., and Perry, I. F., "Acceptance of Overage Children by Their Classmates," *Elementary School Journal,* 1956, *57:*217–220.
52. Neugarten, B. L., "Social Class and Friendship Among School Children," *American Journal of Sociology,* 1946, *51:*305–313.
53. Northway, M. L., and Detweiler, J., "Children's Perception of Friends and Non-Friends," *Sociometry,* 1955, *18:*271–275.
54. Ohlsen, M. M., and Dennis, C. E., "Factors Associated with Education Students' Choices of Classmates," *Educational Administration and Supervision,* 1951, *37:*277–290.

55. Polansky, N., Lippitt, R., and Redl, F., "The Use of Near-Sociometric Data in Research on Group Treatment Processes," *Sociometry,* 1950, *13:*39–62.
56. Potashin, R., "A Sociometric Study of Children's Friendships," *Sociometry,* 1946, *9:*48–70.
57. Precker, J. A., "Similarity of Valuings as a Factor in Selection of Peers and Near-Authority Figures," *Journal of Abnormal and Social Psychology,* 1952, *47:*406–414.
58. Raths, L., and Schweikart, E. F., "Social Acceptance Within Inter-Racial School Groups," *Educational Research Bulletin,* 1946, *25:*85–90.
59. Reader, N., and English, H. B., "Personality Factors in Adolescent Friendships," *Journal of Consulting Psychology,* 1947, *11:*212–220.
60. Segoe, M., "Factors Influencing the Selection of Associates," *Journal of Educational Research,* 1939, *27:*32–40.
61. Smith, G., "Sociometric Study of Best-Liked and Least-Liked Children," *Elementary School Journal,* 1950, *51:*77–85.
62. Smith, M., "Some Factors in Friendship Selections of High School Students," *Sociometry,* 1944, *7:*303–310.
63. Stendler, C. B., *Children of Brasstown,* University of Illinois Bulletin, Urbana, Illinois, The Bureau of Research and Service, College of Education, 1949.
64. Thompson, G. G., *Child Psychology,* Boston, Houghton Mifflin Company, 1952.
65. Thorpe, J. G., "Factors in Friendship Formation," *Sociometry,* 1955, *18:*207–214.
66. Young, L. L., and Cooper, D. H., "Some Factors Associated with Popularity," *Journal of Educational Psychology,* 1944, *35:*513–535.

PART III

APPLYING SOCIOMETRIC RESULTS TO EDUCATIONAL PROBLEMS

CHAPTER 8

IMPROVING SOCIAL RELATIONS IN THE CLASSROOM

One of the most common uses of sociometric results in the classroom is that of aiding in the improvement of pupils' social relations. A study of pupils' sociometric choices aids the teacher in identifying undesirable cliques and cleavages, in locating pupils who are isolated or rejected by their peers, and in discovering other detrimental elements in the classroom social structure. When such data are supplemented by the other information a teacher has about the personal and social development of his pupils, a firm base is established for arranging socially integrative classroom groups and for planning classroom experiences which contribute to improved social relations.

IMPORTANCE OF SOCIAL RELATIONS IN THE CLASSROOM

Teachers have always been aware of the importance of pupils' social relations in maintaining a classroom free from interpersonal conflicts and tensions. However, social relations among pupils attain special significance from the fact that they influence the personal-social development of individuals, the effectiveness of group work, and the classroom learning of individual pupils.

SOCIAL RELATIONS AND PERSONAL-SOCIAL DEVELOPMENT

Psychologists generally agree that personality is a product of interpersonal relationships (*26*). For the preschool child this refers mainly to the types of relationships children have with their parents. However, from the time a child enters school until he reaches adulthood a large share of his interpersonal relationships are with his peers. Other things being equal, the types of relationships a child develops with his peers will determine to a large extent how he views the world about him and how he views himself. If he has secure and satisfying relationships with his age mates, he will tend to view the world as a warm and friendly place and will develop feelings of confidence in himself and others. He will tend to seek further social contacts with his peers, and he will find it easier to make heterosexual adjustments when adolescence is reached. The security arising from being accepted by others and the increased social experience obtained with age mates will enable him to develop the social skills and the social attitudes necessary for establishing and maintaining effective interpersonal relationships in adulthood.

In contrast, children who feel isolated or rejected among their peers are more likely to develop feelings of inadequacy and self-doubt. They are more apt to view the world as a cold and threatening place and to respond by withdrawing from social contact or by showing aggressive hostility toward others. The conflicts and emotional tension resulting from poor social relations retard the child's personal development and make it increasingly difficult for him to adjust to others. The lack of satisfying social relationships with age mates also restricts the social experiences of the child and hampers the development of social skills and social attitudes which are so important in the modern adult world.

Although the school does not have the sole responsibility for the personal-social development of children, it is in a strategic position to provide assistance. This is especially evident regarding the unique role of the school in providing experiences in social relations. For some children, such as those living on farms, the school is the only place where the child can obtain extensive experience in social interaction with age mates. Although other children may have greater opportunities for social contact in neighborhood groups, the majority of their waking hours is spent in school. Thus, the availability of social contact and the sheer amount of time children spend in school groups puts the school in a unique position for improving the ability of children to develop satisfying social relationships.

The diversified composition of school groups also provides an exceptional opportunity to provide new experiences in the area of social relations. Children of different races, religious beliefs, and socioeconomic levels are brought together in the school. Because of the social stratification in our society and the parental restrictions on out-of-school companions, social interaction with age mates of varying backgrounds is an experience that most children can obtain *only* in the school. Improving children's social relations in this area, to the point where they have an understanding, appreciation, and acceptance of individuals who differ from themselves, should make a unique contribution to their personal and social development.

SOCIAL RELATIONS AND GROUP EFFECTIVENESS

Since much of the learning that occurs in school takes place in groups, the improvement of group effectiveness is of major concern to the classroom teacher. The type of social relations existing among pupils influences group effectiveness in several ways. Poor social relations, characterized by cliques and cleavages in the social structure and by a disproportionate number of pupils who are isolated and rejected, generally results in a hostile emotional climate, in lowered group morale, and in poor communication among group members. This may appear in the classroom in the form of bickering among pupils, attention-getting behaviors, and open rebellion against classroom procedures, or it may appear in the form of passive, apathetic response to the classroom situation. Neither atmosphere is conducive to the learning of constructive group roles, to the achievement of group tasks, or to the learning of subject-matter content. Energy that should be directed into rewarding and satisfying learning experiences is dissipated by emotional conflicts.

In a classroom where the pupils have feelings of acceptance toward each other, where the social structure indicates a cohesive social group, and where feelings of isolation and rejection are reduced to a minimum, working and learning together become an enjoyable and productive experience. The security arising from mutual acceptance in an integrated group frees the group members from emotional conflicts and enables them to direct their energies toward the group task. They are more apt to take pride in the accomplishments of the group and to feel responsible for working toward the achievement of group goals. This increases the unity of group effort and provides individuals with experience in a variety of constructive group roles.

Generally, both the quantity and the quality of group discussion increase as the group moves toward a more cohesive group structure. The informal and relaxed atmosphere that accompanies group cohesiveness enables the pupils to express their ideas more freely. The security provided by such an atmosphere also enables the pupils to evaluate the ideas expressed by group members in terms of the value of the ideas rather than in terms of the prestige of the pupils stating them. Thus, group discussion tends to become more idea-centered as the pupils are freed from concern with personal acceptance and rejection by their classmates. This tends to result in greater group productivity and more effective group learning.

SOCIAL RELATIONS AND CLASSROOM LEARNING

It has already been pointed out that social relations among pupils influence the feelings and attitudes they develop toward themselves and others, the types of social experiences they have, and the effectiveness of group work in the classroom. All of these should have direct, or indirect, effects on the classroom learning of individual pupils. Although there is little evidence on this point, improved social relations would appear to have the following beneficial effects on individual learning:

1. The security that arises from satisfying social relationships frees the pupil of emotional tension and enables him to concentrate more on his assigned learning tasks.
2. The social pressure arising from the feeling of being accepted by classmates increases the pupil's motivation to learn. This is partly due to the pupil's desire to maintain status in the group and partly due to his feeling of loyalty and responsibility to the group members.
3. The increased social contact accompanying peer acceptance aids in clarifying and reinforcing the pupil's classroom learning experiences, by providing greater opportunity to exchange ideas with age mates.
4. The improved morale derived from satisfying social relationships in the classroom helps create in the pupil a favorable attitude toward the learning experience and toward the school in general.

The importance of peer acceptance to children and adolescents and the pressure of the peer group on individual pupils are frequently overlooked by teachers. These factors can be disruptive and disturbing influences in the classroom, or they can contribute to more effective learning experiences. The effect they have on the learning of individual pupils is determined largely by the extent to which teachers attempt to understand and improve the pupils' social relations.

GROUP APPROACHES TO IMPROVED SOCIAL RELATIONS

The development of a cohesive classroom social structure which provides satisfying social experiences for each pupil involves working with both classroom groups and individual pupils. Methods of assisting individual pupils to improve their social relationships will be considered in the next chapter. Here, the discussion will be confined to group approaches for improving pupils' social relations in the classroom.

Although sociometric results provide the basic data for diagnosing and improving pupils' social relations, an effective classroom program in this area is not limited to sociometric procedures. The grouping procedures used in the classroom, the classroom environment provided by the teacher, and the classroom activities themselves can all be used as constructive forces for the improvement of pupils' social relations. The essential steps a teacher should take in these areas are briefly described in the following paragraphs. These will be elaborated upon in the remainder of this chapter.

1. Provide a social arrangement in the classroom which permits pupils to be near others with whom they feel most comfortable in social interaction. The security resulting from such an arrangement (sociometric grouping) enables pupils to participate more freely and effectively in the group. The increased social experience improves social skills and develops self-confidence, which enables pupils to expand their network of social relationships.
2. Provide for social interaction among pupils of various subgroups (e.g., boy-girl, rural-urban, racial, religious, and socioeconomic). Both in the arrangement of groups and in the performance of classroom activities, an attempt should be made to intermix the pupils from the various subgroups. This provides security for the minority group members; develops in the pupils an understanding and appreciation of individuals belonging to different subgroups; and reduces the social cleavages commonly found between subgroups.

3. Provide a classroom environment that is conducive to harmonious interpersonal relationships. This implies socially integrative behavior on the part of the teacher; a democratic atmosphere in the classroom; and the provision of frequent opportunities for pupil interaction. Such a classroom environment creates socially integrative attitudes on the part of the pupils and enables them to experience the benefits of coöperative group work.
4. Provide a variety of classroom activities that contribute to an understanding of social interaction and to the development of social relations skills. The advantage of using a variety of activities lies in the fact that the pupils can obtain *knowledge* about social interaction, they can discuss their *feelings* about social relations problems, and they can obtain *practice* in social relations skills. Experience in all three areas is necessary for the optimum social development of pupils.

SOCIOMETRIC GROUPING

After a sociometric test has been administered to a classroom group and the results have been analyzed, the first step toward improving social relations is that of putting the pupils' choices into effect. If the pupils were asked to choose seating companions, the classroom seating arrangement should be changed in accordance with their preferences. If the pupils were asked to select work companions, work groups should be organized along sociometric lines. This does not imply that the teacher should ignore all other known facts about the pupils, but rather that the pupils' preferences should be used as the guiding basis for arranging or rearranging the groups. Effective sociometric grouping is that which places each individual in the most favorable position for developing satisfying social relationships and which results in the most generally cohesive and integrated group structure. Thus, both the welfare of the individual and the welfare of the group must be considered. Within this general framework are a number of specific steps to be taken which will aid the teacher in using sociometric grouping.

FORMING SOCIOMETRIC GROUPS

For the purpose of illustration, let's assume that a teacher wants to organize work groups along sociometric lines. The pupils have been asked to name the five classmates with whom they would most prefer to work. With this number of choices allotted to each pupil, the teacher can usually expect to satisfy at least two of the choices made by each pupil. Using this as a minimum goal, the following procedures will aid in the organization of the groups:

1. Decide on the size of the groups. A work group of five is usually most effective for small group discussion. Although it may be necessary to vary the size of the groups for special purposes, care should be taken not to make the groups too large.
2. Start with the unchosen pupils (isolates) and place them with their highest choices. Give isolates their first two choices if possible, but do not place two isolates in the same group unless it is necessary. Never place more than two isolates in a group.
3. Next, consider those pupils who received only one choice (neglectees). If the choice a neglectee received was reciprocated by him, place the neglectee with the person with whom he has the mutual choice, regardless of the level of choice. Then attempt to satisfy his first choice, or the highest level of choice it is possible to satisfy without disrupting the groups that are already being formed.
4. Continue to work from the pupils receiving the smallest number of choices to the pupils receiving the largest number of choices. In each instance, attempt to satisfy the chooser's mutual choices first and his highest level of unreciprocated choices next.

Although this is the general procedure in forming sociometric work groups, a number of other factors should be considered as the groups are being formed. The following guiding principles illustrate some of the basic considerations in developing work groups which provide maximum security for the individual and the greatest potential for improving social relations:

1. If it is possible to satisfy more than two choices for each pupil, attempt to give isolates and neglectees more of their choices. If less than two choices can be satisfied for each pupil, give the highly chosen pupils only one of their choices. This is based on the assumption that highly chosen pupils are secure in their social relationships and that they can readily adjust to others, while the isolates and neglectees have a greater need to be with those with whom they feel secure.
2. Where cleavages (i.e., socioeconomic, sex, race, rural-urban, etc.) exist in the sociometric results, arrange the groups so that the cleavages will be diminished. For example, where rural and urban pupils tend to choose members of their own subgroups, the work groups should be arranged so that each group contains some rural and some urban pupils. However, there should always be *at least* two pupils from each subgroup in the resulting work groups. Placing two urban pupils in with a group of rural pupils, two boys in with a group of girls, and the like, provides additional security for the members of the subgroups. In attempting to reduce cleavages in this manner, keep in mind the pupils' choices and place pupils from different subgroups together where there is the best opportunity to satisfy the largest number of choices. You will probably find that this is also the best arrangement for bringing about an integration of the subgroups and thereby reducing the social cleavage.
3. If closely knit cliques appear in the social structure, it is usually necessary to estimate the possible influence of these cliques on the social relations of the class members. If a clique seems undesirable in terms of the social development of its members or in terms of its influence on the classroom group, it is best to attempt to broaden the social contacts of the members of the clique. This may be done by placing two, or more, of the members of the clique in different work groups. As with other subgroups, a member of a closely knit clique should have at least one other member of the clique in the same work group.
4. Where rejection choices were used, check to be sure that pupils who reject each other are not in the same group. If rejection

choices were not used, make your best guess concerning rejection and adjust the groups accordingly.

It will be noted that these suggestions for forming sociometric groups are based mainly on the sociometric results obtained from the pupils. They are designed to place isolated and rejected pupils in the most favorable position for developing satisfying social relationships; to reduce cleavages between subgroups; to broaden the social contacts of closely knit cliques; and in general to arrange work groups that will contribute to a more integrated and cohesive group structure. As pointed out previously, however, this does not imply that teachers should arrange groups solely on the basis of sociometric results. Teachers have numerous insights into the interests, abilities, and behavior of their pupils which should also be considered when forming sociometric work groups. If a pupil has special interests which indicate that one work group would be better than another, the teacher should arrange the work groups so that his special interests, as well as some of his sociometric choices, are satisfied. If a pupil has a specific skill or ability that is needed by some work group, this should likewise be considered. If two pupils continuously cause a disturbance when working together, it may be desirable to place them in separate work groups. All factors which have an influence on the improvement of social relations and on the effectiveness of the group activity should be taken into account.

When all of the factors have been considered and the final work groups are formed, it is usually necessary to check the choices of each pupil to be certain that all group members have some of their choices satisfied; that as many mutual choices as possible have been honored; and that members of subgroups are in the best position for integration into the social structure. The resulting work groups usually have one or two isolated or neglected pupils, one highly chosen pupil, and two or more pupils of average choice status. Some variation in the composition of the groups is expected, however, due to variations in the distribution of choices from one classroom group to another.

USES AND RESULTS OF SOCIOMETRIC GROUPING

Sociometric grouping has been used in a variety of ways in school settings. In addition to the formation of work groups, described above, teachers have used sociometric grouping to arrange seating in the classroom, to organize groups for laboratory work, to organize groups for field trips, to form classroom committees, to arrange seating in the school cafeteria, to organize play groups, and to organize groups for other curricular and extracurricular activities. Some high schools have assigned pupils to homerooms on the basis of sociometric choices. At the college level, sociometric choices have frequently served as a basis for selecting dormitory roommates.

Teachers usually report that they notice an immediate change in pupils' attitudes when the sociometric choices are put into effect. The isolated pupils tend to feel accepted, since they are placed with some of their choices. They have no way of knowing that they were unchosen. The members of minority groups tend to feel less tension, since they are placed with majority group members and the cleavage they feared did not appear in the sociometric grouping. These feelings tend to be reflected in improved morale and more active participation in classroom activities. Thus, the groundwork is laid for improving social relations.

Although teachers' reports are generally favorable concerning the results of sociometric grouping, to evaluate the influence of sociometric grouping on pupils' social relations is a difficult problem. Sociometric grouping is usually combined with other methods of improving social relations, and the influence of the grouping method can not be isolated. In addition, studies in this area are generally limited to a few classroom groups, and procedures are not carefully enough controlled to permit general conclusions.

Despite these difficulties and limitations, however, it seems worth while to review some illustrative studies in this area. The findings at least suggest the possible effects that might be expected from sociometric grouping.

Atkinson (*3*) used sociometric grouping to organize work groups for an elementary school social studies program. Over a two-year period she noted that the number of isolated children in the classroom was reduced when sociometric groups were organized and the children were permitted to demonstrate special skills to the class. Similar results were reported by Minnis (*24*), Shoobs (*28*) and Zeleny (*36*) for other elementary classrooms. In all cases, however, sociometric grouping was accompanied by special efforts on the part of the teacher to attract favorable attention to the isolated pupils. This was generally done by having the isolated pupil demonstrate some special skill before his classmates or by assigning him to some classroom responsibility where he would receive recognition from his peers.

A study by Kerstetter and Sargent (*17*) illustrates how sociometric grouping may have beneficial effects, if factors other than the pupils' choices are also considered. A sociometric test, based on the choice of seating companions, was administered periodically to a fifth-grade class. The results of the first test indicated a closely knit subgroup of five pupils. They were seated together in the classroom, without regard to other factors. In a retest a few months later, it was noted that the choices given by these pupils all went to the members of their own subgroup and that no choices were received from pupils outside of the subgroup. Since this subgroup was virtually a "social island" in the classroom and its members were involved in a number of delinquent-type escapades, it was decided to separate the members of the subgroup. Study groups were organized on the basis of pupils' choices and two members of the subgroup were placed in one study group and the three remaining members were placed in another study group. The delinquent-type behavior declined, and a sociometric test given a month later indicated that the members of the subgroup had become integrated into the general classroom structure.

Dineen and Garry (*10*) attempted to evaluate the effectiveness of sociometric grouping in reducing a cleavage between children from the upper and the lower social classes. They requested pupils in grades one through six to choose seating companions. In grades one, three, and five, seating was rearranged on the basis of the pupils' choices. A special effort was made to seat upper- and lower-class children near each other, wherever possible. In grades two, four, and six, no changes in seating were made. After a sixteen-week period the same sociometric test was again administered to all classes. The results indicated that in those classes where sociometric seating was used there was a greater reduction in the cleavage between upper- and lower-class pupils. These results are encouraging, since sixteen weeks is a relatively short time to expect changes in anything as pervasive as the social cleavage between children from different social classes.

Buck (*6*) experimented with sociometric grouping in an eighth-grade science program. Two classroom groups were equated on the basis of age, intelligence, and years in the school. One group was taught in the normal manner while the other group was organized on the basis of sociometric choices. Seating arrangements, work groups, and laboratory partners were all determined by sociometric preferences. A comparison of sociometric results at the end of one semester indicated that the distribution of sociometric status scores was similar in both groups. However, in the classroom where sociometric grouping was used there were sixteen mutual choices as compared with eleven mutual choices in the other group. This would suggest a more cohesive group structure where sociometric grouping was used. Although the difference in the number of mutual choices was not large, it should be noted that the study was limited to a three-month period.

Moreno and Jennings (*25*) also described a study where sociometric grouping was compared with arbitrary placement. They organized dining groups in a girls' training school on the basis of sociometric choices and retested the groups about six months later. The second test showed an increase in the number of mutual choices and a decrease in the number of isolated girls. A similar control group, whose members were arbitrarily assigned seats in the dining hall, showed a decrease in the number of mutual choices over the same period of time.

Although few details were given, Amundson (*1*) reported that assigning high school pupils to homerooms on the basis of sociometric choices improved their social relations. In the spring of their freshman year, all pupils were asked to indicate their preferences for homeroom classmates for the following year. During their sophomore year pupils were placed in the homeroom which satisfied the largest number of their sociometric choices. A sociometric test administered at the end of the sophomore year indicated a higher degree of social acceptance among the pupils than was present at the end of the previous year. To what extent the increased social acceptance of pupils was due to the homeroom activities and to what extent it was due to the sociometric grouping could not be determined from the data. However, organizing homerooms on the basis of sociometric choices may contribute to the effectiveness of other socializing experiences included in the homeroom program.

Two studies at the college level also reflect on the possible effects of sociometric grouping. Zeleny (*35*) compared three different methods of improving students' social acceptance in college classes. In one class the students worked on problems in arbitrarily assigned groups; in another class the work groups were arranged on the basis of sociometric choices; and in a third class he interviewed the students and gave them suggestions for improving their behavior. Changes in sociometric results over a four-week period indicated that students gained most in social acceptance where sociometric work groups were used. The next most effective procedure was that of individual interviews with the students. The least effective was that of working in arbitrarily assigned groups, although even this method improved the social acceptance of some students. Thrasher and Kerstetter (*32*) also described how sociometric grouping improved the social acceptance of students in a college class, but they did not compare the changes with classes not using sociometric grouping.

As pointed out previously, the findings of these studies are merely suggestive due to the limitations in research design and the limited number of groups used. However, it should be noted that the results are consistent in indicating the possible beneficial effects of sociometric grouping. This should encourage the classroom teacher to experiment with sociometric grouping in his own classroom.

INTRODUCING SOCIOMETRIC GROUPING

Teachers who have not previously used sociometric grouping would probably feel most comfortable in using it in the arrangement or rearrangement of classroom seating. This does not involve changes in the on-going activities in the classroom and therefore would not involve a change in teaching procedure. Sociometric seating arrangements may be made at the beginning of the school year or any time during the year. If it is done at the start of the school year, special efforts should be made to help the pupils become acquainted with each other. It would also be desirable to administer a second sociometric test approximately six weeks later and rearrange the seating in terms of changes in choice resulting from increased acquaintanceship among the pupils.

In using sociometric choices to organize work groups in the classroom, the teacher inexperienced with sociometric techniques may wish to start with groups that are temporary in nature or those that meet only occasionally. This procedure would seem to be especially important if the teacher is also inexperienced in small group work. Organizing groups for short-term classroom projects, arranging temporary discussion groups or classroom committees, or organizing discussion groups that meet only once a week would be sufficient to introduce the teacher to both sociometric grouping and to small group work. As the teacher becomes more experienced in organizing sociometric groups and in working with small groups, he will be able to determine the most effective use of sociometric grouping procedures in the classroom.

Introducing sociometric grouping on a school-wide basis at the junior and senior high school level would probably be most effective in assigning pupils to homerooms. The choice of classmates to be with in a homeroom would be a natural choosing situation for the pupils, and it would not require changes in the remainder of the school program. Organizing homerooms on the basis of pupils' sociometric preferences should contribute to the guidance function of the homeroom, should help counteract the undesirable social effects of ability grouping in the school, and should help to reduce social cleavages in the school. To achieve these purposes, of course, factors other than the pupils' choices must also be considered when the homerooms are organized. An arrangement which satisfies some of the choices of all pupils and still provides for maximum social integration is generally most desirable.

Other opportunities to initiate sociometric grouping procedures may be found in the school's extracurricular program, in group guidance courses, and in activity programs designed to improve the personal and social adjustment of pupils. Since sociometric grouping contributes directly to the purposes of these activities, it is easily and naturally introduced in these areas.

SOCIOMETRIC GROUPING IN PROPER PERSPECTIVE

As teachers obtain experience in using sociometric grouping, they will be better able to determine where sociometric grouping is most effective. It should be recognized, however, that sociometric grouping should not be used as the sole method of grouping in the classroom, or throughout the school. The needs of the pupils and the purposes of the school are more adequately met when a variety of grouping methods are used. Sociometric grouping is designed primarily to improve the social relations among pupils. For this purpose it is an excellent method of grouping and if used wisely will make a valuable contribution to the development of individual pupils and to the effectiveness of the school program. However, for other purposes, ability grouping or grouping in terms of pupils' special interests may be most effective. The "either-or" arguments concerning the best method of grouping pupils are usually meaningless. The skillful teacher will find uses for a variety of grouping methods. Within this setting, sociometric grouping will be recognized for its unique contribution to the improvement of pupils' social relations.

In addition to the need for a variety of grouping methods in the school, special benefits are derived from combining sociometric grouping with other grouping procedures. The emotional security and increased social interaction that pupils experience in sociometric groups will enable them to participate more effectively in other types of groups. In return, experience in ability and special-interest groups will provide for an extension in acquaintance and association that contributes to the pupils' network of interpersonal relationships. In this way, the various grouping methods complement each other in contributing to the social development of pupils (*12*).

CLASSROOM ENVIRONMENT

In discussing the role of sociometric grouping in the improvement of pupils' social relations, there is a danger in overemphasizing the importance of a single procedure. Although sociometric grouping is an excellent technique for improving social relations, its value will be limited unless the teacher creates the type of classroom environment that fosters the social development of pupils.

The classroom environment which is most conducive to the improvement of social relations among pupils is that in which a friendly, relaxed atmosphere exists. Although sociometric grouping can contribute to such an atmosphere, the attitude and the behavior of the teacher are also extremely important. If the teacher reflects warmth, understanding, and acceptance toward his pupils; if he permits pupils to participate in the planning of classroom experiences; and if he provides for interaction among pupils, the opportunity for improving pupils' social relations is greatly enhanced.

INFLUENCE OF TEACHER'S BEHAVIOR

How the behavior of the classroom teacher influences the pupils' behavior toward each other was demonstrated in a series of studies by Anderson and his associates (*2*). Using carefully controlled observation techniques, they compared the effects of teachers' dominative and integrative behavior on the classroom behavior of pupils. Dominative behavior was characterized by the use of force, commands, threats, shame, blame, and attacks against the personal status of individual pupils. In general, such behavior reflected attempts on the part of the teacher to make pupils behave in terms of his own standards and purposes without consideration of the experiences, desires, purposes, or judgments of the pupils. In contrast, socially integrative behavior was described as that which considered the experiences, desires, purposes, and judgments of pupils. Commands were replaced by requests, with sufficient explanation to make the requests meaningful, so that voluntary coöperation was made possible. Integrative behavior was also characterized by flexible and adaptive teacher behavior which encouraged the expression of individual differences among pupils.

The findings of these studies are comprehensive and detailed. However, the results indicate that teachers with dominative behavior tended to reduce social participation and to increase interpersonal conflicts among pupils. In contrast, the pupils who were with socially integrative teachers showed more spontaneity and initiative in their behavior and more voluntary, constructive social responses toward each other. The behavior of both types of teachers seemed to be contagious and to spread throughout the classroom, with the dominative teacher inciting domination and conflict in the pupils' social responses and the socially integrative teacher inducing socially integrative behavior among his pupils.

The findings of these studies highlight the importance of the teacher's attitude and behavior in setting the stage for improved social relations. The vicious circle of domination and interpersonal conflict must be broken, if the teacher is to encourage socially integrative responses among pupils. Teacher behavior which shows an understanding and appreciation of the feelings, attitudes, and values of pupils helps create a classroom environment which discourages domination and conflict and encourages constructive social interaction.

INFLUENCE OF TEACHER-PUPIL PLANNING

Both sociometric grouping and the socially integrative behavior of teachers, discussed above, are in harmony with the principles of teacher-pupil planning. Essentially teacher-pupil planning involves pupil participation in determining classroom policies and procedures that affect the pupils. Arranging classroom groups on the basis of sociometric choices is actually a form of teacher-pupil planning, since the pupils help decide how the groups should be arranged. One way to take into account the experiences, desires, purposes, and judgments of pupils, which characterize socially integrative behavior on the part of the teacher, is to have pupils participate in classroom decisions. A series of studies by Lewin, Lippitt, and White suggest that such participation on the part of pupils creates a social climate which is conducive to the development of improved social relations.

In a study typical of those in this area (*21*), four groups of ten-year-old boys were carefully observed under different types of group leadership. The primary aim was to determine the effects of "democratic," "authoritarian," and "laissez-faire" leadership upon individual and group behavior. The four groups of pupils were equated on patterns of interpersonal relationships, and intellectual, physical, and personality characteristics. The leaders and the type of leadership control were rotated for each group. Trained observers kept detailed records of the social interactions of the children, of changes in the group structure, of incidents reflecting the atmosphere of the group, and of all conversation during the group meetings.

Under democratic group control all policies were decided by group discussion, with the encouragement and assistance of the leader. Children participated in decisions concerning the procedures to be followed and were free to choose their companions for work. The leader worked closely with the group and attempted to remain objective in his praise and criticism. In essence, this method involved leader and group members planning and working together toward a common group goal.

The authoritarian leader determined all policies, dictated all techniques and activity steps one at a time, and indicated which children should work together on work tasks. He remained aloof from active participation in the group activities and tended to be personal in his blame and criticism of the work of each group member.

The laissez-faire leader gave the group members complete freedom to make decisions and to direct their own activities. He made materials available and supplied information only when requested. He made no attempt to appraise or direct the work of the group. In short, he let the group members plan and carry out their activities without adult guidance or direction.

A comparison of the three types of group control indicated that the democratic method, characterized by coöperative planning, resulted in higher group morale, more friendly remarks exchanged among group members, greater group cohesiveness, and more constructive group work. In the autocratic and laissez-faire groups, there were more expressions of discontent, more personal conflicts between individual group members, and in general less satisfactory social interaction and group effort. The members of both the autocratic and the laissez-faire groups seemed to be restricted in their efforts toward constructive social interaction. The autocratic group members were restricted by the dominative behavior of the leader while the laissez-faire group members were restricted by their own ineptness in planning and carrying out group activities.

Although this study was not conducted in a classroom setting, it indicates how teacher-pupil planning, based on democratic principles, can contribute to a desirable classroom environment. The social interaction of pupils under the guidance and direction of the teacher enables them to practice social skills in an atmosphere free from tension and conflict. Participation in planning classroom activities also enables pupils to experience the fruits of constructive social interaction in the form of classroom accomplishments. As group plans are carried out and group tasks are achieved, pupils become more aware of the advantages of coöperative interaction with peers.

This study also illustrates the undesirable effects of unguided group activity. All too frequently, teachers view teacher-pupil planning as letting the pupils do as they please. Pupils at all age levels want, and need, some guidance and direction. The amount of direction, of course, will depend on the purpose of the activity and the maturity of the pupils. However, lack of direction lowers group productivity and limits the opportunity pupils have to learn constructive group skills and to develop satisfying social relationships.

INFLUENCE OF OPPORTUNITIES FOR PUPIL INTERACTION

Closely related to the principles of teacher-pupil planning is that of providing numerous opportunities for pupil interaction. This is generally done through the use of small work groups and committees, discussed earlier. As pupils experience a larger number of social interactions with their classmates, they tend to express more feelings of acceptance and fewer feelings of rejection toward them. Thus, a multiplicity of contacts on the part of pupils seems to aid in creating a social climate that favors improved social relations.

Kinney (*18*) compared three fifth-grade classes using small flexible groups with two classes using fixed ability groups, and two classes which did not use groups. Sociometric results obtained four months apart indicated a reduction in the number of isolated pupils and in the number of lowly chosen pupils in the classes using small flexible groups. In the classes using ability grouping and in the classes which remained as an entire grade group, the number of isolated and lowly chosen pupils increased over the same period of time. A comparison of the pupils' achievement showed no differences for the various grouping procedures used. The improved status of isolates and lowly chosen pupils, where flexible grouping procedures were used, was attributed directly to the increased opportunities for pupil interaction.

Similar results were reported for the junior high school level, although the results were contaminated by other efforts to improve pupils' social relations. Spector (*29*) used small work groups of increasing size in an eighth-grade classroom. First he placed two pupils in each group. He then periodically increased the size of the groups by one until he finally had five pupils in each group. This had the effect of putting pupils in contact with a number of different classmates. In addition to the grouping procedures, however, special efforts were made to provide an informal classroom atmosphere; the pupils discussed factors related to social acceptability; and other attempts were made to improve the social climate of the classroom. At the end of a five-month period, social acceptability scores, based on the Ohio Social Acceptance Scale, had increased by 46 percent and the number of rejections had decreased. In short, pupils' attitudes toward each other moved from that of indifference and rejection toward that of acceptance.

Although Spector's study was limited to one group and the influence of the grouping procedure was not clear, essentially the same results were reported by Forlano (*11*). He studied changes in junior high school pupils' social acceptance scores over a one-semester period. Using an adaptation of the Ohio Social Acceptance Scale as an index of pupils' social acceptability, he compared core classes with regular classes and noted a significant *gain* in mean acceptance scores and a significant *reduction* in mean rejection scores in the core classes. In the regular classes the pupils showed a significant *reduction* in mean acceptance scores and a significant *gain* in mean rejection scores. Thus, the pupils' feelings of acceptance toward others increased in the core classes while their feelings of rejection toward others increased in the regular classes. A comparison of the procedures used in the two classes indicated that in the core classes a less formal classroom climate existed, more teacher-pupil planning was used, and the pupils spent more time in small work groups and in classroom committees. Although the effect of pupil interaction is again contaminated by other factors, this study indicates the combined influence of the classroom social climate, teacher-pupil planning and pupil-pupil interaction on the improvement of pupils' social relations.

It would be easy to attribute the increased social acceptance among pupils, resulting from the opportunity of interacting with a larger number of pupils, to the increased acquaintance volume of each pupil. However, studies by Hartley (*15*) and Gronlund (*13*) both indicate that there is little relationship between a pupil's social acceptance and the number of pupils that know him. It appears more likely that frequent opportunities for interaction break down stereotyped impressions of others based on casual acquaintanceship (*4*).

SPECIAL CLASSROOM TECHNIQUES

In addition to sociometric grouping and the development of a classroom environment which provides constructive experiences in social interaction, teachers have found some classroom techniques especially helpful in improving pupils' social relations. Although some of them may be most useful in a homeroom program or in a group guidance course, others have been used effectively in the regular classroom. These techniques are usually combined with other individual and group efforts to guide and direct the social learning of pupils.

SOCIAL ACCEPTANCE PROJECT

A technique which is especially useful in a homeroom program, or in a group guidance course, is that of studying and discussing the behavior characteristics that are related to social acceptance among peers (*23*). The project may be started by involving the pupils in a study of their own class. The following steps outline the procedure:

1. The class members are asked to indicate the behaviors which they like best in other people. These are listed on the blackboard as they are given, with some combining of suggestions to prevent the list from becoming too long.
2. When the list is complete, the behavior descriptions are placed in "guess who" form, using both positive and negative aspects of the behavior. For example, if one of the behavior descriptions is "people who are happy," the resulting items would be:

   "Here is someone who is *always* happy"

   "Here is someone who is *never* happy"

   The completed form should have a space for about six names under each positive and each negative behavior description.

3. This form can then be administered to the class, with directions to write the names of the classmates who best fit each description.
4. The results of the "guess who" form are then compared to sociometric results (obtained at the same time or previously) and a chart is worked out to show which behaviors are most characteristic of pupils with high sociometric status and which behaviors are most characteristic of pupils with low sociometric status. The pupils' names, of course, should not be included and the results should be presented in such a way that pupils cannot identify themselves.

When the results of such a study are presented to the pupils, they get a clear picture of which behavior characteristics contribute to peer acceptance in their group. Much interest is usually generated by this procedure, and pupils are anxious to compare their results with the results of other studies. For this purpose, studies by Bonney (*5*) and Tuddenham (*34*), at the elementary school level, and by Kuhlen and Lee (*20*) and Tryon (*33*), at the high school level, might be considered. These studies present the behavior characteristics related to peer acceptance at various grade levels for a relatively large number of pupils.

This type of project not only acquaints the pupils with the types of behavior that contribute to peer acceptance but it also helps them understand the feelings, attitudes, and values underlying peer relations. In the discussion of the results the teacher has an opportunity to help pupils recognize which peer values contribute to social growth and which are detrimental to it; to help them develop respect for differences in the values and behaviors of others; and to suggest ways that pupils can improve in their social relations. Thus, both broad social understandings and specific social learnings can result from the discussions.

STUDY OF BIOGRAPHIES

Another technique for helping pupils understand the behavior and values which underlie effective social relations is through the study and discussion of biographies of great people. McCleary (*22*) used this technique in a junior high school English class and noted an improvement in pupils' interpersonal relations. He had the pupils analyze biographical sketches of well-known persons in terms of the personality traits they possessed. Discussions were concerned with how these personality traits developed and how they influenced the person's success. Books on personality development were consulted, and pupils discussed how they could evaluate their own personality characteristics. Following this, pairs of pupils interviewed each other and wrote biographical sketches of each other. For this part of the procedure, pupils were paired with those pupils with whom they had worked least during the year. After the biographical sketches were written, each pupil was requested to write an autobiographical sketch. As a final step, the class was divided into small groups to study a full-length biography of a famous person and to discuss his personality characteristics.

It will be noted that the procedures used by McCleary enabled pupils to better understand the personality factors which contribute to success, to better understand their fellow-pupils, and to better understand themselves. From an academic standpoint, it also provided the pupils with an understanding of personality dynamics that was useful in analyzing biographies.

Sociometric results before the biographical unit was started indicated a social structure that was divided into three closely knit cliques, with five girls isolated from the other class members. At the end of the unit, three weeks later, sociometric results indicated that the five isolated girls had been absorbed into the group and that a more closely integrated group structure had developed. Observers' reports indicated a decrease in tension among the class members, an improvement in communication, and an increase in group harmony. Although these results are based on only one classroom group, the findings suggest the desirability of further explorations with this technique.

STORY DISCUSSIONS

A technique which has received considerable attention in recent years is that of reading and discussing stories which illustrate problems of human relations. Generally, stories are selected which reflect common problems experienced by the pupils or which broaden the pupils' understandings of feelings and attitudes which commonly underlie interpersonal relationships. Topics such as the role of loyalty in friendships, how leadership develops, tolerance toward minority groups, resolving conflicts in loyalty and values, overcoming shyness, cultural differences in behavior, different roles individuals play in social groups, causes of interpersonal conflicts, and methods of improving social acceptance illustrate the types of themes that might be found in the stories.

Through reading and discussion, it is expected that the pupils will identify with the characters in the story and develop a sensitivity to the feelings and attitudes of persons in different social situations. This identification is generally fostered by having the pupils relate the experiences of the characters in the story to personal experiences they have had. Besides improving the pupils' social sensitivity and broadening their understanding of factors which motivate and direct social behavior, this procedure helps them to internalize values which contribute to social effectiveness. The discussion of solutions to problems arising in social interaction also provides insights which assist them in resolving their own difficulties in social relations.

One of the important considerations in using this technique, of course, is that of selecting a story which illustrates the problem or theme which the pupils should discuss. Several guides have been developed for this purpose. Heaton and Lewis (*16*) present an analysis and arrangement of stories by problem areas and by level of maturity, ranging from primary grades to college. Kircher (*19*) has prepared a bibliography of books for children which illustrates experiences and problems in character formation. Both the content of the stories and the level of difficulty of the stories are given in the annotations. The Illinois Curriculum Program (9) recently issued a handbook entitled *Reading for Living,* which arranges stories by problem area. The problem areas include family and home relationships, personality development, physical and health handicaps, school and teacher relationships, social relationships, and related areas. The content and level of difficulty of each story is briefly described. All of these guides will aid the teacher in selecting the most appropriate story for a given situation.

Probably the most comprehensive program designed to use literature in improving pupils' personal adjustment and human relations skills is that originated by Bullis and O'Malley (8). They developed detailed lesson plans and teaching aids for a human relations class to be taught at various grade levels in the elementary and junior high school program. The prepared discussion material is based on stories which illustrate emotional problems pertinent to human relations. Experiences in the stories are related to the pupils' personal experiences during the discussion period, and attempts are made to help pupils better understand their own behavior. The materials and methods developed by Bullis have been extensively used in the Delaware Human Relations Class Program and in cities throughout the United States, as well as in some foreign countries (7). Although the materials are specifically designed for use in a human relations class, they provide helpful suggestions which can aid the classroom teacher in using the story discussion technique.

The discussion of literary materials shows great promise as a classroom technique for assisting pupils with their interpersonal problems. However, systematic evaluation of its influence on pupils' social relations has been limited. Descriptions of a study by Taba and Elkins (*30, 31*) present a comprehensive account of the use and evaluation of this technique in an eighth-grade English and social studies class. In general, their results indicate that story discussions have a positive influence on pupils' social relations.

More specific results from their study will be discussed in a following section which describes their program in considerable detail.

ROLE PLAYING

A technique especially useful in helping pupils improve their social understandings and their social relations skills is that of role playing. In simple terms, role playing is the acting out of a social situation with individuals assuming the roles of the participants involved. Role playing is usually oriented toward problems of interpersonal relationships and generally includes the following steps:

1. Identification of the problem.
2. Description of the situation and the roles to be played.
3. The selection of participants.
4. Acting out the problem and the various solutions to the problem.
5. Discussion of the role-playing scenes.

The problem may be obtained from the experiences of the pupils themselves, or it may be obtained from stories illustrating problems in interpersonal relationships. The opportunities for role-playing situations frequently arise spontaneously from group discussions or from classroom events. However, it is sometimes desirable for the teacher to plan role-playing sessions which illustrate problems not suggested by the class. Where this is done, the teacher must make special efforts to arouse the pupils' awareness of their need to learn ways to solve the problem. This may be done by describing the problem and asking the pupils to indicate any similar experiences they have had. Another effective method is to read a problem story which illustrates a typical social relations problem and then ask the pupils to act out possible solutions to it (*27*).

Before the participants are selected, the situation should be clearly defined and the roles carefully described. The details of the setting, the role each person is to portray, and what the role playing is to illustrate should be understood at the beginning. Most of this can be done through discussion with the class. Involving the pupils in describing the setting and defining the roles to be played brings the problem closer to the pupils' needs and arouses their interest in the role playing.

The discussion of the problem, the discussion of various solutions to the problem, and the descriptions of the setting and the various roles to be played usually generate considerable enthusiasm among the pupils, and volunteers for the various roles are easy to obtain. Pupils who have different viewpoints on how the problem should be approached may be selected for different role-playing sessions. There should be no reluctance to permit pupils to role-play an inadequate solution to a problem, since this enables pupils to better understand the shortcomings of the solution. When an inadequate solution has been suggested, it is usually best to role-play that solution first. This arouses the pupils' interest in searching for better ways of solving the problem and increases their enthusiasm for further role playing.

Before beginning the role playing, the pupils make general plans as to what they are going to do in the role-playing session. However, they do not decide specifically what they are going to say nor do they practice their roles. The actual role playing is a spontaneous enactment of how they feel the role should be played. Mistakes are expected and no one is criticized for the way the role is played. Actually, misinterpretations and errors in playing a role frequently stimulate discussion concerning different ways the role could be played. This generally leads to constructive suggestions concerning ways to react in social situations.

The discussion following the role playing is probably the most important step. It is here that the pupils analyze the feelings, attitudes, and behaviors that seem effective and ineffective in dealing with the problem. The various solutions that have been portrayed are discussed in detail, and their consequences on social relations are considered. The actual acting out of solutions makes the situation seem real to the pupils and discussion is readily obtained. Sometimes the discussion brings out new solutions to the problem, and the group wants to try out the new solutions in a reënactment of the role-playing scenes. Where this is done, the reënactment should be followed by further analysis and discussion.

In the final discussion and summary of the role-playing experiences, it is important that general principles be derived which have implications for dealing with similar situations in the future. Pupils should be able to identify factors in the role-played situation which contributed to the problem and to recognize the reasons some solutions worked better than others. The impression should not be created that there is only one solution to a human relations problem, but rather the pupils should be helped to acquire attitudes, values, and understandings which expand their skills in social interaction with others.

Although role playing is used for a variety of educational purposes (*14*), it has several unique advantages as a means of improving social relations. First, it permits pupils to act out solutions to problems of social interaction rather than to merely discuss them. This helps them understand their own, and others', feelings in interpersonal situations. Second, pupils gain insight into a variety of ways of dealing with human relations problems. In the permissive atmosphere of role playing they can explore more appropriate ways of reacting to social situations without the fear of failure that is present in real-life situations. Third, role playing provides practice in social skills. Pupils can obtain experience in social interaction with peers in a "psychologically safe" environment. Fourth, observations and discussions of role-playing situations contribute to a general understanding of the factors which influence human behavior. Increased awareness of the role of feelings, beliefs, and actions in social relations situations aids in the development of general principles which guide and direct the pupils in their own future patterns of social behavior.

A COMPREHENSIVE CLASSROOM PROGRAM

Up to this point, methods for improving the social relations of pupils have been discussed separately. However, the various methods may be interrelated into a comprehensive classroom program. Such a program is illustrated in an exploratory study by Taba and Elkins (*30, 31*). They investigated the role of the classroom teacher in improving pupils' social relations in an eighth-grade classroom. An effort was made to emphasize social relations in the classroom arrangements, in the teaching methods used, and in the subject-matter content. The following outline indicates the main features of their program and the influence it had on the pupils' social relations.

CLASSROOM ORGANIZATION

Several school subjects were combined into a two and a half hour block-of-time sequence. These subjects included social studies, literature, and guidance. Reading and discussion of topics in these areas attempted to integrate intellectual understandings, emotional insights, and practical skills by relating the course content to the pupils' own experiences.

CLASSROOM ENVIRONMENT

The teacher attempted to develop a permissive and relaxed classroom atmosphere where the expression of feelings was encouraged. Feelings were discussed as objectively as any other facts which explained and controlled human conduct.

Democratic procedures, based on teacher-pupil planning, were used in determining the actual classroom work. The teacher determined the main ideas to be covered, the skills to be developed, and the type of content to be considered. However, these were general in nature, and the pupils assisted in determining the specific plans and procedures to be used in their daily activities.

Work groups and committees were arranged and rearranged along sociometric lines. Other grouping procedures were used to integrate new members into the classroom group and to expand the pupils' existing networks of interpersonal relations. New pupils were placed on committees to care for the room, so that they could build contacts with the entire classroom membership. Other committees were organized to care for the bulletin board, to check books in and out, to plan social events, and to work on specific classroom projects. Study and discussion groups were organized around specific topics. The flexibility of the grouping procedures provided for inclusiveness and belonging on the part of each pupil.

Thus, a classroom environment was arranged which enabled pupils to learn social relations skills by practicing democratic procedures in a supportive emotional climate. As their skills increased their range of social interaction was gradually extended. Throughout the year pupils' responses were examined, their skills diagnosed, and their difficulties analyzed. Within this setting, both individual guidance and group discussions were utilized to aid pupils in their intellectual, emotional, and social growth.

DIAGNOSTIC TECHNIQUES USED

In addition to the periodic administration of sociometric tests, a number of supplementary diagnostic techniques were used. Information on the pupils' intelligence and achievement was obtained from standardized tests. The emotional atmosphere and the socioeconomic status of the pupils' homes were determined by parent interviews. Value patterns underlying the pupils' sociometric choices were explored by asking pupils to give reasons for their choices. Feelings and attitudes were diagnosed, and deficiencies in social skills were identified, through the use of themes concerning pupils' aspirations and experiences. Significant events related to individual and group development were recorded in the form of anecdotal records. Pupils' perceptions of their social environment were obtained through diaries, kept for several days, in which the pupils recorded what they did, with whom they did it, and how they felt about what they did. An analysis of these data was used to diagnose pupils' needs, to assist in planning classroom experiences, and to assess individual and group growth.

USE OF STORY DISCUSSIONS

In addition to the classroom procedures described above, special efforts were made to improve the pupils' social sensitivity and understanding of problems of human relations through the use of fiction dealing with problems of social relationships. This involved reading and discussing stories which illustrated values, behaviors, and solutions to social problems which were beyond the current experiences of the pupils. Such topics as parent-child relationships, sibling relationships, and peer relationships were included in the stories. The specific stories were selected in terms of diagnosed gaps in the pupils' social insights and social skills.

Discussion of the stories followed a general pattern illustrated by the following questions:

1. What happened in the story?
2. Why did the people in the story behave as they did?
3. How do you think the people in the story felt?
4. Have you ever had experiences similar to those in the story?
5. How could the people in the story change the situation?

It will be noted that these steps not only enabled pupils to obtain a better understanding of human behavior and its causes but it also provided them with an opportunity to share their feelings and values concerning problems of social relationships. The suggested solutions at the end of the story discussions were sometimes acted out in role-playing sessions to increase the pupils' social sensitivity and social relations skills.

RESULTS OF THE PROGRAM

An evaluation of the effects of this program on pupils' social relations indicated a change in the social structure of the group and in the social attitudes and understandings of the pupils. The sociometric results at the end of the school year indicated a more even distribution of sociometric choices, a decline in the number of isolated pupils, an increase in group cohesiveness, and a larger number of intersex choices. Informal evaluation, based on classroom observation and the diagnostic techniques used in the study, indicated that pupils showed more consideration of each others' feelings, were more sensitive to problems of social relations, and had a better understanding of human motivation and its role in interpersonal relationships.

The exploratory nature of this study prevents any firm generalizations concerning the influence of the specific techniques on the pupils' social relations. However, this study does illustrate how a variety of procedures for improving pupils' social relations can be incorporated into a regular classroom program.

SUMMARY

Sociometric results are most frequently used by the classroom teacher as an aid in the improvement of pupils' social relations. This use is especially important, since the type of social relations existing in the classroom influences the personal-social development of pupils, the effectiveness of group work, and the classroom learning of individual pupils.

General procedures for improving pupils' social relations include sociometric grouping, the development of a socially integrative classroom environment, and the use of special classroom activities.

Sociometric grouping involves the arrangement of classroom groups on the basis of sociometric choices. In the formation of these groups an attempt is made to place each pupil in the most favorable position for developing satisfying social relationships. An arrangement is also sought which reduces cleavages between subgroups and which results in the most integrated group structure. The relatively widespread use of sociometric grouping has led to a number of studies evaluating its use in improving pupils' social relations. Although the studies tend to lack careful research controls, the findings are consistent in indicating the value of sociometric grouping as a technique for improving sociometric status and structure.

The classroom environment which seems most conducive to improved social relations is one where the teacher reacts toward the pupils in a socially integrated manner, where teacher-pupil planning is used, and where frequent opportunities are provided for pupil interaction. Studies of an exploratory nature tend to support the significance of a socially integrative classroom environment for improving pupils' social relations.

A number of special classroom techniques have also been used for the purpose of improving pupils' social relations. Classroom projects concerned with the factors related to social acceptance, the study of biographies, story discussions, and role playing have all been used effectively, for this purpose, by classroom teachers. Although there is insufficient evidence to indicate the contribution of each of these techniques to improved social relations, the findings suggest that they warrant further exploration by the classroom teacher.

A comprehensive classroom program for improving pupils' social relations would include a variety of the above procedures. The effectiveness of using a multiplicity of methods was illustrated in an exploratory study by Taba and Elkins.

REFERENCES

1. Amundson, C. L., "Increasing Interpersonal Relationships in the High School with the Aid of Sociometric Procedures," *Group Psychotherapy,* 1954, *6:*183–188.

2. Anderson, H. H., and Brewer, J. E., "Studies of Teachers' Classroom Personalities, II (Effects of Teachers' Dominative and Integrative Contacts on Children's Classroom Behavior)," *Applied Psychology Monographs,* No. 8, American Psychological Association, Stanford University Press, 1946.
3. Atkinson, G., "The Sociogram as an Instrument in Social Studies Teaching and Evaluation," *Elementary School Journal,* 1949, *50:*74–85.
4. Allport, G. W., *The Resolution of Intergroup Tensions,* New York, National Conference of Christians and Jews, 1952.
5. Bonney, M. E., "Personality Traits of Socially Successful and Socially Unsuccessful Children," *Journal of Educational Psychology,* 1943, *34:*449–472.
6. Buck, J. V., "The Sociometric Technique and the Teaching of General Science," *School Science and Mathematics,* 1952, *52:*456–461.
7. Bullis, H. E., "An Educational Program for Development of the 'Normal' Personality," *American Journal of Psychiatry,* 1952, *109:*373–377.
8. Bullis, H. E., and O'Malley, E. E., *Human Relations in the Classroom,* Wilmington, Delaware, The Delaware State Society for Mental Hygiene, 1947.
9. DeBoer, J. J., Hale, P. B., and Landin, E., *Reading for Living,* Illinois Curriculum Program Bulletin No. 18, Springfield, Illinois, Office of the Superintendent of Public Instruction, 1953.
10. Dineen, M. A., and Garry, R., "Effect of Sociometric Seating on a Classroom Cleavage," *Elementary School Journal,* 1956, *56:*358–362.
11. Forlano, G., "Measuring the Quality of Social Acceptance in Some Ninth Grade Core and Noncore Classes," *High School Journal,* 1954, *38:*12–16.
12. Grambs, J. D., *Group Processes in Intergroup Education,* New York, National Conference of Christians and Jews, 1952.
13. Gronlund, N. E., "Acquaintance Span and Sociometric Status," *Sociometry,* 1955, *18:*62–68.
14. Haas, R. B., *Psychodrama and Sociodrama in American Education,* New York, Beacon House, 1949.

15. Hartley, R. E., *Sociality in Preadolescent Boys,* New York, Bureau of Publications, Teachers College, Columbia University, 1946.
16. Heaton, M. M., and Lewis, H. B., *Reading Ladders for Human Relations,* Washington, D.C., American Council on Education, 1955.
17. Kerstetter, L. M., and Sargent, J., "Re-Assignment Therapy in the Classroom," *Sociometry,* 1940, *3:*293–306.
18. Kinney, E. E., "Study of Peer Group Social Acceptability at the Fifth Grade Level," *Journal of Educational Research,* 1953, *47:*57–64.
19. Kircher, C. J., *Character Formation Through Books,* Washington, D.C., Catholic University of America Press, 1945.
20. Kuhlen, R. G., and Lee, B. J., "Personality Characteristics and Social Acceptability in Adolescence," *Journal of Educational Psychology,* 1943, *34:*321–340.
21. Lippitt, R., and White, R. K., "The Social Climate of Children's Groups," Chapter 28, in R. G. Barker, J. S. Kounin, and J. F. Wright (eds.), *Child Behavior and Development,* New York, McGraw-Hill Book Company, 1943.
22. McCleary, L., "Restructuring the Interpersonal Relations of a Junior High School Class," *School Review,* 1956, *69:*346–352.
23. McClelland, F. M., and Ratcliff, J. A., "The Use of Sociometry as an Aid in Promoting Social Adjustment in a Ninth Grade Home-Room," *Sociometry,* 1947, *10:*147–153.
24. Minnis, N. I., "Sociometry as a Guidance Technique," *National Elementary Principal,* 1954, *34:*180–183.
25. Moreno, J. L., and Jennings, H. H., "Sociometric Methods of Grouping and Regrouping with Reference to Authoritative and Democratic Methods of Grouping," *Sociometry,* 1944, *7:*397–414.
26. Shaffer, L. F., and Shoben, E. J., *The Psychology of Adjustment,* Boston, Houghton Mifflin Company, 1956.
27. Shaftel, G., and Shaftel, F. R., *Role Playing the Problem Story,* New York, National Conference of Christians and Jews, 1952.
28. Shoobs, N. E., "Sociometry in the Classroom," *Sociometry,* 1947, *10:*154–164.

29. Spector, S. I., "Climate and Social Acceptability," *Journal of Educational Sociology,* 1953, *27:*108–114.
30. Taba, H., *With Perspective on Human Relations,* Washington, D.C., American Council on Education, 1955.
31. Taba, H., and Elkins, D., *With Focus on Human Relations,* Washington, D.C., American Council on Education, 1950.
32. Thrasher, F. M., and Kerstetter, L. M., "Sociometry and an Activity Program on the University Level," *Sociometry,* 1947, *10:*178–185.
33. Tryon, C. M., "Evaluations of Adolescent Personality by Adolescents," *Monographs of the Society for Research in Child Development,* No. 4, Washington, D.C., National Research Council, 1939.
34. Tuddenham, R. D., "Studies in Reputation, III: Correlates of Popularity Among Elementary-School Children," *Journal of Educational Psychology,* 1951, *42:*257–276.
35. Zeleny, L. D., "Status: Its Measurement and Control in Education," *Sociometry,* 1941, *4:*193–204.
36. Zeleny, L. D., "The Value of Sociometry to Education," *Sociometry,* 1943, *6:*247–248.

CHAPTER 9

IMPROVING THE SOCIAL RELATIONSHIPS OF INDIVIDUAL PUPILS

The improvement of pupils' social relations can be achieved to a large extent through the use of group procedures discussed in the last chapter. Despite the teacher's skill in this area, however, some pupils will also require individual help in their attempts to develop satisfying social relationships. These are usually the isolated and rejected pupils who, for a variety of reasons, seem unable to attain acceptance among their peers. A study of the pupil and the reasons for his difficulty will usually suggest the type of remedial action to be taken. Although some causes of isolation and rejection are easily detected and easily remedied, the causes are frequently so complex and so interrelated that a multiplicity of diagnostic and remedial procedures are necessary.

METHODS FOR UNDERSTANDING THE ISOLATED AND REJECTED PUPIL

Attempts to understand the factors which have prevented an individual pupil from developing satisfying relationships with his peers may vary from informal classroom observation to a complete case study. The intensity of the investigation will depend to a large extent on the seriousness of the pupil's problem and the time the teacher has available for the study of individual pupils. Even the busy classroom teacher, however, can obtain considerable information concerning the pupil's difficulties in his social relationships by reviewing the pupil's school record, by careful observation in the classroom, by conferences with the pupil, and by conferences with his parents. Additional information may also be obtained from the pupil's classmates, through the use of sociometric interviews and "guess who" techniques.

In seeking the reasons for a pupil's social isolation or rejection by his peers, the teacher should keep in mind that a number of factors are usually operating. To explain a pupil's lack of acceptance by the group in terms of a single factor, such as low school achievement, poor physical coördination, unkempt appearance, or nonsocial behavior is usually inadequate. Although one factor may be more conspicuous than others, the degree of social acceptance a pupil obtains among his peers is based on his total pattern of personal and social characteristics. Thus, all aspects of the pupil's intellectual, physical, and social behavior should be considered.

In searching for the reasons for low peer acceptance, it is also important to look beyond the pupil's surface behavior. An isolated pupil's lack of acceptance may be attributed to the fact that he is quiet and withdrawn, but what is the cause of his withdrawn behavior? Does he merely lack knowledge of how to make social contacts? Does he lack skill in interpersonal relationships? Does he prefer to work alone? Does he have deep-seated feelings of inferiority which prevent him from interacting with others? Is his withdrawal so extreme that he needs psychiatric care before he can be helped with his social relations? Questions such as these should be considered when looking beneath the surface behavior for reasons for lack of acceptance. Some of the causes may be simple and obvious, and thus be easily determined by the classroom teacher. However, others may be so complex and subtle that the child should be referred to a specialist for more intensive study.

Although attention should be directed toward the behavior of the isolated or rejected pupil, the teacher should also give consideration to factors in the pupil's school and home environment. Are the class members ignoring or rejecting a pupil because he differs from the group in intelligence, interests, race, religion, or socioeconomic status? It is sometimes as important to help the group understand and respect differences in people as it is to help the individual pupil change his behavior. Is there anything in the classroom arrangement or the teaching procedure that contributes to the pupil's social isolation or rejection? What factors in the home situation might be contributing to the pupil's lack of peer acceptance? Modifying factors in the child's environment may be necessary before individual efforts to help the child are effective. The multiplicity of factors operating in social acceptance and rejection requires observation and study of both the individual child and the social environment in which he lives.

EXAMINING THE PUPIL'S SCHOOL RECORD

Information on the pupil's age, intelligence, achievement, special skills, and interests can usually be obtained from the school records. How an isolated or rejected pupil compares with his classmates in these areas may provide clues to his difficulty in social relations. Too great a deviation in any of these areas might help to explain why he prefers to work alone or why the class members exclude him from their activities. A past record of low school achievement might partly account for his attitude toward school in general and his classmates in particular. A record revealing retention or acceleration in his school progress might clarify why he is out of step with his present classmates. These and many other facts can be obtained from the school records by the insightful teacher.

In addition to obtaining a better understanding of isolated and rejected pupils, an examination of the school records might provide clues for helping them improve their status among peers. Special skills and interests of the isolated or rejected pupil may suggest classroom activities in which favorable recognition from peers can be obtained. Such special skills and interests may also serve as a basis for encouraging the pupil to participate in certain extracurricular activities where he can obtain peer recognition and desirable social experiences. Although information from a variety of sources is necessary if a firm basis for remedial action is to be established, school records provide a good starting point.

OBSERVING THE PUPIL IN GROUPS

Observations of the isolated or rejected pupil as he interacts with classmates provide a rich source of information concerning the apparent reasons he is having difficulty in his social relations. In these observations, the teacher should note incidents which reveal both the pupil's behavior toward his classmates and the class members' reaction to his behavior. Since the problem is one of ineffective interpersonal relationships, both the behavior of the individual pupil and the behavior of those responding to him will provide significant clues. Although the teacher's observations will vary somewhat in terms of the nature of the pupil's difficulty, general questions concerning the pupil's social relationships will aid in directing the teacher's observations.

OBSERVING ISOLATED PUPILS. Isolated pupils are generally low in social aggressiveness and tend to be ignored by their classmates. The following questions illustrate the areas of observation that will prove helpful in analyzing and understanding the isolated pupil.

1. Does the pupil voluntarily withdraw from social interaction or does he attempt to establish social contacts with other pupils?
2. Are there any obvious reasons for the pupil's social isolation (e.g.,

physical handicap, inadequate attention to cleanliness, lack of social skill, etc.)?

3. Does the isolated pupil enjoy constructive, individual activities or does he appear unhappy in his position of isolation?
4. Does the pupil reflect a need and desire for social acceptance by making excessive efforts to obtain the approval of the teacher?
5. Do any of the class members initiate social interaction with the isolated pupil? How does he react to their efforts?
6. How do the class members react to the isolated pupil's attempts to initiate social interaction with them?
7. What type of social contacts does the isolated pupil seem to have outside of the classroom? Does he play alone on the playground? Does he walk home alone? Does he have friends in other classes?
8. Is there anything notable in the isolated pupil's social behavior that can be used as a basis for helping him build better social relationships?

OBSERVING REJECTED PUPILS. Rejected pupils are generally overly aggressive in social situations and are actively disliked by their classmates. The following questions will aid the teacher in observing the social relationships of the rejected pupil.

1. Does the rejected pupil have any obvious behavior characteristics which might lead to rejection (e.g., attention-seeking behavior, being overly critical of others, being quarrelsome, etc.)?
2. Does the rejected pupil belong to a minority group that is rejected in the community? To what extent can the group's values be changed?
3. Does the rejected pupil seem to be aware that he is rejected by others? How does he react when pupils exclude him from their activities?
4. How do the class members react to the rejected pupil's persistent attempts to gain social recognition?
5. What type of social behavior does the rejected pupil exhibit on the playground, in the halls, and in other out-of-class situations?
6. What personal and social qualities does the rejected pupil exhibit

that can be used as a starting point in improving his social relationships?

Answering these and similar questions, through classroom observation, will guide the teacher in forming hunches concerning the reasons for a pupil's social isolation or rejection, will aid in identifying causal areas needing more intensive study, and will provide clues for remedial action.

CONFERENCES WITH THE PUPIL

In attempting to understand the reasons for a pupil's isolated or rejected position in the group, it is usually helpful to hold individual conferences with the pupil. These may be part of a regularly scheduled series of conferences with all pupils or they may be held on a more informal basis. Care should be taken, however, to make the conferences a natural outgrowth of the classroom activity, so that special significance is not attached to the conferences.[1]

In such conferences the teacher can determine how the pupil feels about his peers, how he feels about himself, and what value he attaches to social acceptance by peers. The pupil's attitude toward his social relationships is an important factor in understanding his social behavior and his social position in the group. Some pupils consciously withdraw from peer activities because they have little interest in social interaction and prefer to pursue constructive, individual interests. Other pupils withdraw from peer activities because they fear rejection by peers. Although they pursue individual tasks, they are unhappy and insecure due to

[1] An excellent basis for arranging such conferences is provided by the administration of a problem check list such as the SRA Junior Inventory (grades four to eight) or the SRA Youth Inventory (grades seven to twelve). These inventories enable the pupils to check the personal problems of emotional and social adjustment that are of greatest concern to them. Such information provides a good starting point for individual conferences and contributes valuable insight into the pupil's perception of his problems of adjustment. These inventories are distributed by Science Research Associates, 57 West Grand Avenue, Chicago 10, Illinois.

their inability to achieve the peer acceptance they value so highly. Still others are overly anxious about their status in the peer groups and try too hard to please their peers in attempts to gain status. Knowing whether the pupil is self-sufficient and happy in his isolated position, whether he is using social isolation as a means to protect himself against rejection, or whether he is too anxious about his social relations will aid the teacher in understanding his social interaction with classmates.

In discussing with the pupil his attitudes toward peer relationships, the teacher should not make the pupil aware of the fact that he is isolated or rejected by his classmates. The focus should be on how the pupil perceives his role in the group and the extent to which his feeling of acceptance is in harmony with his aspirations for social status. Individual differences in social awareness and in social aspiration make the pupil's perception of his social relationships an important consideration in the teacher's selection of remedial procedures.

CONFERENCES WITH PARENTS

Another basic method of obtaining helpful information concerning the isolated or rejected pupil is that of informal conferences with parents. These conferences can provide information on the pupil's out-of-school life, the atmosphere of the pupil's home environment, and the parents' perception of the pupil's social adjustment.

Asking parents about the pupil's behavior at home, his leisure-time interests, his peer relationships in the neighborhood, and his other out-of-school activities and interests will aid the teacher in determining the pervasiveness of the pupil's adjustment difficulties and will provide clues for remedial action. Careful observation and questioning during the conference will also reveal the type of parental control used in the home, the parents' aspirations for the pupil, and the extent to which the parents are aiding or hindering the pupil's attempts to develop satisfying social relationships. Both the out-of-school life of the pupil and the parents' attitude toward his social relationships have significance for understanding and guiding the pupil's social behavior in the classroom.

Although the teacher is interested in obtaining information from the parents, the conference should not be considered a one-way process. There should be a mutual exchange of information concerning the pupil's social adjustment in the school and in the home. In discussing the pupil's social adjustment in school, however, the teacher should not attract attention to his isolated or rejected position in the classroom. It is better to discuss the pupil's need for help in relating to others in terms of actual classroom incidents. This places the emphasis on the pupil's social behavior rather than on his social position. The latter may be easily misinterpreted by parents and may actually interfere with efforts to help the pupil.

During such conferences the parents of isolated and rejected pupils frequently seek suggestions for helping the pupil make friends in the neighborhood. This is an opportune time for planning with the parents a remedial program that permeates both the home and the school.

OBTAINING INFORMATION FROM PEERS

There is little value in attempting to obtain information from peers concerning the isolated pupil. He tends to be ignored by his classmates, and their neutral attitude toward him makes it difficult to obtain peer evaluations of his personal and social characteristics (*10*). Information concerning the rejected pupil is readily obtained from peers, however, because the rejected pupil has aroused negative feelings among his classmates. Pupils are very much aware of his presence and would like to reject him from the group. Determining the reasons for their feelings of rejection toward him can aid the teacher in understanding his difficulties in interpersonal relationships and can also provide insights into the standards and values held by the class members. These reasons are commonly obtained through the use of the sociometric interview and the "guess who" technique.

The sociometric interview is a technique for obtaining the reasons for acceptance and rejection as perceived by the pupils themselves. Each pupil is asked to indicate why he selected and rejected each of the pupils recorded on his sociometric test. This may be done by asking the pupil to write his reasons after each name on the sociometric form, or it may be done through individual interviews with each pupil. Although the latter method tends to be more time-consuming, it generally yields much more information. It can also be used as a good starting point for teacher-pupil conferences concerned with pupils' social relations. Questions concerning the reasons for a pupil's sociometric choices lead naturally into discussions of the pupil's attitude toward his peers, his perception of his own role in the peer group, and his need for help in improving his social relationships.

The "guess who" technique, which was described in Chapter 1, can also be used to obtain information concerning the way the peer group views the rejected pupil. With this method, a list of behavior characteristics is presented to the pupils and each pupil writes the names of those classmates who best fit the descriptions. An analysis of the number of times the rejected pupil is mentioned for each characteristic provides insight into how his classmates evaluate his behavior. The effectiveness of this technique is determined to a large extent by the type of behavior characteristics selected. These may be based on published forms (*12*), or they may be based on the behavior characteristics deemed important by the pupils and the teacher. Procedures for developing a "guess who" test based on pupils' suggestions may be found in Chapter 9.

Although the reasons pupils give for their sociometric choices, and their responses to the "guess who" test, may be distorted by their feelings toward the rejected pupil, they are nevertheless valuable. The pupils' responses indicate their perceptions of the rejected pupil's shortcomings and thus reveal the reputation the rejected pupil has among his classmates. If the teacher is going to be effective in helping the rejected pupil gain acceptance in the group, he must not only attempt to change the behavior of the rejected pupil but he must also attempt to change the rejected pupil's reputation among his peers. Thus, peer evaluations of the rejected pupil aid the teacher in understanding the reasons for his rejection and provide clues for changing the group's attitude toward him.

GENERAL PROCEDURES FOR HELPING THE ISOLATED AND REJECTED PUPIL

The specific remedial procedures to be used in helping an isolated or rejected pupil will be determined largely by the teacher's study of the reasons for the pupil's lack of acceptance. However, a number of general procedures can be suggested that will aid the classroom teacher in planning an effective remedial program. Although many of these procedures can be used while the isolated or rejected pupil is being studied more intensively, or where the reasons for isolation or rejection cannot be clearly determined, an understanding of the pupil is usually necessary for their most effective use.

Since multiple factors usually underlie social isolation and rejection, single procedures are generally ineffective in helping isolated or rejected pupils achieve satisfying social relationships. Thus, the following general procedures, or some modification of them, should be included in a comprehensive remedial program (*2, 15, 16, 18, 19*).

SOCIOMETRIC PLACEMENT

In the sociometric arrangement of seating, and in the formation of other sociometric groups, it is especially important that isolated and rejected pupils be placed with their first choices. This places them in the position in the classroom social environment where they feel most secure and where they have the greatest opportunity for establishing satisfying social relationships. Care should be taken to see that classmates who have rejected the unchosen pupils are not placed near them in the seating arrangement and are not placed in the same work group with them.

These suggestions, of course, apply only to the original placement of the pupil. Further study of the individual pupil and therapeutic efforts to improve his social relationships may indicate the desirability of placing him in situations with a variety of different classmates. This may be found helpful in expanding the interpersonal contacts of isolated pupils and in breaking down the barriers between rejected pupils and their classmates. Such procedures should not be attempted, however, until the unchosen pupil has developed security in the group and his social behavior indicates he is ready to broaden his social contacts. In short, sociometric placement is a safe starting point. Other therapeutic group arrangements must be based on the teacher's evaluation of the social progress of the unchosen pupil and of the progress the total group is making toward improved social relations.

MAINTAINING AN ACCEPTING ATTITUDE

The attitude the teacher has toward the isolated or rejected pupil is an essential factor in helping him improve his social relationships with his peers. Maintaining an attitude of personal warmth and acceptance toward the unchosen pupil adds to his feeling of security and belonging in the classroom. It also helps him recognize that the teacher understands him and values him as a person. This builds a firm base for the type of teacher-pupil rapport necessary for effective individual guidance. Suggestions for modifying social behavior and for improving relationships with others are more readily acted upon by the pupil who views the teacher as a warm and accepting person.

It is generally not difficult for the classroom teacher to maintain an accepting attitude toward the quiet, withdrawn isolate. He does not disturb the classroom decorum, and his shyness in social interaction arouses natural sympathy on the part of the teacher. However, the noisy, rebellious, rejected pupil who constantly disrupts the class is a different matter. His behavior is personally disturbing to the teacher and feelings of antagonism and hostility toward the pupil are easily aroused. The same factors which contribute to his rejection by peers tend to arouse attitudes of rejection on the part of the teacher (9).

The best defense against the development of unhealthy attitudes toward the rejected pupil comes from an understanding of the pupil and the reasons for his behavior. Recognizing that a rejected pupil's classroom antics are attempts to get the attention of peers, rather than to antagonize the teacher, will help in maintaining a more tolerant and objective attitude toward his behavior. This, of course, does not imply that the teacher must accept the unsocial behavior of the rejected pupil. It merely means that he can handle the behavior without feeling or showing resentment toward the pupil. Understanding the rejected pupil's difficulties in obtaining satisfying social relationships makes it easier for the teacher to communicate to the pupil, by both word and gesture, that his classroom behavior is not acceptable but that he is both liked and accepted as a person.

HELPING PUPILS MODIFY BEHAVIOR

Frequently pupils are isolated or rejected because they are unaware of the modes of behavior which contribute to peer acceptance, they lack insight into the adverse effects of their behavior on peer relations, and they lack the social skills necessary for making friends. They can generally be helped to develop the necessary knowledge and skill in these areas through group discussions, role playing, and other group techniques discussed in Chapter 9. However, the group procedures should be supplemented by individual attention from the classroom teacher.

Individual conferences following class discussions of the types of behavior which peers value most highly are generally fruitful. Here, the teacher can explore with the isolated or rejected pupil his own strengths and weaknesses in the areas of behavior considered important by peers. Although helping the pupil develop insight into his undesirable behavior characteristics is an important part of the process (*19*), extreme care must be taken not to overwhelm the pupil with unfavorable evaluations of his conduct. Letting the pupil take the lead in discussing his behavior, starting with the desirable behavior characteristics of the pupil, and gradually directing the pupil's attention to behavior which should be modified, is usually effective.

During the conference, the teacher should help the pupil make plans for modifying his behavior and for practicing the new modes of behavior. These plans should be concerned with definite behavioral acts and specific situations rather than with generalities. To plan to practice "courteousness toward others" usually brings discouraging results. Changes in behavior are more apt to occur if the plans refer to specific actions, such as listening without interrupting, when another pupil is talking in class. The younger the pupil, the more important it is that the behavior changes be discussed in specific terms. However, even high school and college students are more likely to modify their behavior if the plans for change are definite (*23*).

In the classroom, the teacher should arrange situations where the isolated or rejected pupil can try out his new plans and can practice the accompanying social skills. For example, plans in the area of "being more helpful to others" should be followed up by classroom opportunities for being helpful to others. During the practice of new modes of behavior, teacher guidance and the frequent use of judicious praise and reassurance will increase the probability of success. The teacher should expect neither large nor immediate changes in behavior, however, since the building of new behavior patterns is a gradual and difficult process.

HELPING PUPILS ATTRACT FAVORABLE RECOGNITION FROM PEERS

Both the isolated and rejected pupil can be made more acceptable to the group if some way is found to attract favorable attention to them. This is frequently done by arranging situations where the pupil can demonstrate a skill which is highly valued by the group. Skill in such areas as art, music, sports, and dancing can all be used effectively in the elementary school classroom. At the secondary school level, special courses such as art, music, agriculture, industrial education, home economics, and physical education provide numerous opportunities for the demonstration of highly valued skills. Laboratory work in science courses also provides opportunities to demonstrate important skills. In some secondary school courses skill in making maps, charts, graphs, and diagrams can be used effectively. Although it is not expected that every isolated and rejected pupil will have some skill in which he can excel, this method of attracting favorable recognition from peers is one that should be carefully considered.

In addition to capitalizing on an isolated or rejected pupil's special skills, several other methods can be used effectively. Arranging classroom situations which enable the pupil to provide special knowledge desired by the group, or to share experiences that are interesting and valuable to the group members, is frequently useful in helping him gain recognition. Hobby displays such as stamp collections, insect collections, coin collections, and rock collections can also be utilized, where they coördinate with the classroom activities. Appointing the isolated or rejected pupil to positions of responsibility in the classroom (e.g., caring for the bulletin board, the biology aquarium, etc.) is likewise helpful in attracting the favorable attention of peers (*13*).

The alert classroom teacher will note numerous opportunities to use the isolated or rejected pupil's skills, abilities, and interests to help him gain favorable attention in the classroom. Care should be taken, however, to prevent attracting so much attention to the unchosen pupil that it appears that he is getting special recognition from the teacher. The label of "teacher's pet" can only lead to further rejection by peers. Another caution in this area is to be certain that the isolated or rejected pupil is socially ready for the situations arranged for him. Starting out with situations where he can gain favorable attention from another class member, or from a small group, may be necessary with some pupils. As his confidence and social skills improve, he can be led to make contributions which enable all of his classmates to see him in a more favorable light.

HELPING PUPILS BUILD SELF-CONFIDENCE

Lack of satisfying social relationships generally create feelings of inadequacy. Thus, efforts must be directed toward providing success experiences which build up the unchosen pupil's self-confidence. Proper sociometric placement, help in improving the pupil's social relations skills, and gradual induction into positions of recognition in the classroom all contribute to this end. However, helping the pupil achieve success in his academic work, in physical games and sports, and in social activities can also contribute to the isolated or rejected pupil's development of self-confidence.

At the beginning it may be necessary for the teacher to arrange situations where success is assured, and to depend on the use of praise and reassurance to encourage participation. For the most effective results, however, efforts must also be directed toward improving the basic skills needed in academic, physical, and social activities. If an unchosen pupil is low in school achievement, special help should be provided by the classroom teacher or by a remedial specialist. If the pupil lacks proficiency in games, sports, dancing, or other activities highly valued by the peer group, special help should be provided through physical education classes and extracurricular activities. Increased knowledge and skill in these areas enable the pupil to participate with his peers on a more equal basis and to experience success more frequently. With each successful experience, he will develop increased confidence in himself and in his ability to participate effectively in peer activities.

IMPORTANCE OF MODIFYING THE VALUES OF THE GROUP

In working with isolated and rejected pupils, the teacher should not overlook the importance of attempting to modify the values of the group (*5, 21*). As pointed out in Chapter 7, children tend to ignore or reject others who differ from themselves in intelligence, achievement, interests, values, personality characteristics, socioeconomic status, and racial and cultural background. Helping pupils to increase their acceptance of differences in themselves and others should accompany special efforts to help the isolated or rejected pupil. This will aid in removing some of the barriers which prevent isolated and rejected pupils from gaining acceptance in the group. It will also have a therapeutic effect on the behavior of the unchosen pupils. Their withdrawn or aggressive behavior is frequently caused or aggravated by the intolerant attitudes of the peer group.

Changes in the values of the peer group may be brought about through individual conferences with the pupils and through the group methods discussed in Chapter 9. It is mentioned here merely to stress the importance of devoting attention to the peer group as well as to the individual pupil. Fruitless attempts to help isolated and rejected children gain social acceptance are frequently due to the lack of attention to unhealthy standards and values held by the members of the peer group.

USING THE RESOURCES OF THE SCHOOL, HOME, AND COMMUNITY

Most of the suggestions up to this point have been concerned with the remedial procedures the classroom teacher can apply directly in the classroom. However, isolation or rejection in the classroom is usually indicative of a general lack of acceptance among peers (*11*). Since the pupil's difficulties in peer relationships tend to pervade all aspects of his life sphere, special help should not be limited to that which can be provided by the classroom teacher. By utilizing the total resources of the school, the home, and the community, the teacher can initiate an integrated series of constructive experiences that contribute to the pupil's ability to develop satisfying social relationships with his peers.

One resource of the school that is seldom used by the isolated or rejected pupil is that of the extracurricular program. A study of 2500 high school pupils has shown that less than 50 percent of the pupils least accepted by their peers belonged to any school organization (*3*). Similar results were obtained in another study of 2000 high school pupils (*8*). In this latter study, it was reported that isolated and rejected pupils devoted most of their free time to individual hobbies, reading, movies, and other activities that could be pursued in isolation. For the majority of such pupils, feelings of inadequacy prevent them from joining in the activities of their peers. They will usually not participate in school organizations unless encouraged to do so by some influential person such as the classroom teacher. Guiding them in the selection of school clubs, sports, or other extracurricular activities in harmony with their abilities and interests is sometimes all that is needed to encourage participation. For the most effective results, however, this probably should be done after the pupil has begun to develop increased social relations skills in the classroom. Being a member of a school organization has little beneficial social effect, unless the pupil has sufficient self-confidence and social skill to establish effective social relationships with the group members. Enlisting the help of the teacher in charge of the school organization can also aid in ensuring that the pupil's experience will be a socially beneficial one.

If the school has guidance and counseling services available, referring the isolated or rejected pupil for individual or group counseling may prove effective. Individual counseling can aid the pupil in understanding and coping with personal problems of adjustment that are interfering with his ability to relate effectively to others. Group counseling and other forms of group therapy have also been found useful in helping isolated and rejected pupils (*4, 6*). Where the pupil has deep-seated feelings of inferiority or hostility underlying his behavior, the help of a professional counselor is usually necessary before the classroom teacher can effectively aid the pupil with his social relationships. Even the less severe cases of isolation and rejection, however, can be made more responsive to remedial classroom procedures by individual and group counseling.

The guidance activities of the homeroom program can also be utilized to aid the isolated or rejected pupil. Group discussions of problems of interpersonal relationships, instruction in courtesy and manners, special units on grooming and cleanliness, and practice in social skills are examples of the types of activities that can be carried on effectively in the homeroom program. Such activities are especially useful at the high school level where the peer group places increased emphasis on physical appearance and social skills.

Working with the parents of an isolated or rejected pupil also may provide fruitful results. Most parents are anxious to help their children develop satisfying social relationships and welcome the suggestions of the teacher. One way the teacher can be helpful to parents is to guide them in finding ways of providing increased social contact for the child. Suggestions concerning the use of in-school and out-of-school activities that are available to the child; pointing out the value of encouraging the child to invite schoolmates to his home after school; and in some cases urging the parents to give their children more freedom in their selection of friends and in their participation in peer activities may be useful. The aid of the parents can also be enlisted in the development of the pupil's abilities, skills, and interests. Special tutoring in school subjects, private music lessons, summer camp programs, and the like, might be suggested where appropriate.

Most communities have a variety of organized activities available to children. The beneficial effects of scouting, YMCA and YWCA programs, 4-H clubs, recreational programs, and other community activities should not be overlooked in searching for socializing experiences for the isolated and rejected pupils. As with school organizations, however, isolated and rejected children tend to shun such activities unless they are encouraged to participate by both teachers and parents. A personal invitation from the adult leader in charge of the activity, or from one of the active members, is also usually effective in encouraging participation. This can frequently be arranged by the classroom teacher or the parent.

Despite the number of school and community facilities that are available for helping pupils improve their social relations, the classroom teacher still remains the central person in the remedial program. If school organizations are going to benefit the isolated or rejected pupil, it is the teacher who must encourage the pupil to participate; if the guidance services are to be properly used, it is the teacher who must make the referral; if parents are to contribute most effectively, it is the teacher who must seek their coöperation; and if community resources are to be used effectively, it is the teacher who must initiate the action. Thus, it is the teacher who must take the initiative in focusing the resources of the school, the home, and the community on the problems of the isolated or rejected pupil. The teacher's daily contact with the pupil in a group setting also places the teacher in the most strategic position for integrating the pupil's various out-of-class experiences into constructive forces for improved social relations.

ADAPTING REMEDIAL PROCEDURES TO SPECIFIC CASES OF ISOLATION AND REJECTION

An effective remedial program for helping an isolated or rejected pupil establish satisfying social relationships should be firmly grounded on an understanding of the individual pupil and the reasons for his social difficulty. Although the general procedures discussed in the previous section may be helpful in designing such a program, individual patterns of social isolation and rejection demand modifications in procedure and variations in emphasis.

PATTERNS OF SOCIAL ISOLATION AND REJECTION

Classroom patterns of social isolation and rejection vary from one individual to another. However, the following general patterns of isolation and rejection are sufficient to illustrate the importance of adapting remedial classroom procedures to each individual case.

THE "SELF-SUFFICIENT" ISOLATE. Some children enjoy pursuing individual interests and they are happy and self-sufficient in their solitary pursuits. They are alone a great deal but they are happily occupied with constructive activities. They may welcome peer recognition of their individual accomplishments and may enjoy sharing their activities with one or two other children, but they have neither the desire nor the inclination to become "social stars." They appear to be confident and happy in their limited social sphere. Helping such pupils develop mutual relationships with one or two other children who have similar interests and helping them share their ideas effectively in group work may be sufficient to assure them an adequate and satisfactory social position in the group. To convey to such a child that he should be more socially active will only tend to make him dissatisfied with his otherwise satisfactory social position and to distract him from his healthy interests in individual activities.

THE "WITHDRAWN" ISOLATE. Some children withdraw from

social contact because they fear that others will reject their attempts to gain peer acceptance. They want to be accepted by the group but they lack the confidence and the skill to establish satisfying social relationships. Although the withdrawn isolate may engage in individual activities similar to those of the self-sufficient isolate, he can usually be identified by his lack of self-confidence and his general unhappiness. He finds little satisfaction in individual pursuits, since his need for social acceptance is a dominating force in his life. A comprehensive program will include activities which help him establish a feeling of security, which provide for gradual induction into the group, which build up his self-confidence, and which improve his social skills.

THE "AGGRESSIVE" REJECTEE. Some children react to lack of social acceptance among peers by aggressive reactions rather than withdrawal. They make frequent attempts to attract the attention and recognition of peers. Through fighting, teasing, quarreling, and various attention-getting devices, they express their unmet needs for social acceptance. Their unsocial behavior leads to further rejection by the group members and the vicious circle of rejection-aggression-rejection evolves. This pattern of social rejection will require a remedial program that puts considerable emphasis on the development of more effective social behavior, the attainment of recognition through socially acceptable channels, and the reduction of hostility.

THE "CULTURAL" ISOLATE OR REJECTEE. Some children tend to be isolated or rejected because of the group members' prejudice toward the cultural or racial group to which they belong. Their lack of acceptance may contribute to their withdrawal from group activities or to more aggressive reactions toward the group members. Thus, the remedial procedures suggested above may be helpful in working with the individual. However, attempts to change the attitudes of the group members toward cultural and racial differences must also constitute an important part of the remedial program.

THE "EMOTIONALLY DISTURBED" ISOLATE OR REJECTEE. Some children have such severe emotional problems underlying their difficulties in social relations that they are unresponsive to any remedial program in the classroom. Such children, usually characterized by extreme withdrawal or uncontrollable hostility, require referral to a competent psychologist or psychiatrist. For such a child, the remedial classroom program should be developed in coöperation with the specialist under whom the child is receiving treatment.

GUIDES TO AN EFFECTIVE REMEDIAL PROGRAM

Variations in the patterns of social isolation and rejection suggest several important considerations in developing a remedial program for a specific isolated or rejected pupil. These may best be stated in terms of general principles which should guide the teacher in planning a remedial program that is adapted to the individual needs of each pupil.

1. The teacher should recognize and consider individual differences in drive for social activity and need for social acceptance by peers. Although social acceptance is considered a basic social need, individuals vary in the pattern of social relationships that satisfactorily meet their needs. Some individuals require extensive social contact to meet their social needs, while others feel adequate and satisfied with a few close friends. Clues to an individual's level of social aspiration can be obtained from interviews and classroom observations.
2. The teacher should recognize and consider individual differences in the pattern of factors causing and contributing to an individual's social position. Although two isolated pupils may have a single conspicuous causative factor in common (e.g., unkempt appearance), the network of related personal and social factors contributing to their isolation will usually vary considerably. A search for multiple causes will generally reveal the unique pattern of factors operating in each individual case.
3. The teacher should recognize and consider individual differences

in skills, abilities, and interests that can be used for improving an individual's social position. Although some pupils have considerable potential for developing highly valued skills, others may be generally weak in this area. Using what potential the pupil has, capitalizing on special interests, and creating classroom situations which attract recognition to the pupil's personal assets may partly compensate for weaknesses in skill and ability.

4. The teacher should recognize and consider the standards and values held by the group members. Although individuals tend to choose associates who are similar to themselves in personal and social characteristics, they can be helped to extend their capacity to accept differences in others. This will not only help the isolate and rejectee achieve acceptance but it will also contribute to a broader understanding of human relations on the part of the group members.
5. The teacher should recognize and consider individual differences in the degree of emotional disturbance underlying an individual's social difficulty. Although most isolates and rejectees have only mild feelings of inferiority and hostility underlying their social behavior, others may have such extreme emotional disturbances that they require treatment from a specialist before their social relations can be improved. Extreme withdrawal or aggression which is unresponsive to remedial classroom procedures provides clues for referral.
6. The teacher should recognize and consider individual differences in responsiveness to remedial procedures. Although some isolates and rejectees may be helped to attain acceptance in the group in a relatively short time and with fairly simple techniques, changes in social relations are generally gradual and require a multiplicity of procedures. Improvement in individual cases should be viewed in terms of the pupil's social aspirations, his social potential, the complexity of factors causing and contributing to his social position, and the comprehensiveness of the remedial program.

PROBLEMS OF THE SOCIALLY ACCEPTED PUPIL

In this chapter considerable emphasis has been placed on helping the isolated and rejected pupil achieve satisfying social relationships. This is as it should be, since the unchosen pupil has the greatest need for individual guidance from the classroom teacher. The fact that the socially accepted pupil may also have problems in the area of social relationships, however, should not be overlooked. Both the inspection of sociometric results and classroom observations will provide clues to some of their problems. Although the specific problems of individual pupils are numerous and varied, the following types of problems require special attention from the classroom teacher.

LACK OF MUTUAL RELATIONSHIPS

Mutual choices on a sociometric test have special significance in evaluating the social position of individual pupils. They serve as an index of the extent to which each pupil is developing satisfying mutual relationships with the group members. One close friendship may contribute more to an individual's feeling of security and acceptance in the group than several choices from pupils whom he himself does not choose. Thus, the teacher should devote special attention to those pupils who are accepted by some of their classmates but who have no mutual choices.

Since the number of mutual choices an individual receives is closely related to his choice status, the pupil who is chosen by a relatively small number of classmates is usually the one who lacks mutual relationships (*1*). There are some surprising exceptions to this, however. Occasionally highly chosen individuals have been noted to lack mutual relationships. Although they attract a large number of choices among their peers, their own choices of preferred associates remain unreciprocated. This lack of close friendship with desired associates can contribute to feelings of isolation, even among the highly chosen leaders of the group (*14*).

The pupil who is accepted by his peers but lacks mutual choices is usually aided by sociometric grouping (*17*). Arranging seating, work groups, and other opportunities for social contact with those of his preferred companions who have similar interests and abilities is generally sufficient to establish some satisfying mutual relationships. Where sociometric arrangement fails to bring about the desired results, efforts should be made to identify the personal and social factors preventing the development of friendship patterns. So many unique difficulties arise in the social relationships between specific individuals that appropriate remedial techniques must be based on a careful study of the situation.

DECLINE IN SOCIOMETRIC STATUS

Another type of socially accepted pupil that requires special attention from the classroom teacher is one whose sociometric status is declining (7). Although minor fluctuations in choice status are expected, a sudden large drop in choice status or a continuous decline over a period of time is a clue to difficulty in the pupil's social relationships. After ruling out obvious causes for the loss of status (i.e., prolonged period of absence, illness, etc.), the teacher should make a careful search for the factors causing and contributing to the pupil's decline in choice status.

Downward shifts in choice status may signify a temporary upset in the pupil's home or school life, the onset of a severe emotional difficulty, or some other factor influencing his behavior toward others. However, loss of choice status may also indicate changes in the values of the peer group rather than changes in the individual pupil. For example, Moreno (*14*) has shown that minority group members who were accepted by their peers at the third-grade level tended to lose status in the fourth grade as a result of the greater influence of racial prejudice. Similarly, a study by Tryon (*22*) has indicated that changes in the values of the peer group during adolescence may cause both temporary and permanent losses in choice status for some pupils. Late-maturing boys and girls may temporarily decline in status, due to a lack of physical development and the lack of heterosexual interests. A permanent loss of status may also result during adolescence, if a pupil fails to make the heterosexual adjustments necessary for acceptance in the adolescent peer group.

Whether a pupil's decline in choice status is due to some temporary situational factor, to changes in the individual's behavior, or to changes in the values of the peer group can only be determined by an intensive study of the situation. Likewise, remedial action, or referral, must be determined by the factors causing the pupil's loss of status. However, it should be noted that helping a pupil develop a few close friends can frequently compensate for a declining choice status and can add greater stability to the pupil's social relationships with his peers (*22*).

UNREALISTIC SOCIAL ASPIRATIONS

Every individual desires and needs social acceptance among peers. However, some pupils seem to have an exaggerated need for social acceptance and social recognition. They want to be liked and admired by everyone and no amount of attention from peers seems to satisfy them. These are generally pupils who have experienced little social success in the past. Previous experiences of social rejection or lack of acceptance have magnified the importance of peer acceptance, and a level of social aspiration has emerged which is wholly unrealistic. Their idealized goal prevents them from enjoying the recognition and acceptance tendered them by some of their classmates. They want to be the center of attention and a preferred associate of all of their peers.

Helping such pupils to experience the satisfaction of close interpersonal relationships and to appreciate the value of a few loyal friends may aid in reducing their irrational drive for peer acceptance. However, if they are to achieve satisfaction in their social relationships, they must also be helped to see the futility of trying to win the admiration and acceptance of everyone. Evidence from sociometric studies which show that even the most popular individual is seldom preferred by the majority of the group members and that lack of expressed preference toward an individual usually means a feeling of indifference toward him, rather than rejection, may be helpful in this regard (*17*). Where routine attempts to help the pupil develop a more realistic attitude toward peer acceptance are unsuccessful, referral for special help is generally desirable. A professional counselor can usually aid the pupil in the development of insight into his exaggerated need for peer acceptance and can help him set more realistic social goals.

EXTREME DEPENDENCE ON THE PEER GROUP

Although most pupils who are accepted by their peers strike a happy balance between conformity to the values of the peer group and independent self-direction, some pupils seem to be completely dependent on the peer group for guidance and direction. They are unable to satisfactorily pursue individual activities, to do independent thinking, or to make individual decisions. Their goals, activities, and standards of conduct are determined largely by the dictates of the peer group. In group decisions they will not commit themselves until they are able to determine how the majority of the group members feel, and then they will go along with the majority opinion. As Stendler (*20*) has pointed out, they seem unable to distinguish between "getting along with others" and "going along with others."

Pupils who show such extreme dependence on the peer group are generally those who have relatively low status among their peers and lack the knowledge and skill needed for improving their social relationships. They assume that if they submit completely to the desires of the peer group they will be rewarded for their loyalty. In addition to helping such pupils learn more effective methods for attaining peer status, the teacher should provide a healthy balance of individual and group activities. Encouraging and recognizing independent judgments and individual efforts will assist in counteracting the undesirable effects of extreme dependence on the peer group.

SUMMARY

Pupils who are isolated or rejected by their peers generally have the greatest need for individual help in improving their social relationships. A remedial program for such pupils should be based on a careful study of the reasons for their isolated or rejected position in the group. Information from school records, classroom observations, teacher-pupil conferences, teacher-parent conferences, and peer evaluations can all be useful in this regard. Since a combination of personal and social factors usually underlie social isolation and rejection, a search for multiple causes is generally most fruitful.

A comprehensive remedial program for improving the social relationships of isolated and rejected pupils should include a variety of classroom procedures. Sociometric placement and an accepting attitude toward the pupil should be supplemented by classroom experiences that help the pupil modify his behavior, attract favorable recognition from peers, and build up his self-confidence in social interaction. In working with individual pupils, the teacher should not overlook the importance of modifying the values of the peer group and of utilizing the resources of the school, the home, and the community.

Variations in individual patterns of social isolation and rejection suggest the desirability of adapting the remedial procedures to each specific case. Such a remedial program should take into account the pupil's social aspirations, the pattern of factors causing the pupil's social difficulty, the pupil's skills, abilities, and interests, the values held by the group members, the degree of emotional disturbance underlying the pupil's social behavior, and the pupil's social potential. When the pupil does not respond to the teacher's remedial efforts, he should be referred to a professional counselor for special help.

Although isolated and rejected pupils are in obvious need of help with their social relationships, some socially accepted pupils also have problems requiring remedial action. The lack of mutual relationships, a decline in sociometric status, unrealistic social aspirations, and extreme dependence on the peer group are types of problems which warrant special attention from the classroom teacher. In each case, a study of the factors causing the pupil's social difficulty will suggest the type of remedial action necessary.

REFERENCES

1. Bonney, M. E., "The Relative Stability of Social, Intellectual, and Academic Status in Grades II to IV, and the Inter-Relationships Between These Various Forms of Growth," *Journal of Educational Psychology,* 1943, *34:*88–102.
2. Bonney, M. E., "Values of Sociometric Studies in the Classroom," *Sociometry,* 1943, *6:*251–254.
3. Brown, D., "Helping Adolescents Win Social Acceptance," *High School Journal,* 1955, *38:*157–162.
4. Cox, F. N., "Sociometric Status and Individual Adjustment Before and After Play Therapy," *Journal of Abnormal and Social Psychology,* 1953, *48:*354–356.
5. Cunningham, R., *Understanding Group Behavior of Boys and Girls,* New York, Bureau of Publications, Teachers College, Columbia University, 1951.
6. Davis, R. G., "Group Therapy and Social Acceptance in a First-Second Grade," *Elementary School Journal,* 1948, *49:*219–223.
7. DeVault, M. V., "Sociograms in High School Classes," *High School Journal,* 1955, *38:*300–303.
8. Feinberg, M. R., "Relation of Background Experience to Social Acceptance," *Journal of Abnormal and Social Psychology,* 1953, *48:*206–214.
9. Gronlund, N. E., "Relationship Between the Sociometric Status of Pupils' and Teachers' Preferences For or Against Having Them in Class," *Sociometry,* 1953, *16:*142–150.
10. Gronlund, N. E., and Anderson, L., "Personality Characteristics of Socially Accepted, Socially Neglected, and Socially Rejected Junior High School Pupils," *Educational Administration and Supervision,* 1957, *43:*329–338.

11. Gronlund, N. E., and Whitney, A. P., "Relation Between Pupils' Social Acceptability in the Classroom, in the School, and in the Neighborhood," *School Review,* 1956, *64:*267–271.
12. Laughlin, F., *The Peer Status of Sixth- and Seventh-Grade Children,* New York, Bureau of Publications, Teachers College, Columbia University, 1954.
13. McClelland, F. M., and Ratcliff, J. A., "The Use of Sociometry as an Aid in Promoting Social Adjustment in a Ninth Grade Home-Room," *Sociometry,* 1947, *10:*147–153.
14. Moreno, J. L., *Who Shall Survive?* New York, Beacon House, 1953.
15. Nedelsky, R., "The Teacher's Role in the Peer Group During Middle Childhood," *Elementary School Journal,* 1952, *52:*325–334.
16. Northway, M. L., *A Primer of Sociometry,* Toronto, University of Toronto Press, 1952.
17. Northway, M. L., and Weld, L., *Sociometric Testing,* Toronto, University of Toronto Press, 1957.
18. Olson, W. C., "The Improvement of Human Relations in the Classroom," *Childhood Education,* 1946, *22:*317–325.
19. Roberts, J. D., "Improving the Status of Isolates," *National Elementary Principal,* 1952, *32:*183–188.
20. Stendler, C. B., *Teaching in the Elementary School,* New York, Harcourt, Brace and Company, 1958.
21. Taba, H., "Acceptance and Rejection," *Childhood Education,* 1954, *30:*423–426.
22. Tryon, C. M., "Evaluations of Adolescent Personality by Adolescents," *Monographs of the Society for Research in Child Development,* No. 4, Washington, D.C., National Research Council, 1939.
23. Zeleny, L. D., "Status: Its Measurement and Control in Education," *Sociometry,* 1941, *4:*193–204.

CHAPTER 10

SOCIOMETRY IN THE SCHOOL

In the last two chapters the emphasis has been on the use of sociometric results in the improvement of pupils' social relations in the classroom. Although this is probably the most common use of sociometric results in educational settings, sociometric theory, research, and practice have suggested a number of useful purposes for which sociometric procedures might be used in the school. In this chapter, those educational applications which seem to have the greatest potential for improved school practice will be considered. Since many of the suggested uses are of an experimental nature, a systematic method of applying and evaluating sociometric procedures will also be presented.

SOCIOMETRY AND PUPIL LEADERSHIP

The school provides numerous opportunities for the development of pupil leadership. Informal positions of leadership in the classroom and formal leadership positions in school clubs, sports, and other extracurricular activities enable pupils to obtain experience in various leadership roles. In addition, it has been indicated that approximately three-fourths of all high schools have some provision for pupil leadership in the form of student councils (*36*). Despite the extensive opportunities for leadership development in the school and the importance of the school's role in training leaders for society, the identification and development of pupil leadership is generally haphazard and unplanned (*15*).

The sociometric test can contribute to leadership training in the school in two ways. It can aid in the identification of pupils with leadership potential, and it can provide an equitable basis for nominating pupils for formal leadership positions in the school.

IDENTIFICATION OF LEADERSHIP POTENTIAL

The value of the sociometric test for identifying individuals with leadership potential was recognized early in the development of the sociometric test. Both Moreno (*35*) and Jennings (*23, 24*) described its use in the identification of leaders in a training school for girls. Later studies have also indicated the value of sociometric procedures for identifying leadership potential in other group situations (*19*). Although most of the studies in this area are exploratory in nature, they have consistently indicated a positive relationship between high sociometric status and other leadership qualities (*19*).

The significance of sociometric status scores for identifying leadership potential among school pupils was indicated in a follow-up study by Gronlund and Holmlund (*22*). They obtained sociometric status scores for 1073 sixth-grade pupils in a large Midwestern city. Seven years later the high school records of fifty-three pupils with high sociometric status (stars) and forty-nine pupils with low sociometric status (neglectees) were examined for evidence of leadership activity in high school. The results indicated that forty-six of the high status pupils completed high school and that eleven of these pupils were elected to twenty-nine high school leadership positions. These included the president of the freshman class, the president of the senior class, the treasurer of the junior class, two members of the board of directors of the sophomore class, four members of the board of directors of the junior class, five members of the board of directors of the senior class, three vice-presidents of school clubs, one secretary of a school club, and eleven members of the student council. This array of high school leadership positions was held in two large high schools whose combined graduating classes included approximately 1000 pupils.

In contrast to the pupils with high sociometric status, only twenty-seven of the low status pupils completed high school. Of these, only one pupil held any type of leadership position. This was a girl who was elected secretary and treasurer of a school club and chairman of the student counseling program.

These findings are especially impressive when viewed in light of the fact that sociometric status was based on one sociometric test; that the test was administered at the sixth-grade level; and that choices were confined to classroom preferences for seating companion, work companion, and play companion. Even under these limited circumstances, sociometric status scores were predictive of leadership activity in high school. It would appear that with frequent sociometric testing, on a variety of criteria and under various conditions, the sociometric test could make a valuable contribution to the identification of leadership potential among pupils.

The sociometric test, of course, merely indicates the possession of social leadership qualities. Those pupils who are highly chosen on a sociometric test have the ability to maintain harmonious social relationships with a large number of peers and tend to have considerable influence over them (*20*). Whether or not they have formal leadership skills or constructive social attitudes cannot be determined from sociometric data. However, since individuals with high sociometric status are frequently elected to formal leadership positions, it would seem desirable to identify them early and to provide them with opportunities to develop the skills and attitudes necessary for effective group leadership. This may be done through informal leadership positions in the regular classroom, in the homeroom program, and in various extracurricular activities. Despite the type of leadership experiences provided, the sociometric test can make a unique contribution to the identification of pupils with potential leadership ability.

NOMINATION OF PUPILS FOR FORMAL LEADERSHIP POSITIONS

Although pupils are generally elected to formal leadership positions in the school in a democratic manner, the nomination of candidates for these positions is sometimes far from democratic. Small cliques and organized pressure groups frequently nominate candidates and close the nominations before the majority of pupils have time to decide whom they would most prefer as candidates. As a consequence, pupils who represent a minority of the group members are sometimes elected to leadership positions. Such procedures generally favor pupils from the higher socioeconomic classes (*32*) and deprive some capable pupils from attaining formal leadership experiences (*2*).

An adaptation of the sociometric technique has been found useful as a method for correcting the inequities in the nomination of pupils for formal leadership positions in the school. The procedure is relatively simple and easily administered. On a secret ballot, each pupil is asked to nominate the two or three pupils whom he would most prefer for each leadership position. These nominations are then tallied and the pupils receiving the largest number of votes become the candidates for the positions. Thus, every pupil participates in the nomination of candidates, and those pupils who are nominated tend to represent the majority of group members.

The obvious advantage of using the sociometric method of nominating candidates is that it screens the entire group for leadership ability. This generally results in the most effective group leadership and provides leadership experience for those pupils with the greatest leadership potential. Although socioeconomic class affiliation and other extraneous factors will still operate to a certain degree, the influence of these factors will tend to be minimized.

The sociometric method of nominating candidates for leadership positions has special advantages in selecting members for the student council. Since the council members serve as representatives of a given group of pupils, every pupil in the group should have a voice in his selection. The sociometric method provides this opportunity. In addition, the broader social contacts of pupils who are sociometrically selected as council representatives enable them to work more effectively with the pupils whom they are representing and their social relation skills enable them to be more effective council members.

Sociometric nominations for the student council, or for other leadership positions in the school, are most effective when the pupils have a clear understanding of the nature and requirements of the position for which they are nominating candidates. Discussing with the pupils the qualities which the candidates for the position should possess will increase the likelihood of their naming pupils who have the abilities, as well as the social relation skills, necessary for effective leadership performance.

SOCIOMETRY AND SPECIAL SCHOOL PROBLEMS

In attempts to meet the needs of pupils with varying abilities and from diverse home backgrounds, a number of special problems have arisen in the school. How to best meet the academic, emotional, and social needs of exceptional children; how to reduce the drop-out rate among high school pupils; how to deal effectively with discipline problems in the school; and how to prevent juvenile delinquency among school pupils are some of the more challenging and persistent problems faced by the modern school. Although the complexity of these problems defies any simple or single solution, recent sociometric studies have indicated the contribution sociometric results can make to more effective educational decisions in these areas.

SOCIOMETRY AND THE EXCEPTIONAL CHILD

In recent years considerable attention has been directed toward the type of school program which can best meet the needs of the exceptional child. Various provisions in the regular classroom, in special classes, and in combinations of regular and special classes have been considered. The extensive research in this area, however, has not conclusively indicated the superiority of any one type of program (*28*). One of the difficulties has been to arrange a school program which meets the academic needs of the exceptional child without interfering with his social adjustment. This concern with the social adjustment of exceptional children has resulted in the increasing use of the sociometric test in evaluating the influence of the school program on the exceptional child's social adjustment pattern. A review of some of the major studies in this area will illustrate the utility of sociometric procedures for this purpose.

A series of studies by Gallagher (*17*) and Gallagher and Crowder (*12, 18*) have demonstrated how sociometric results can be used to evaluate the extent to which the social needs of gifted children are being met in the regular classroom. Their results indicated that, as a group, the gifted children tended to be well accepted by their classmates and were frequently recognized as leaders in classroom activities. They noted, however, that some of the gifted children were socially isolated among their peers. Through a series of case studies, they indicated how a knowledge of the sociometric position of the gifted child could aid in making curriculum adjustments for him (*12*).

Sociometric studies by Johnson (*25*), Johnson and Kirk (*26*), and Miller (*34*) were concerned with the extent to which mentally handicapped children were accepted in the regular classroom. In general, their results indicated that mentally handicapped children tended to experience low social acceptance among their normal peers and that a disproportionate number of them were socially isolated or rejected. Similar results were reported by Cruickshank (*13*) and Force (*16*) concerning the sociometric position of physically handicapped children in the regular classroom. Force suggested that the physically handicapped child held a minority status position in the classroom similar to that of members of various racial, religious, and cultural groups. However, the fact that physically handicapped children can attain normal social relations in the classroom was indicated in a study by Soldwedel and Terill (*38*). They reported that ten physically handicapped children in a class of thirty pupils had sociometric status scores which were equivalent to those of the nonhandicapped children.

Although there is indirect evidence concerning the influence of special classes on pupils' social relations (*1*), there have been relatively few sociometric studies in this area. One by Mann (*31*) is of special significance, since it illustrates the use of the sociometric test in the evaluation of a special program designed to meet both the academic and the social needs of the gifted. In this program, gifted pupils spent half of their school day in regular classes and the other half day in special classes limited to the gifted. It was assumed that such a school program would enable the gifted pupils to maintain normal peer relations while obtaining the benefits of special classes. All elementary school children were included in this program of partial segregation, but the study was limited to grades four, five, and six. The results of the sociometric choosing indicated that both the gifted and the typical children gave the majority of their sociometric choices to the members of their own group. This sociometric cleavage between gifted and typical children appeared at all grade levels, indicating that the program of partial segregation did not contribute to normal peer relations as had been intended.

These studies demonstrate the value of sociometric results for testing some of the assumptions concerning the best placement of the exceptional child. For years educators defended the practice of placing the exceptional child in the regular classroom on the basis that this would enable him to maintain normal peer relations. However, the above studies show that the exceptional child may be socially segregated among his typical peers, despite the fact that he is physically present in the regular classroom group. Thus the sociometric test gets beneath the surface of physical placement and evaluates the social placement of the child.

The use of sociometry in evaluating the social relationships of exceptional children is relatively new. Consequently, the studies in this area are too few to make any firm generalizations concerning the type of school program which best meets their social needs. However, the studies do indicate that, despite the type of educational provisions made for exceptional children, the sociometric test is a valuable instrument for evaluating the influence of the school program on their social relationships. Where the sociometric results indicate a detrimental influence, the sociometric choices of exceptional children can also provide clues concerning the most favorable social placement for them.

SOCIOMETRY AND SCHOOL DROP-OUTS

One of the most persistent problems in education is the large drop-out rate among school pupils. It is estimated that approximately 50 percent of the pupils who start school in the first grade do not graduate from high school. Although there are numerous reasons for pupils dropping out of school, recent sociometric studies have indicated that lack of social acceptance among peers might be a contributing factor.

Studies by Kuhlen and Collister (*29*) and Ullmann (*44*) have shown that pupils who drop out of school have lower sociometric status than those who graduate. Similar results were reported by Gronlund and Holmlund (*22*). They compared the drop-out rate among fifty-three pupils with high sociometric status and forty-nine pupils with low sociometric status. Only seven of the high status pupils dropped out of high school before graduating, while twenty-two of the low status pupils dropped out of high school before graduating. Since none of the above studies reported on the socioeconomic class level of the pupils, it would be easy to interpret these results in terms of the fact that pupils with low sociometric status more frequently come from lower socioeconomic classes, where the drop-out rate is higher. However, there is some evidence to indicate that social acceptance by peers is a factor independent of socioeconomic class level. McGuire (*33*) noted a tendency for pupils from low socioeconomic classes to remain in school if they had high social acceptance among their schoolmates and to drop out if they had low peer acceptance.

These studies indicate the contribution sociometric results can make to the early identification of potential school drop-outs so that special provisions can be made to meet the social as well as the academic needs of these pupils. Although there is no assurance that special efforts toward improving the social relationships of pupils with low peer acceptance will reduce the drop-out rate to any great extent, such efforts should contribute to the retention of those pupils from the lower social classes who have above average academic ability but who lack a feeling of belonging in the school. Improving the retention rate among these pupils, even to a limited degree, would be well worth the effort.

SOCIOMETRY AND DISCIPLINE PROBLEMS

The classroom teacher and the school administrator are confronted with a wide array of discipline problems in the school. Some are of a transitory nature and easily handled with simple control techniques. These are generally of little concern to the teacher and are so common that they are considered a normal aspect of group behavior. However, other discipline problems are of a persistent and serious nature and require considerable attention from the teacher and the administrator alike. Many of these problems can be traced to conflicts between racial and cultural groups, to undesirable clique formations, and to the hostile reactions of pupils who are rejected by their peers. Although there are no simple solutions to such problems, sociometric procedures can aid in diagnosing the problems and can provide clues for remedial action.

Where conflicts between subgroups in the classroom, or in the school, result in discipline problems, the network of positive and negative feelings revealed by the sociometric test can contribute to an understanding of the nature and scope of the problem. Noting the exchange of positive and negative sociometric choices between the subgroups will aid in detecting whether a relatively few pupils are involved in the conflict or if it pervades the entire group. Sociometric results can also be used to determine the most influential pupils in each subgroup. Concentrating remedial efforts on the informal leaders of the conflicting subgroups and providing sociometric arrangements which emphasize the positive relationships between the members of the subgroups, and which separate the pupils who reject each other, should contribute to fewer interpersonal conflicts and should increase the effectiveness of other procedures for developing greater harmony between the subgroups.

Frequently a small clique of pupils is responsible for many of the discipline problems in the classroom or in the school. In such cases, sociometric results can be used to indicate the nature of the relationships between the various members of the clique and the relation of the clique members to the other pupils in the group. Identifying and working with the leader of the clique is sometimes effective in changing the attitude and the behavior of all of the members of the clique. Sociometric grouping procedures which separate the members of a disturbing clique have also been found effective in reducing their undesirable influence in the group (27). The separation of clique members is usually most effective when they are distributed throughout the group in terms of the sociometric choices they have directed toward nonclique members. This enables them to have some of their sociometric preferences satisfied, and it provides the best opportunity for absorbing them into the total group.

In dealing with individual pupils who are chronic discipline problems, sociometric results can contribute insight into their undesirable behavior and can aid in determining their best social placement in the group. A pupil who is a chronic discipline problem generally has low sociometric status and is most frequently rejected by his peers. Noting which pupils he chooses on the sociometric test and discussing with him the reasons for his choices can aid in understanding the attitudes and values which underlie his behavior difficulties. Making arrangements for him to work with those of his chosen associates who would seem to have the most desirable influence on his behavior and assisting him to obtain greater acceptance among the group members should contribute to the effectiveness of other remedial efforts.

Although the sociometric test can contribute to the diagnosis and treatment of specific discipline problems in the school, its greatest contribution in this area is of a preventive nature. Much of the teasing, fighting, bullying, quarreling, impertinence, and the like, which occurs in schools, is an indication of insufficient attention to social relations among pupils. By using sociometric results to analyze and improve pupils' social relations in the school, many of the minor interpersonal conflicts among pupils can be alleviated, and some of the more serious discipline problems can be prevented. Even more important, emphasis on improved social relations can lead to attitudes of friendliness and coöperation among pupils which transcend the mere prevention of overt expressions of interpersonal strife.

SOCIOMETRY AND JUVENILE DELINQUENCY

The role of the school in the prevention of juvenile delinquency is receiving increased emphasis. A comprehensive study by Glueck and Glueck (*21*) has indicated that delinquent tendencies can be detected at an early age in the school and that much future delinquency can be averted through a preventive school program. Since pupils who drop out of school before graduation and pupils who are discipline problems in the school more frequently become delinquent, the sociometric procedures discussed in these two areas have implications for a preventive program in the school. However, sociometric studies have also indicated the possible contribution of sociometric results where attention is focused directly on pupils identified as potential delinquents.

The most significant identifiable characteristic of the potential delinquent is truancy. The Gluecks (*21*) found, in their study of 500 delinquents and 500 nondelinquents, that 95 percent of the delinquents had been truants and that the majority had played truant before the age of eleven. Although the truant's dislike for school may be based on a number of factors, recent sociometric studies have indicated the importance of studying the social relationships of the truant in attempting to understand and improve his social adjustment in the school. Both Croft and Grygier (*11*) and McGuire (*33*) reported that truants tended to have low sociometric status among their schoolmates and that they were frequently socially isolated in the school. It is not inconceivable that this lack of acceptance by schoolmates contributes to the truant's desire to escape what he perceives as an intolerable situation. Nor is it inconceivable that some truants seek membership in delinquent gangs to obtain the recognition and acceptance that were not afforded them in their normal school relations. Thus, special efforts toward improving the social relationships of truants may contribute to a reduction in truancy and thereby to the prevention of later delinquency. For this purpose, the sociometric test can aid in determining the social position of the truant among his peers, and it can provide clues for improving his social relationships in the school.

When pupils with delinquent tendencies band together into an informal gang, the sociometric test can contribute to the detection and destructuring of the delinquent group. A study by Cook (7) has illustrated how the sociometric test may be used for this purpose. At the beginning of the study there was a closely knit group of pupils who had been involved in various types of delinquent escapades. Sociometric results indicated the leader of the group and the relationships among the various group members. During the two-year period of the study, various procedures were used in an attempt to destructure the delinquent group. Social arrangements in the classroom, group activities, individual counseling, and group guidance methods were all included in the program. As various procedures were used, sociometric analyses were made to determine the effect of the procedures on the destructuring of the group. At the end of the study, sociometric results indicated that the delinquent group was disintegrating and that its members were developing associations with other subgroups of pupils whose behavior was more socially desirable. Although a variety of procedures were used in this study, the sociometric test made a number of valuable contributions. It provided insight into the social structure of the delinquent group, it assisted in the identification of pupils for individual and group guidance, it contributed to the remedial process, and it provided the main basis for periodically evaluating the progress being made toward the destructuring of the delinquent group.

Throughout this section, an attempt has been made to describe and illustrate the utility of the sociometric test in dealing with special school problems. Since the discussion was confined to sociometric procedures, a word of caution is in order. School programs designed to meet the needs of exceptional children, to reduce school drop-outs, to maintain effective discipline, and to reduce juvenile delinquency must take into account numerous factors besides those of the pupils' social relations. Likewise, a variety of preventive and remedial procedures are necessary for an effective program. Thus, the sociometric test should not be viewed as a panacea for these school problems. Rather, it should be viewed as a useful technique which can supplement and complement other methods for meeting the special needs of children who are having difficulty in adjusting to the regular school program.

USES OF SCHOOL-WIDE SOCIOMETRIC RESULTS

Although the sociometric test is most frequently administered on an informal basis, when some specific purpose arises for its use, there are special advantages in an annual administration of a sociometric test on a school-wide basis. If properly planned, the results can be used for arranging homeroom classes, for identifying potential cases of maladjustment, and for evaluating the social structure of the school. In addition, the sociometric results for each pupil can be included in his cumulative guidance record for future use by teachers, counselors, and administrators.

An effective method of introducing school-wide sociometric testing is to have pupils choose the boys and girls they would most prefer as classmates in their homeroom the following year. If students are permitted to choose any of the pupils at the same grade level, the sociometric choices would cut across classroom lines. This would provide a basis for rearranging homeroom groups, and an analysis of the sociometric results would provide information on the social acceptance of individual pupils and their social relationships in the school.

The administration of the sociometric test on a school-wide basis would be relatively simple, since each teacher could administer it to his own pupils during the homeroom period. If the sociometric test was administered in the spring of the year, the results could be analyzed and recorded before the school year ended and the homeroom classes could be organized for the following fall.

ARRANGING HOMEROOM CLASSES

In arranging homeroom classes on the basis of sociometric results, an attempt should be made to intermix the pupils from various socioeconomic, racial, religious, and cultural groups, as well as to satisfy some of the sociometric choices of each pupil. A fairly even distribution of boys and girls must, of course, also be considered. In general, the organization of the homeroom classes should provide a social arrangement which is most conducive to the social integration of pupils along sociometric lines.

When homeroom classes are organized on the basis of pupils' sociometric preferences, each pupil is placed in the most favorable position for satisfying his need for belonging to the peer group. The increased emotional security resulting from such an arrangement should contribute to the social development of individual pupils, should help counteract the undesirable social effects of ability grouping in the school, and should increase the effectiveness of homeroom activities designed to improve pupils' social relations. Thus, sociometrically arranged homerooms should enable the homeroom program to become a dynamic force for developing harmonious social relations in the school. The extent to which it is effective in this regard can, of course, be evaluated at the end of each school year when the annual sociometric test is administered.

IDENTIFYING MALADJUSTED PUPILS

As indicated in previous chapters, the number of sociometric choices a pupil receives on a sociometric test cannot be used as a direct indication of his personal and social adjustment. However, the disproportionate number of adjustment problems among socially isolated and rejected pupils makes sociometric results valuable for identifying those pupils who are most apt to have adjustment difficulties. Thus, when school-wide sociometric results are combined with the results of other diagnostic measures, they can serve as a screening device for locating potential cases of maladjustment.

The feasibility of such a screening program has been demonstrated in a study by Ullmann (*43*). He combined sociometric results with self-rating inventories and teachers' ratings of adjustment and noted that the several measures tended to complement each other in identifying potentially maladjusted pupils. The sociometric test seems to be especially helpful in identifying the quiet, withdrawn child who may be experiencing adjustment difficulties not readily apparent to the classroom teacher. Thus, sociometric results can make a unique contribution to a mental health screening program. When used for this purpose, those pupils identified as potential cases of maladjustment must, of course, be followed up by more intensive study.

Obtaining annual sociometric results for each pupil in the school will have special value in identifying potential cases of maladjustment. The cumulative record of each pupil's social relationships will make it possible to note sudden drops in social acceptance, radical changes in patterns of choice and other possible indications of adjustment problems. Following up such leads may make it possible to prevent more serious problems of adjustment from developing.

EVALUATING THE SOCIAL STRUCTURE OF THE SCHOOL

The increased emphasis on the role of the school in improving intergroup relations (*8, 40*) has indicated the importance of the sociometric technique for evaluating the social structure of the school. Analyzing the results of a sociometric test administered on a school-wide basis will aid in determining how well the various school activities, as well as the homeroom program, are contributing to a socially integrated school population. Cleavages between pupils representing various socioeconomic classes (*37*), and different racial (*10*), religious (*6*), and ethnic groups (*30*), can be determined readily from the sociometric results. Where such cleavages exist, special efforts can be directed toward improving intergroup relations, and the annual school-wide sociometric results can contribute to a periodic evaluation of the effectiveness of the program.

Evaluating the social structure of consolidated schools has particular value because of the possible social cleavage between rural and urban pupils (*4*) and pupils from different communities (*5*). Although such cleavages are more likely to be present in newly consolidated schools, a socially integrated school population will generally not evolve unless special efforts are made to provide socially integrating experiences (*3*). As with other social cleavages in the school, annual school-wide sociometric results can contribute to an evaluation of the progress being made toward integrating the pupils into a unified school population.

OTHER USES OF SCHOOL-WIDE SOCIOMETRIC RESULTS

Sociometric results obtained on a school-wide basis will provide information on the social relationships of each pupil in the school. This information can be recorded on forms, such as those suggested in Chapter 3, and included in each pupil's cumulative guidance record. This would contribute to a permanent record of each pupil's social development and would provide valuable information for teachers, counselors, and administrators.

School-wide sociometric results could be useful to teachers in a number of ways. First, the teacher would be provided with information concerning the social relationships of his pupils before the school year began. This would contribute to a better understanding of the pupils and thereby contribute to more effective plans for the homeroom program. Second, school-wide sociometric results could provide a basis for arranging classroom seating and work groups, before the teacher was able to obtain classroom sociometric choices. Third, pupils who had low acceptance among their peers could be identified before the beginning of the school year and could receive special attention as soon as school started. Fourth, school-wide sociometric results could aid in the interpretation of classroom sociometric results by indicating the extent to which a pupil's social acceptance in the classroom was related to his more general social acceptance in the school. This would enable the teacher to obtain a fairly reliable index of each pupil's social acceptance by peers, and remedial efforts could be directed toward those pupils who had the greatest need for remedial help.

Counselors should find school-wide sociometric results especially useful in understanding pupils referred for counseling. The degree to which a pupil is accepted by his peers, the types of pupils he chooses as associates, and the types of pupils who choose him should contribute valuable insights into his problems of social and emotional adjustment. It is also possible that a pupil's social relationships, recorded over a period of years, might aid in vocational counseling. Ability to maintain effective social relationships with a large number of peers, or inability to establish satisfying peer relationships, would seem to have implications for certain types of vocations. When viewed in the light of other information, sociometric results could thus contribute to more effective vocational planning.

School-wide sociometric results could also aid in administrative decisions concerning the school program. Modifications in the school curriculum, changes in the extracurricular program, revision of the school's bus schedule, arrangements for the school lunch program, and the like, all have implications for pupils' social relations. Decisions in such areas are more apt to be in harmony with the social needs of pupils, if evidence is available on the pupils' social relations in the school. With annual sociometric testing, the influence of changes in the school program on pupils' social relations could, of course, be evaluated at the end of each school year.

In this section, some of the more obvious uses of school-wide sociometric results have been mentioned. As teachers, counselors, and school administrators become familiar with sociometric procedures in the school, they will probably recognize other valuable uses of school-wide sociometric results obtained on an annual basis.

APPLYING SOCIOMETRIC RESULTS IN THE SCHOOL

Throughout the last part of this book, an attempt has been made to indicate the various educational areas in which sociometric testing might be found useful. Some of the suggestions have been based on research findings, some on the practical experiences of classroom teachers, and others on the apparent utility of sociometric measures. In general, however, much remains to be learned about how to apply sociometric results appropriately and effectively to educational problems. Until more sufficient evidence is available, it would seem advisable to use an experimental approach in applying sociometric results in the school. For this purpose, the methods of action research are especially appropriate.

Essentially, action research refers to the systematic study of school problems by those persons in a position to put the findings into action (*9*). Using modified research techniques, teachers, supervisors, counselors, and school administrators identify practical school problems, select and try out promising solutions, and evaluate the consequences of the action taken. Through careful recording of the procedures used and systematic interpretation of the results, generalization for improved school practices evolve. The action research process provides an approach that can be used effectively by the individual classroom teacher or can be used in a coöperative study of school-wide problems. In either case, it provides a systematic method for applying sociometric results to educational problems (*14, 39, 41, 42*).

ACTION RESEARCH PROCEDURES FOR APPLYING SOCIOMETRY IN THE CLASSROOM

When the classroom teacher uses action research procedures in the application of sociometry to classroom problems, he has two objectives in mind. The first is to use the most effective procedures for solving the immediate classroom problem; the second is to obtain information which will guide future actions with similar classroom problems. These objectives can be most effectively attained if the action research procedures follow an orderly series of steps. Although these steps will vary somewhat with the nature of the problem and the degree of refinement desired in the research design, the following basic steps are usually included in a comprehensive design for typical social relation problems in the classroom.

IDENTIFYING THE PROBLEM. The first step in action research is that of identifying the problem and stating it as clearly as possible. In the social relations area, a problem may come to the teacher's attention through classroom observation or through sociometric testing. The problem may be concerned with an individual pupil (e.g., a social isolate) or with a classroom group (e.g., a social cleavage). Regardless of how the problem was first identified, or how pervasive it is, an attempt should be made to define the problem in specific terms. This can usually be done most effectively by stating it in question form. The following questions illustrate how a problem of social isolation and of social cleavage might be stated:

1. How can a socially isolated girl who is new in class be helped to improve her social relationships?
2. How can a classroom social cleavage between two racial groups be reduced?

ANALYZING THE PROBLEM. When the problem has been identified and stated as clearly as possible, the next step is to analyze the difficulty and to attempt to identify the factors causing and contributing to the problem. Procedures such as those suggested in Chapter 9 may be useful for this purpose. At this stage, it is also helpful to examine research studies concerned with the same problem. These studies should not be examined for simple solutions to the problem, but for suggestions concerning the most probable causal areas and for types of remedial action that might be considered.

As the problem is diagnosed more fully, a detailed record should be made of the procedures used and of the findings pertinent to an understanding of the problem and its most probable causes. This will provide information for the formulation of hypotheses, or scientific hunches, concerning the best solutions to the problem and for developing a plan of action.

FORMULATING HYPOTHESES AND DEVELOPING A PLAN OF ACTION. As noted in the above descriptions, the first two steps of action research are similar to the procedures a classroom teacher would use in attempting to solve any classroom problem in the area of social relations. The unique characteristic of action research is the systematic method of designing a plan of action and of gathering, recording, and interpreting evidence regarding the success of the action. This process requires that the proposed action be stated in the form of a hypothesis so that the effects of the action can be clearly determined. The statement of the hypothesis should include both the goal to be achieved and the procedure, or action, for achieving that goal. The following examples indicate how hypotheses might be stated for the illustrative problems referred to above:

1. Assigning a socially isolated girl who is new in class to some classroom responsibility which puts her in contact with the majority of the class members (action) will improve her social relationships (goal).
2. Sociometric grouping procedures in the classroom which intermix pupils from two different racial groups (action) will reduce the social cleavage between them (goal).

Each hypothesis stated above is, of course, just one of the many that could be stated in each area. Each has been deliberately confined to a simple statement of action for the sake of clarity. In actual practice, a series of such hypotheses might be stated and tested for each problem, or a multiple approach to action might be included in one hypothesis. Regardless of the complexity of the practice included in the hypothesis, care must be taken to state the hypothesis so that it clearly denotes the action to be taken and the goal to be achieved.

Although the action hypothesis structures the procedures to be followed, a plan of action should be much more detailed. It should include the specific types of action to be taken, the method to be used in recording the procedural steps, and the techniques to be used for evaluating the extent to which the goal has been achieved. In essence, these steps constitute a formulation of the action research plan, and they should all be carefully considered before the plan is put into action.

CARRYING OUT THE ACTION RESEARCH PLAN. When the research plan is put into action, an attempt should be made to control as many elements in the situation as possible without disrupting the natural activities of the classroom. For example, during a study of the influence of sociometric grouping on a classroom racial cleavage problem other experiences which may influence the results should not be introduced at the same time. If it becomes necessary, or desirable, to do so, the hypothesis should be revised and the research plan expanded to include the modifications. Action research in the classroom must be flexible because numerous unforeseen circumstances may arise. However, when changes in procedure are made, they should be carefully recorded and the research plan changed accordingly.

The complexity of factors operating in a classroom situation and the flexibility of action research procedures make a careful record of the on-going process extremely important. This record should include a description of the action taken, the teacher's subjective impressions of the effectiveness of the action, and a description of any uncontrolled events that might have influenced the effectiveness of the procedures used. This information will aid in the interpretation of the results, and it will also provide a rich source of new hypotheses for future action.

DETERMINING RESULTS. In determining the degree to which the goal has been achieved in action research, both objective and subjective methods of appraisal should be used. Although an attempt should be made to use objective measuring instruments wherever possible, outcomes which elude objective measurement should not be omitted. For example, the influence of sociometric grouping on a classroom racial cleavage can be objectively evaluated by comparing sociometric results obtained at the beginning and at the end of the research period. However, the teacher may be equally concerned with the influence of sociometric grouping on the observable interaction of the pupils, on changes in the emotional climate of the classroom, and on changes in the behavior of a particular child. Recorded observations and subjective judgments may be necessary to evaluate these outcomes. Despite the limitations of such subjective procedures, they generally provide useful evidence concerning important aspects of the problem. The inadequacies of subjective evidence in the evaluation process can be allowed for when the results are interpreted and generalizations are drawn.

INTERPRETING THE RESULTS. An analysis of the results of action research will indicate whether a change in the predicted direction has occurred. For example, the prediction that sociometric grouping will reduce a social cleavage between two racial groups can be evaluated by noting the change in the number of sociometric choices exchanged between the members of the two groups. If there is an increase in the number of sociometric choices between the members of the two groups after sociometric grouping procedures have been used, the findings are in the predicted direction. Inferences can then be drawn concerning the practical significance of the results and the extent to which the results are due to the action taken (i.e., sociometric grouping).

Generalizations based on action research in the classroom must, of course, be stated cautiously and tentatively. The complexity of factors operating in the classroom, and especially in the social relations area, makes it extremely difficult to generalize concerning the relationship between a desirable result and a specific action or group of actions. The generalizations that are drawn should be considered guides to future action which can be further tested in other situations.

CONTINUOUS RETESTING OF GENERALIZATIONS. Action research in the classroom is more or less a continuous process. Problems are identified, hypotheses are developed, action is taken, the effectiveness of the action is evaluated, and general suggestions for future action are indicated. These suggestions provide new hypotheses for improved practice and the process is repeated. Thus, the effectiveness of classroom procedures for handling specific classroom problems is continuously being evaluated. Although generalizations evolve which guide and direct classroom practice, these generalizations are regarded as tentative and are retested in each new situation. In essence, then, action research in the classroom is a form of controlled action which works toward the continuous improvement of classroom practices.

This continuous retesting of generalizations concerning effective classroom practices is especially important in applying sociometric results to classroom problems. The complexity of social relation problems, and the diversity of factors causing and contributing to such problems, makes it desirable to use a systematic but flexible approach. Procedures that assisted one isolated pupil gain acceptance in a classroom group may be ineffective with a different pupil. Procedures that helped to reduce a social cleavage in one classroom group may bring about no change in another group. Thus, procedures for improving pupils' social relations should be regarded as hypotheses to be tested, rather than sure-fire solutions.

Through continuous retesting under various conditions, the teacher will build up a working knowledge of the most effective procedures for applying sociometric results to classroom problems.

COÖPERATIVE ACTION RESEARCH AND SCHOOL-WIDE PROBLEMS

The same action research procedures that are used by individual teachers in the classroom can be used in applying sociometric results to school-wide problems. In the latter case, however, the action research is usually conducted on a coöperative basis. Teachers, supervisors, counselors, and administrators coöperatively identify the problems that are of greatest concern to them and they jointly develop, carry out, and evaluate the plan of action.

One of the main advantages of coöperative action research is that it is possible to develop more carefully controlled studies for evaluating the application of sociometry to educational problems. For example, the influence of sociometric grouping on pupils' social relations can be compared to the influence of ability grouping and arbitrary grouping, by using each method in several classrooms and comparing the results. Similarly, the effectiveness of the sociometric method of nominating pupils for leadership positions in the school can be evaluated by using it with some pupils and not with others. This ability to compare the results of different school practices with a relatively large number of pupils in each group makes it possible to draw more firm generalizations concerning the effectiveness of the practices.

Where action research procedures are designed to compare two different school practices, both practices are usually included in the hypothesis. The following statements illustrate hypotheses for the experimental application of sociometric procedures to educational problems:

1. Sociometric grouping of pupils in the homeroom (action) will

improve pupils' social relations (goal) to a greater degree than ability grouping (alternate action).

2. Student council members who are sociometrically nominated (action) will be more effective (goal) than those who are appointed (alternate action).
3. School programs which include special efforts to improve pupils' social relationships (action) will be more effective in reducing truancy, discipline problems, school drop-outs, and juvenile delinquency (goal) than school programs which do not devote special attention to pupils' social relationships (alternate action).

These hypotheses illustrate how sociometric procedures can be introduced into the school on an experimental basis so that their effectiveness in various areas of school practice can be determined rather than assumed. By using sociometric procedures with one group of pupils and not with another, a comparison of results makes it possible to evaluate systematically the contribution of sociometric procedures to improved school practice. This assumes, of course, that all factors which might influence the results are controlled as carefully as possible. Thus, the two groups of pupils should be similar; the procedures used in the two groups should be the same, except for the differences in practice that are being evaluated; and the same evaluation procedures should be used in both groups. Although it is impossible to control all factors in action research in the school, an attempt to control the main factors which might influence the results and a careful record of the procedures used will contribute to more adequate interpretations of the contribution of sociometric procedures to improved school practice. Through the repeated application and evaluation of sociometric procedures under controlled conditions, generalizations will result which can serve as guides to the most effective application of sociometric procedures in the school.

The complexity and variety of social relation problems in the school and their inextricable relationship to the educative process would seem to indicate an ugent need to explore further the potentialities of sociometric procedures in educational practice. Although published sociometric studies provide useful suggestions for this purpose, much of the exploration will need to be done by teachers, supervisors, counselors, and administrators, in their own schools. A cautious and intelligent approach, based on action research procedures, will provide rich rewards in the form of improved school practices and improved social relations in the school.

SUMMARY

The use of sociometry in the school is relatively new and much remains to be learned concerning its most effective use. However, there appears to be a number of useful purposes for which sociometric procedures might be used in the school.

Sociometric results can contribute to a leadership training program in the school, by assisting in the early identification of leadership potential among pupils and by providing an equitable basis for nominating pupils for formal leadership positions. Sociometric results have also been found useful in studying the special needs of children who are having difficulty in adjusting to the regular school program. The inadequate social relationships of some exceptional children indicate the importance of using the sociometric test in evaluating the extent to which the school program is meeting the social needs of the exceptional child. The low sociometric status of school drop-outs, truants, and pupils who are discipline problems in the school also suggests that sociometric procedures can contribute to special programs designed to alleviate such problems.

Although sociometric results are usually obtained when some special need arises for their use, there are several advantages in obtaining school-wide sociometric results on an annual basis. Such results can be used for arranging homeroom classes, for identifying potentially maladjusted pupils, and for evaluating the social structure of the school. In addition, they can be used for special purposes by teachers, counselors, and administrators.

The lack of sufficient evidence on how to apply sociometric results appropriately and effectively to educational problems indicates the desirability of using an experimental approach. The systematic methods of action research seem to be ideal for this purpose. Through the application of sociometric procedures under the controlled conditions of action research, the potentialities of sociometric procedures for improved school practices can be systematically evaluated in various areas of the school.

REFERENCES

1. Barbe, W. B., "Evaluation of Special Classes for Gifted Children," *Exceptional Children,* 1955, *22:*60–62.
2. Bass, B. M., Wurster, C. R., Doll, P. A., and Clair, D. J., "Situational and Personality Factors in Leadership Among Sorority Women," *Psychological Monographs,* No. 16, Washington, D.C., American Psychological Association, 1953.
3. Becker, M. G., and Loomis, C. P., "Measuring Rural-Urban and Farm and Non-Farm Cleavages in a Rural Consolidated School," *Sociometry,* 1948, *11:*246–261.
4. Blanchard, B. E., "A Social Acceptance Study of Transported and Non-Transported Pupils in a Rural Secondary School," *Journal of Experimental Education,* 1947, *15:*291–303.
5. Bonney, M. E., "A Sociometric Study of the Peer Acceptance of Rural Students in Three Consolidated High Schools,"*Educational Administration and Supervision,* 1951, *37:*234–240.
6. Bonney, M. E., "A Study of Friendship Choices in College in Relation to Church Affiliation, In-Church Preferences, Family Size, and Length of Enrollment in College," *Journal of Social Psychology,* 1949, *29:*153–166.
7. Cook, L. A., "An Experimental Sociographic Study of a Stratified Tenth Grade Class," *American Sociological Review,* 1945, *10:*250–261.
8. Cook, L., and Cook, E., *Intergroup Education,* New York, McGraw-Hill Book Company, 1954.
9. Corey, S. M., *Action Research to Improve School Practices,* New

York, Bureau of Publications, Teachers College, Columbia University, 1953.

10. Criswell, J. H., "A Sociometric Study of Race Cleavage in the Classroom," *Archives of Psychology,* No. 235, 1939.
11. Croft, I. J., and Grygier, T. G., "Social Relationships of Truants and Juvenile Delinquents," *Human Relations,* 1956, *9:*439–466.
12. Crowder, T., and Gallagher, J. J., "The Adjustment of Gifted Children in the Regular Classroom: Case Studies," *Exceptional Children,* 1957, *23:*353–363.
13. Cruickshank, W. M., and Medve, J., "Social Relations of Physically Handicapped Children," *Journal of Exceptional Children,* 1948, *14:*100–106.
14. Cunningham, R., *Understanding Group Behavior of Boys and Girls,* New York, Bureau of Publications, Teachers College, Columbia University, 1951.
15. DeHaan, R. F., "Social Leadership," in Part II, the 57th Yearbook, National Society for the Study of Education, *Education for the Gifted,* Chicago, University of Chicago Press, 1958.
16. Force, D., "Social Status of Physically Handicapped Children," *Exceptional Children,* 1956, *23:*104–107.
17. Gallagher, J. J., "Social Status of Children Related to Intelligence, Propinquity, and Social Perception," *Elementary School Journal,* 1958, *59:*225–231.
18. Gallagher, J. J., and Crowder, T., "The Adjustment of Gifted Children in the Regular Classroom," *Exceptional Children,* 1957, *23:*306–312, 317–319.
19. Gibb, C. A., "Leadership," Chapter 24, in G. Lindzey (ed.), *Handbook of Social Psychology,* Cambridge, Massachusetts, Addison-Wesley Publishing Company, 1954.
20. Gibb, C. A., "The Sociometry of Leadership in Temporary Groups," *Sociometry,* 1950, *13:*226–243.
21. Glueck, S., and Glueck, E., *Delinquents in the Making: Paths to Prevention,* New York, Harper & Brothers, 1952.
22. Gronlund, N. E., and Holmlund, W. S., "The Value of Elementary School Sociometric Status Scores for Predicting Pupils' Adjustment in High School," *Educational Administration and Supervision,* 1958, *44:*255–260.

23. Jennings, H. H., *Leadership and Isolation,* New York, Longmans, Green and Company, 1950.
24. Jennings, H. H., "Sociometry of Leadership," *Sociometry Monographs,* No. 14, New York, Beacon House, 1947.
25. Johnson, G. O., "A Study of the Social Position of Mentally-Handicapped Children in the Regular Grades," *American Journal of Mental Deficiency,* 1950, *55:*60–89.
26. Johnson, G. O., and Kirk, S. A., "Are Mentally-Handicapped Children Segregated in the Regular Grades?" *Journal of Exceptional Children,* 1950, *17:*65–68.
27. Kerstetter, L. M., and Sargent, J., "Re-Assignment Therapy in the Classroom," *Sociometry,* 1940, *3:*293–306.
28. Kirk, S. A., Chairman, "The Education of Exceptional Children," *Review of Educational Research,* 1953, *23:*389–554.
29. Kuhlen, R. G., and Collister, E. C., "Sociometric Status of Sixth- and Ninth-Graders Who Fail to Finish High School," *Educational and Psychological Measurement,* 1952, *12:*632–637.
30. Lundberg, G., and Dickson, L., "Inter-Ethnic Relations in a High School Population," *American Journal of Sociology,* 1952, *58:*1–10.
31. Mann, H., "How Real Are Friendships of Gifted and Typical Children in a Program of Partial Segregation?" *Exceptional Children,* 1956, *23:*199–201.
32. Martin, W. E., Gross, N., and Darley, J. G., "Studies of Group Behavior: Leaders, Followers, and Isolates in Small Organized Groups," *Journal of Abnormal and Social Psychology,* 1952, *47:*838–842.
33. McGuire, C., "Adolescent Society and Social Mobility," Ph.D. Dissertation, University of Chicago, 1949.
34. Miller, R. V., "Social Status and Socio-empathic Differences Among Mentally Superior, Mentally Typical, and Mentally Retarded Children," *Exceptional Children,* 1956, *23:*114–119.
35. Moreno, J. L., *Who Shall Survive?* New York, Beacon House, 1953.
36. National Association of Secondary-School Principals, *The Student Council Handbook,* Washington, D.C., National Education Association, 1955.

37. Neugarten, B. L., "Social Class and Friendship Among School Children," *American Journal of Sociology,* 1946, *51:*305–313.
38. Soldwedel, B., and Terill, I., "Sociometric Aspects of Physically Handicapped and Non-Handicapped Children in the Same Elementary School," *Exceptional Children,* 1957, *23:*371–372, 381–383.
39. Taba, H., *With Perspective on Human Relations,* Washington, D.C., American Council on Education, 1955.
40. Taba, H., Brady, E. H., and Robinson, J. T., *Intergroup Education in Public Schools,* Washington, D.C., American Council on Education, 1952.
41. Taba, H., and Elkins, D., *With Focus on Human Relations,* Washington, D.C., American Council on Education, 1950.
42. Taba, H., and Noel, E., *Action Research: A Case Study,* Washington, D.C., Association for Supervision and Curriculum Development, N.E.A., 1957.
43. Ullmann, C. A., *Identification of Maladjusted School Children,* Public Health Monograph No. 7, Washington, D.C., Government Printing Office, 1952.
44. Ullmann, C. A., "Teachers, Peers and Tests as Predictors of Adjustment," *Journal of Educational Psychology,* 1957, *48:*257–267.

INDEX OF NAMES

INDEX OF SUBJECTS

Set in Intertype Garamond
Format by Nancy Etheredge
Published by HARPER & BROTHERS, *New York*